In Search of the Promised Land
The Collected Papers of Burton Blatt

Edited by

Steven J. Taylor, PhD
Syracuse University

and

Steven D. Blatt, MD
State University of New York Health Science Center

David L. Braddock, PhD
AAMR Books and Research Monographs Editor

AAMR
American Association on Mental Retardation

© 1999 by the American Association on Mental Retardation

Published by
American Association on Mental Retardation
444 North Capitol Street, NW, Suite 846
Washington, DC 20001-1512

The points of view herein are those of the authors and do not necessarily represent the official policy or opinion of the American Association on Mental Retardation. Publication does not imply endorsement by the editor, the Association, or its individual members.

Printed in the United States of America.

Library of Congress Cataloging-in-Publication Data
Blatt, Burton, 1927–
    In search of the Promised Land: the collected papers of Burton Blatt / edited by Steven J. Taylor, Steven D. Blatt, David L. Braddock.
        p.   cm.
    Includes bibliographical references.
    ISBN 0-940898-63-2
    1. Mentally handicapped—Institutional care. 2. Mentally handicapped—Civil rights. 3. Blatt, Burton, 1927– . I. Taylor, Steven J., 1949– . II. Blatt, Steven D., 1957– . III. Braddock, David L. IV. Title.
HV3004.B59 1999
362.3'85—dc21
                                                  99-21914
                                                     CIP

Dedication

As a teacher, scholar, author and advocate,
your actions have enriched society
for generations to come.

As our friend, brother, uncle, husband and father
you have enriched our lives forever.

With love and appreciation
we dedicate this book to Burton Blatt.

Table of Contents

Preface by Burton Blatt vii
Acknowledgments ix
Foreword by Stanley S. Herr xi
Foreword by Seymour B. Sarason xv
Introduction by Steven J. Taylor and Steven Blatt . xix

PART 1: In and Out of Purgatory 1
   Editors' Introduction 3
   Christmas in Purgatory 5
      "I Sometimes Wish That God Were Back…" ... 7
      "Suffer the Little Children…" 8
      Postscript 9
   The Dark Side of the Mirror 11
   Leaves From a European Diary 15
   The Family Papers: A Return to Purgatory 23

PART 2: In and Out of Poetry 29
   Editors' Introduction 31
   Poems and Aphorisms 33
      Verse 33
      Reformation of Pandemonium 33
      Aphorisms of a Burned-Out Pessimist 38
      Primary Connections 40
      On Institutions 41
      Humanness 41
      Point-Counterpoint 42
      Strange Allies 44
      Benchmarks of Civilization 45
      Antecedents and Consequences of Evil 46
      The Smells of Hell 49
      Victims and Victimizers 49
      Human Abuse and Personal Responsibility 50
      Faith 52
      Horror 53
      Law 57
      Love 59
      Civilization 60
      Glory 65

PART 3: In and Out of Human Policy 67
   Editors' Introduction 69
   Man Through a Turned Lens 71
   How to Destroy Lives by Telling Stories 83
      God and Popeye 83
      Invented Abuses for Invented Diseases 85
      What Practitioners Should Know 86
      Preventing Abuses 88
      Rediscovering the 19th Century 88
      Other Stories and Other Dilemmas 91
      How to Reduce Human Abuse 95
   Aspirations and Values 99
      Moral Goals and Technical Means 99
      Naderism and the Bureaucratization
         of Values 101
   The Controversies 105
      Nature/Nurture 105
      Cure/Permanence 109
      Pathology/Variance 111
      Institutionalization/Communitization
         Normalization/Mainstreaming 112

PART 4: In and Out of the Professions 121
   Editors' Introduction 123
   This Crazy Business 125
      Dreams and Means 125
      Ideas 125
      All Ideas Have Histories 127
      Mainstreaming, the Community, and
         the Teachers' Union 130
      The Year of the Child and Other
         Indecencies 133
      Innovation Is the Name of the Game 138
      Definitions, Labels, Incidence, and Prevalence:
         Wedged by Executive and Squeezed by
         Academic Views 139
      Concepts of Mental Retardation 142
      Reform or Revolution 142
   The Industries 145
      Treatment, Research, and Training
         Professionals 147
      Builders and Architects 149
      Merchants and Manufacturers,
         Organized Labor, and Bankers 150
      Pork Barrels and Politicians 151
      Lawyers 152
      Advocacy 153
      Life With the Decision Makers 156
   If People Could Heed Good Advice 159
      Lessons From the Street Lectures 159
      How to Change Yourself 162

Afterword by Steven D. Blatt 169
Biographical Sketch of Burton Blatt 171
Source Credits and Notes 175
References 177
About the Editors 181

PREFACE[1]
TO *EXODUS FROM PANDEMONIUM*

Burton Blatt

Now this volume is, for all practical purposes, completed, I have permitted myself the time to think about why I wrote it. There are many different reasons why people write books, and I had mine.

I hope this volume does some good. I do not expect it to affect my standard of living, but I do hope more than a few people will read it. Why did I write it? I wrote it for myself, which may not be a very good reason, but it's my reason. The preparation of this volume has forced me to attempt to understand a little better one of the truly puzzling and frightening aspects of our civilization: the nature and conditions of human abuse. I had become so confused and so frightened by what I had seen and had heard about man's treatment of his fellow man that I could no longer ignore the probability that, unless I struggled to understand inhuman treatment of humans, I would become either insensitive to such treatment (as I believe I had become) or I would not be able to tolerate my own relatively pleasurable life in the face of the Holocaust surrounding those of us unaffected. Therefore, foremost of my personal objectives was the need to give expression to my bewilderment and unhappiness with the very painful and slow progress of the humane in mankind. For this basically selfish act, I do hope that I had other unselfish motivations. That is, I do hope this book will contribute, in its own way, to the alleviation of some pain or suffering for some people and to the clearer appreciation of the concept of human abuse by other people. I do hope that it will be more valuable than, merely, as my catharsis.

…As I began to write and to think, I discovered that "mental retardation" is incidental to the purpose of this volume and the pathology it seeks to understand. By this I mean, it's subject is not so much "mental retardation" as it is those who offend the mentally retarded. It is not so much about the retarded personality as it is about our retarded civilization. It is not so much about people who are incapable of changing as it is about public policy which does not permit those people opportunities for changing. Early in the writing of this volume, I realized that its central focus might have been on innumerable groups, other than the mentally retarded, such as: American Indians, Blacks, people in jails, possibly even certain college students or ordinary children in schools. I realized that I chose the mentally retarded for, essentially, two reasons: first I have more interest in mental retardation and more experience in meeting them than other groups; second, the mentally retarded appear to be the "least of the least," the abused of the abused, the least able to advocate for themselves and the most in need of advocates. I will admit that, at one time, my specific interest in mental retardation was much more pronounced than my general interest in human abuse. Now, my specific interest remains deep but my general interest in the nature and origins of abuse has become dominating. Consequently, although some will view this volume as one concerned with the essential plight of the institutionalized mentally retarded, and as one written for the concern of professional workers and parents who must deal with the mentally retarded, I have written it for people who are troubled about our civilization, especially as public policy condones, excuses, and sometimes requires the cruel and inhuman treatment of certain individuals.

Reference

Blatt, B. (1970). *Exodus from pandemonium: Human abuse and a reformation of public policy.* Boston: Allyn & Bacon.

Acknowledgments

We would like to acknowledge the people who contributed directly or indirectly to the publication of this book. We want to express our sincere appreciation to David Braddock, editor of AAMR's Monograph Series, for his interest in and support of this project. We also appreciate the willingness of Seymour Sarason and Stanley Herr to write Forewords to this book. Special thanks to Rachael Zubal, Cyndy Colavita, and Debbie Simms for excellent secretarial and editorial support in the preparation of this book and to Peggy Seiter for the final copy editing of this work. We should also acknowledge that partial support for the compilation and editing of this book has been provided by the National Institute on Disability and Rehabilitation Research, Office of Special Education and Rehabilitation Services, U.S. Department of Education, through grants awarded to the Center on Human Policy. (Need it be said that the opinions expressed in this book are those of the person who expressed them and no endorsement by the U.S. government should be inferred?) Finally, we thank Douglas Biklen, Robert Bogdan, the staff of the Center on Human Policy, and many other colleagues and former students in the School of Education at Syracuse University with whom we often share memories of Burton Blatt and who help to keep his spirit alive.

Steven J. Taylor

Steven D. Blatt

FOREWORD
THE POWER OF DREAMS AND WORDS

Stanley S. Herr
University of Maryland School of Law
President, American Association on
Mental Retardation (1998-1999)

Burton Blatt—prolific writer, distinguished educator, and exposer of human abuses—was one of the pioneering figures in the disability rights movement. Yet his legacy and its implications for the field of developmental disabilities at a time of transition needs to be more widely shared. When we recall that 50-some years ago the Nazi regime ended only after mass killings that began with the murder of individuals with mental retardation by their medical doctors and culminated in the Holocaust against millions of Jews, gypsies, homosexuals, and labor organizers, one badly needs to reread Burt's works and understand his search for the causes and remedies for the abuse of one human being by another.

Burton Blatt lived his life with painful self-awareness of the costs of good men and women doing nothing. He made sure he was not one of them. In a dazzling array of books and speeches, of acts of unapologetic chutzpah and simple compassion, Professor Blatt was always a prophet and a truth teller. He cast light on the works of good women and men to forestall—or at least remediate —abuse, neglect, indifference, discrimination, and raw cruelty against "the least of the least." Like many of us, he chose to concentrate his life energies on individuals with mental retardation because they were regarded by the public as the least of the least, "the abused of the abused, the least able to advocate for themselves and the most in need of advocates" (Blatt, 1970, p. xvi).

He wrote the preceding words in the year I happened to graduate from Yale Law School, and those sentiments certainly mirrored my own when people asked me why I had turned my back on a judicial clerkship or comfortable corporate law firms. Even a dear adviser and that most liberal lion of the federal judiciary, United States Court of Appeals Judge David L. Bazelon, seemed puzzled why year after year I chose to concentrate on the then obscure area or disability rights and the still more obscure intersection of law and mental retardation.

But Burt Blatt understood the choice perfectly, and in 1972 in a symposium to the *Syracuse Law Review*, he described me as one of his new heroes because as a "legal theorist and practitioner," I had taken up the cause of vindicating the legal rights of people with mental retardation. He recognized a shift in the source of leadership: "Much of the gains being reported originated in the minds and through the efforts of lawyers, and many of the crucial decisions and policy reforms are products of our courts" (*Syracuse Law Review*, 1972).

To be in the pantheon of Burt's heroes as a young lawyer was heady, if not fully deserved. It provoked me to study deeper and work harder to understand the questions that disturbed the sleep and haunted the days of Burton and Gunnar Dybwad and the Danish lawyer N. E. Bank-Mikkelsen and other visionaries, particularly the multifaceted question: What is the nature of and conditions for human abuse? In his wild, sometimes undisciplined, but always searing and illuminating books, he addressed such questions, confessing that he wrote "to protect myself, to save my mind if not my soul" (Blatt, 1970, p. xv). Burt's candor and soul were on remarkable display, as when he acknowledged writing *Exodus From Pandemonium*, because:

> I could no longer ignore the probability that, unless I struggled to understand inhuman treatment of humans, I would become either insensitive to such treatment (as I believe I had become) or I would not be able to tolerate my own relatively pleasurable life in the face of The Holocaust surrounding those of us unaffected (Blatt, 1970, p. xv).

And how did Burt vaccinate himself and the rest of us from insensitivity and indifference? Burt, the exposer and the antithesis of an insensitive man, reminded us that we stand in the debt of, and in a direct line with, all truth tellers who have gone before us. You and I must continue Burt's legacy as we pull aside polite fictions that mask human abuse.

Steven Taylor and Steven Blatt have rendered a great service in bringing Burt's dreams and words to a new and wider audience. The photos—images of horrors past in this country and suggestions of abuses that continue elsewhere—also need to be widely seen. For like the refrain to Sam Cooke's song, too many in our field "don't know much about history." This skillfully woven compilation invites us on both a historical and futuristic tour that we dare not miss. We are guided through purgatory as well as policy conundrums the field has yet to solve. We hear prophetic calls for the closing of institutions as well as cautions in an era when we are legally obligated to become "our brother's treater." We learn of advocacy controversies that still rage and are prodded to work at changing mankind as the preferred path to reducing inhumanity. We are challenged not just to find good lawyers to battle a bad world, but to make a kinder world that has fewer injustices to fight.

In a time when writers in our field seem to know more and more about less and less, when too often the professional's prose squeezes the joy from language, we can turn to this volume for wide vistas and refreshment. A graceful and daring writer, Burt clearly loved turning the memorable phrase and tackling the great moral projects. He offers up no easy answers, reminding us of the searing words of Albert Camus, that "perhaps we can't stop the world from being one in which children are tortured but we can reduce the number of tortured children." In these pages, we have a mix of grand ideas and grandfatherly advice; a meditation on tragic events and heroic figures who struggle in their own way to make their piece of the world better. The tales are both familiar and exotic, like his account of the manager of Indonesia's only cash-starved institution who created a place that "smelled sweet," and was cleaner and more decent than the well-endowed institutions of Burt's homeland. These reports ultimately provoke haunting questions: In relationships with vulnerable people, how does goodness triumph in one place or human abuse take root in another? How do we first change ourselves in order to lead the balanced, humane, and soul-stirring life that Burt allows us to glimpse in this volume's brilliant concluding essay? How do we unlock our imaginations to dream wondrous possibilities, to accomplish great things? Enter these pages and find some of the clues.

Back in the dark days of 1970, at the height of our institutionalization mania, Burt Blatt courageously called for:

> a network of small community-centered residential facilities [linked to a]...total community program of pre-service and inservice training and research, collaborating with our best universities...[to tap students'] idealism, service, and professional skills. (p. 258)

The developmental disabilities field today heeds Burton Blatt's call. Community-based networks of services and value-based staff training programs capture Burt's mobilization of "idealism, service, and professional skills" and are designed to not only avoid the abuses but to recognize and unleash competency and achievement in all our clients.

To ensure that the voices of the poor and homeless, those with disabilities of mind or body, are not overlooked, we must resolve to hold fast to our long-term commitments to them and to our better selves. As I tell my students, from their ranks will come the future Judge Joseph Waddys (the judge in the landmark right to education case, *Mills v. Board of Education*, in 1972), the future Judge Patricia Walds (then cocounsel in that case, now a federal circuit judge), and the Gunnar Dybwads, women and men who will lend their voices and talents for those who are homeless or have disabilities, who will make some time on a *pro bono* or staff attorney basis or in whatever forms their careers take, to represent the underassisted, suffering segments of humanity. It is they who will serve a child in a special-education placement process or an adult in a shelter seeking a disability benefit as if that child's or adult's case is the most important one they will ever face. With their promising careers and capacities for service, with the collective will of good folks, evil will not triumph nor will indifference prevail over those who are homeless or have disabilities.

This is the ultimate triumph of Burton Blatt and all who share his humanist values. Recall his unapologetic chutzpah—a hidden camera on the belt of his collaborator and the photo essays published in 1966 in *Christmas in Purgatory* (Blatt & Kaplan, 1966, 1974) and *Look* magazine (Blatt, 1967)—that helped to shake the "out of sight, out of mind" blindness of the American public to people put away in places like Willowbrook. Now in a time of centrist complacency, in a time of a distracted Congress, we too must have the chutzpah to publicize the images that are tabooed, to reveal the abuses that others try to suppress. Now, in the twilight of the 20th century, we must resist a new era of indifference to human rights abuses abroad and creeping Social Darwinism at home. On this difficult stage of the journey, take Burt Blatt to heart. Gain strength from his words and dreams. Most of all, never become discouraged, and remember his stirring creed (Blatt, 1970, p. 259):

Believe that you are more than your brother's keeper. Believe that, while on this earth, you are his savior and he is yours.

References

Blatt, B. (1967). The tragedy and hope of retarded children. *Look, 31,* 96–103.

Blatt, B. (1970). *Exodus from pandemonium: Human abuse and a reformation of public policy.* Boston: Allyn & Bacon.

Blatt, B. (1981). *In and out of mental retardation: Essays on educability, disability, and human policy.* Austin, TX: Pro-Ed.

Blatt, B. (1984a). *In and out of books: Reviews and other polemics on special education.* Austin, TX: Pro-Ed.

Blatt, B. (1984b). *In and out of the university: Essays on higher and special education.* Austin, TX: Pro-Ed.

Blatt, B., & Kaplan, F. (1966). *Christmas in purgatory: A photographic essay on mental retardation.* Boston: Allyn & Bacon.

Blatt, B., & Ozolins, A., & McNally, J. (1979). *The family papers: A return to purgatory.* New York: Longman, Inc.

Syracuse Law Review. (1972). Symposium on the legal rights of the mentally retarded. *Syracuse Law Review, 23,* 991–1165.

Foreword

Seymour B. Sarason
Yale University

I am appreciative of the opportunity again to write about Burt fifteen years after his death. But before I do I shall start with my remarks at the memorial service for him. Reading his *Collected Papers* without a "picture" of the kind of person he was is a disservice both to Burt and the reader.

"There was a part of me that shrank from the task of writing today about Burton Blatt, because I knew that my powers of description and expression would be inadequate to instill in today's ritual the passion of this man, to convey the consequences of the vast vacuum his death has created, as the passion he engendered in us in his life and his death. Already I am aware how my words are dull brass compared to the gold of his person.

"Whether warranted or not, I am comforted by the thought that, aside from his wife, Ethel, I knew Burt in more ways over a longer period of time than anyone else. I shall endeavor to describe these ways in the hope that it will add depth to your relationship to or observation of Burt. I first met Burt not long after he got his doctorate and became chairman of the Department of Special Education at Southern Connecticut State College. My initial reaction to him was one of caution, indeed disbelief. Here was a guy who was ebullient, expressive of his feelings, friendly and outgoing, quick to praise, obviously ambitious, and yet amazingly uncompetitive. Amazingly uncompetitive, no trace of personal aggrandizement—those are very rare characteristics among academics. So I waited, observed, and tried to discern how and when those characteristics would emerge. They never did.

"I said that Burt was ambitious, and he was in two major ways. He wanted to make a difference in this world, to be recognized as someone who, intellectually and morally, had to be contended with, someone who thought and acted both distinctively and with distinction. But Burt was also ambitious for the setting, and those in it, for which he was administratively responsible. He never, and I repeat never, used the setting and those in it to enhance his personal-intellectual ambitions. Quite the contrary, he had a complete inability and unwillingness to use others for his purposes. I could give you instance after instance—at Southern, Boston University, Syracuse, and the Massachusetts Department of Mental Health—when he tolerated ineptness or inadequacies in others because he saw it as his obligation to try to help them to overcome their failings. In many of these instances he literally rescued people from themselves, and through his warmth, honesty, and support created the conditions that facilitate personal change. And when in other instances he was the bearer of bad news, he was as sensitive and helpful as he was forthright. He had that ability, very rare in administrators who are leaders, to distinguish between the obligations of his role and personal tastes.

"If he did not like someone, if he thought someone was or would be controversial, if he thought a person was critical of him, those were insufficient bases for not hiring that person, or not promoting him or her, or for keeping that person at a social or intellectual distance. What was good for the program, or department, or school—what would give it an air of excitement and ferment—was not necessarily good for Burt's personal equilibrium, but, as he knew, if it is too hot in the kitchen then get out. Burt never got out. On the contrary, the hotter the kitchen, the more he seemed to enjoy it and the more he and the kitchen seemed to thrive.

"What you have to understand is that Burt had a sense of personal and intellectual identity that did not depend on what others said about him. That identity was invulnerable to external judgment. His sense of what was right and what was wrong, what would stand up with time, and what would be consigned to the dust bin of history had a basalt-like strength. He would take seriously what others said about his research and writings, and he was quick to admit where he was wrong. He knew that he was imperfect; that far from knowing everything he wanted to know, what he did know was pitifully little; that what he wanted to grasp would always exceed his reach. Yes, he knew all that. No one was more honest with himself. But if he knew all that and it did not seriously disturb or deter him, it was because of that sense of identity and obligation that said: 'Burt, you know what is right, you know what is trivial and what is important, and you know that waging the right war is more important than if you win all the skirmishes and battles. How you are regarded in the present pales before the judgments of the future.' A poet once said that life takes its final meaning in chosen death. Burt's sense of identity and obligation defined his choice: to give no ground to cruelty, injustice, and other unseemly features of the human animal.

"Another covert characteristic of Burt that needs emphasis is that he was a religious person. Most of us who are Jewish are not religious but rather identify with the cultural-historical traditions that surround Judaism. Burt was religious in that he believed, within the context of formal Judaism, that what he did—what anyone did, Jewish or not—had meaning beyond human comprehension, there was mystery in this world and it was mystery that ultimately judged the worth of our lives. It was mystery that obligated him to revere life, to be intolerant of intolerance, and to constantly judge himself not by the fashions of the moment or by the transient plaudits of the crowd but by the standards of a final, mysterious, unknowable arbiter, however defined. To the secular mind Burt was an anomaly and he knew it, but he never paraded the existence of that internal compass although its existence directed everything he ever did. Because of that religious compass Burt was far harder on himself than he was on anyone else. Precisely because he believed in some ultimate reckoning, he willingly carried a burden that those without faith do not have. He demanded more of himself because of this religious faith. Burt and I rarely discussed religion. I respected and mightily envied him his faith. He never felt alone on this earth, that aloneness that in the modern era has become a curse.

"And now I have to tell you a story that illuminates the quintessential Burt. When *Christmas in Purgatory* had been completed, he sought to have it published by the Kennedy Foundation. Burt did not want to go the route of a commercial publisher; he wanted it disseminated as widely as possible with no material gain to himself. He met with Robert and Ted Kennedy. At that time Robert Kennedy was making (or about to make) a run for the senatorship from New York. I cannot recall accurately whether Ted Kennedy had already become a senator or was about to seek that post in Massachusetts. In any event, in light of the fact that the photographic essay portrayed the inhumane conditions in institutions in New York and Massachusetts, it was obvious that the two Kennedys could make a lot of political hay if the essay received the light of published day. They were eager to support its publication if, and only if, that essay named the institutions. Burt pointed out to them that he had given his word to an official in each of the institutions that he would never reveal the names of the institutions. And for obvious reasons: The careers of these officials would be at an end because they had aided the whistleblowers. The Kennedys tried to persuade Burt to name names. When he related this part of the story to me shortly after the meeting had taken place, Burt laughed softly, but with a trace of sadness, and said: 'Did they really think that I would go back on my word?' The soft laughter—and as you know, Burt rarely laughed softly—expressed his ironic amusement about how the Kennedys misjudged him. The trace of sadness reflected his pity for people who found it too easy to jeopardize others for their self-interest. Burt was ambitious and assertive but never hostile or aggressive. That he had hostile and aggressive thoughts goes without saying, but on the level of action I never saw or heard him say or do a hostile thing—and there were myriad occasions when the incitements to retaliate tested his limits.

"Burt was a romantic and this meant that he saw the world and those associated with him in optimistic terms. Although he did not believe that every day in every way the world was getting better and better, he did believe that it was a person's obligation to act as if he or she were capable of making it better. He did believe in the wish fulfilling prophecy: If you wanted to make the world better, if you acted accordingly, you would make your world a better one. Burt's romanticism explains one of his most endearing weaknesses: the tendency to idealize all who surrounded him, to talk only of their virtues and accomplishments, to play down and to seemingly ignore their all-too-obvious imperfections, however a part of him know otherwise. Early on I learned that if I wanted 'the truth' about anyone or any event in Burt's life, I had to do three things: listen to Burt, then listen to Ethel, and then listen to the two of them together. It was not that Burt was unrealistic and Ethel was realistic but rather that each had an amazingly firm grasp on a different aspect of reality. Burt was incomprehensible apart from his relationship to Ethel and, of course, his sons. But Ethel was the sounding board, the voice of another truth to which Burt listened. Ethel knew well that there was no stopping Burt once he decided that he had to take a certain course of action. He could count on her to speak her mind and not to subject him to the 'I told you so' reaction. Whatever Burt did in which he took pride, whatever recognition and eminence distinguished him, were for Burt symbolic gifts to Ethel and his sons. Family, nuclear and extended, was the centerpiece of Burt's existence.

"I continue to talk to Burt. Secular me, I confess enjoying the fantasy that he is watching and listening to this occasion, deeply touched by our feelings, but characteristically having difficulty believing that he made such a difference in our lives. My favorite book of Burt's is *Exodus From Pandemonium* (1970). His exodus from this world with dramatic poignancy emphasized how our own pandemonium has increased. If we had any doubt that this is not the best of all possible worlds, Burt's death should dispel that doubt."

Those who in the last decade have entered the field of special education are probably unaware how much of their perceptions and conceptions of the field derives from Burt's activities and writings. For example, for all practical purposes there is no controversy today about deinstitutionalization; we do not hear individuals and groups say that individuals with mental retardation should be removed from the community and placed in institutions. Institutionalized people with mental retardation were *always* a very, very small fraction of those who were so diagnosed. That fraction would probably have doubled or tripled if states had had the fiscal resources to build more warehouses. And that is the point: Community attitudes were supportive of these institutions even though every 10 years or so the moral squalor in these institutions would be exposed. Band Aids would be applied, the scandals then forgotten in the belief that wrongs had been righted. No *individual* more than Burt played as crucial a role in changing public attitudes and policy. Despite the historical record, I feel secure in saying that we will never return to the bad old days.

Burt's galactic contribution was primarily moral although by no means restricted to that. I say moral because he had the courage of a biblical prophet to expose evil, to alert his world both to its insensitivity and its obligations to the least of its inhabitants. But it was a morality powered by the belief that the least of us are not as "least" as our practices assumed. Burt took his morality as seriously as he did the possibilities of the educational process. I once heard him say to a critic, "Don't tell me what retarded people cannot do, tell me under what conditions they can learn and do more." That was not the reply of a do-gooder. More than anyone I ever knew, Burt could go on at length referring to studies done over the decades indicating that conventional wisdom about what people with mental retardation could learn under altered conditions did not support conventional wisdom. He was both a moralist and a scholar.

It would be an egregious mistake to talk about Burt only in terms of mental retardation. He was a generalist whose moral and psychological principles led him in his writing to analyze and criticize education in general, including higher education.

The field of education today lacks leaders: people who seek in diverse ways to alert our society to the inadequacies of our educational system, people who are activists and know that writing is but one way to alert the citizenry. Burt was in the best traditions of the muckrakers. When you expose "muck" you expose man's inhumanity to man or, at times, how the best of intentions supports the worst of consequences.

In the last decade I have had occasion to observe many special-education programs in public schools. In my talks with special-class teachers and administrators I would always seek in some way to bring up Burt's name, if only in an effort to indicate that I was knowledgeable about the field. Aside from the few usual exceptions, Burt's name was not known to most of them. I found and still find that incomprehensible. Regardless of our field, we all need and should have role models and heroes. At the very least I expect a professional to know the history of his or her field, because without such knowledge one's own sense of professional identity is an impoverished one. That explains why this collection of Burt's papers is such a source of satisfaction to me. It should be required reading for anyone now in the field or entering it.

Reference

Blatt, B. (1970). *Exodus from pandemonium: Human abuse and a reformation of public policy.* Boston: Allyn & Bacon.

Introduction

Steven J. Taylor and Steven D. Blatt

Do great leaders make history or does history make great leaders? This is probably a question best left to historians to ponder. For the rest of us, it is sufficient to know when history is being made and to appreciate the people who were prominent at the time.

The period from the mid-1960s through the early 1980s was a historical, if tumultuous, era in the field of mental retardation. During this era, events changed the landscape of services for people with mental retardation and their families. New philosophies and service approaches emerged during this time, and we continue to feel the after-effects of the dramatic changes of this period.

Few people figured more prominently in the changes that occurred during the 1960s and 70s in our field than the late Burton Blatt. Professor Blatt—Burt to just about everyone who knew him—was one of the first leaders in the field, along with Gunnar Dybwad and Seymour Sarason, to speak out against the horrific abuses of people with mental retardation in America's institutions in the mid-1960s. Burt did not merely condemn institutional conditions at professional meetings or in academic journals, although he did this. He committed what he sometimes referred to as the ultimate "indiscretion": He aired the profession's and the field's dirty secrets in public view. Through his book *Christmas in Purgatory* (Blatt & Kaplan, 1966), written with photographs taken by Fred Kaplan, and a widely read photographic exposé published in *Look* magazine (1967), he focused *public* attention on the "back wards" of public institutions for people with mental retardation. The institutions, and the field, would never be the same.

For those who are new to the field of mental retardation, it is difficult to describe the changes that have occurred over the past 25 to 30 years. In the 1960s and early 70s, institutionalization was the predominant—and in many places, exclusive—form of "treatment" for people with mental retardation. America's institutions housed nearly 200,000 people. Most institutions contained as many as several thousand people, with living units, called "wards," accommodating as many as 150 people with severe disabilities. Custodial care was poor, and programming was minimal or nonexistent.

Community services during this era were few and far between. Prior to the passage of Public Law 94-142 (now the Individuals with Disabilities Education Act) in 1975, public schools routinely excluded children with mental retardation. Families were faced with two choices: institutionalize their children or care for them 24 hours a day with no help.

The era was ripe for a person such as Burt Blatt, a person of courage and commitment who was willing to confront injustice and inhumanity. Following the publication of *Christmas in Purgatory* (Blatt & Kaplan, 1966) came exposés at Willowbrook State School in New York and eventually at institutions across the country.

Parents took their grievances to court, and federal judges started handing down far-reaching decisions establishing the right to education and ordering institutional reform and deinstitutionalization. The United States Congress passed a series of laws designed to benefit adults and children with disabilities. The parent movement and then self-advocates grew strong and demanded a role in setting public policy. Professionals not only developed new concepts—normalization, integration, inclusion, to name a few—but translated these concepts into new ways of supporting people with mental retardation and their families in the community.

The world is better for people with mental retardation and their families today because of leaders such as Burt Blatt.

It is, therefore, of historical interest to read the words of someone who was so instrumental in bringing about the changes that occurred in the field and the society. But this is more than a history book. Burt Blatt was a person of uncommon wisdom who offered timeless lessons for how we treat our fellow human beings.

As a person and as a Jew, Burt was haunted by the Holocaust. His work in the field of mental retardation was merely one expression of his need to understand "man's inhumanity to man." He was concerned not only about the treatment of people with mental retardation, but with the state of our civilization. As he wrote in the Preface to his book *Exodus From Pandemonium* (1970):

> The preparation of this volume has forced me to attempt to understand a little better one of the truly puzzling and frightening aspects of our civilization: the nature and conditions of human abuse. I had become so confused and so frightened by what I had seen and heard about man's treatment of his fellow man that I could no longer ignore the probability that, unless I struggled to understand inhuman treatment of humans, I would become either insensitive to such treatment (as I believe I had become) or I would not be able to tolerate my own relatively pleasurable life in the face of the Holocaust surrounding those of us unaffected. (p. xv)

Thus, the words of Burt Blatt need to be read—read and mulled over—not merely to understand a certain historical era, but to understand the age-old problem of human abuse, of inhumanity, that continues to plague us today. This is why Burt remains, more than 10 years after his death, one of the most widely cited and quoted authors in the field of mental retardation.

It is tempting to speculate on what Burt might have to say about the state of mental retardation services today. One cannot say with any certainty what he might have thought about our latest service approaches, current controversies, or the condition of our remaining institutions and expanding community service system. His book *The Family Papers: A Return to Purgatory* (Blatt, Ozolins, & McNally, 1979), published 10 years after his original exposé, probably provides the best clue about what he might have observed about the current state of the field of mental retardation: "As you will see, everything has changed during the past decade. As you will see, nothing has changed."

Burt Blatt was a prolific writer, an author of more than 300 articles, chapters, and books. He published not only research articles, essays, and monographs, but poetry and fiction as well.

It is impossible to publish in a single volume more than a small sampling of Burt's many writings. Each person who knows his work well—his former students and his many close colleagues—would make a unique selection of which of Blatt's writings should be published in a book of his collected papers. This volume contains merely one such selection of which of Burt's writings were most significant, meaningful, and inspirational.

Burt was the master of the metaphor and the play on words. As the selections in this book illustrate, his writing was filled with biblical images and quotations from classical writers such as Dante. Several of his books incorporated the phrase *in and out* in the title (*In and Out of Mental Retardation, In and Out of the University, In and Out of Books*). Perhaps this was a reference to the biblical book of Exodus or perhaps this reflected his ability to stand back from the worlds in which he was centrally involved and to view them from a fresh perspective. In any case, we have organized the selections of Burt's writings contained in this volume into four parts reflecting this "in and out" theme: "In and Out of Purgatory," "In and Out of Poetry," "In and Out of Human Policy," and "In and Out of the Professions."

In reprinting the writings contained in this volume, we have resisted the temptation to change Burt's language—specifically, the use of the male pronoun and "man" to refer generally to human beings as well as the lack of "people first" language—in accord with current conventions and sensitivities. Burt's language reflected the eras in which he was raised and in which he wrote. Regarding the lack of "people first" language, we also suspect that Burt might have argued, as he does in the pages that follow, that mental retardation is a metaphor and invented disease and not something that people "have."

The selected writings of Burton Blatt are followed by an Afterword by Steven Blatt, M.D., Burt's son and one of the coeditors of this volume. At the end of the volume, we provide brief a biographical sketch of Burt Blatt.

"There are many different reasons why people write books, and I had mine," wrote Burt in the Preface to *Exodus From Pandemonium* (1970). "Why did I write it?" he continued, "I wrote it for myself, which may not be a very good reason, but it's my reason…to give expression to my bewilderment and unhappiness with the very painful and slow progress of the humane in mankind."

So Burt wrote for himself. Aren't the rest of us extremely fortunate to be the beneficiaries of his need to write?

References

Blatt, B. (1967). The tragedy and hope of retarded children. *Look, 31,* 96–103.

Blatt, B. (1970). *Exodus from pandemonium: Human abuse and a reformation of public policy.* Boston: Allyn & Bacon.

Blatt, B. (1981). *In and out of mental retardation: Essays on educability, disability, and human policy.* Austin, TX: Pro-Ed.

Blatt, B. (1984a). *In and out of books: Reviews and other polemics on special education.* Austin, TX: Pro-Ed.

Blatt, B. (1984b). *In and out of the university: Essays on higher and special education.* Austin, TX: Pro-Ed.

Blatt, B., & Kaplan, F. (1966). *Christmas in purgatory: A photographic essay on mental retardation.* Boston: Allyn & Bacon.

Blatt, B., Ozolins, A., & McNally, J. (1979). *The family papers: A return to purgatory.* New York: Longman, Inc.

PART 1

In and Out of Purgatory

Fred Kaplan

Editors' Introduction to Part 1

Although Burton Blatt had published articles and reviews on the topics of the educability of intelligence and classification systems in mental retardation, it was the 1966 publication of his book *Christmas in Purgatory*, with photographer Fred Kaplan, and a subsequent article in *Look* magazine (Blatt & Mangel, 1967) that thrust him into the professional and public spotlight. The publication of these works represented the first of what Burt would later call his "indiscretion" at exposing the well-kept secret of the horrific conditions in America's institutions. The field of mental retardation would never be the same. It is certainly no coincidence that the populations of public institutions for people with mental retardation reached their peak the year in which the *Look* article was published and then began a steady decline that continues to this day.

Burt's writing was rich in the use of metaphors. He used the image of purgatory to represent the abusive and dehumanizing conditions in institutions. Part 1 starts with excerpts from *Christmas in Purgatory*, with sample photographs published in the book, followed by his subsequent reflections on reactions to this book in a "Postscript" in *Exodus From Pandemonium* (1970) and an address before the Massachusetts legislature.

As Burt noted in his Preface to *Exodus*, his horror at institutional conditions reflected his broader concern with the nature and conditions of human abuse. In a profound sense, institutional abuse was a metaphor for the cruel and inhuman treatment of human beings by human beings. Thus, we also reprint here Burt's "Leaves From a European Diary" in which he described his trip to Germany and attempt to understand the origins of the Nazi Holocaust.

This part concludes with excerpts from *The Family Papers: A Return to Purgatory* (Blatt, Ozolins, & McNally, 1979), a follow-up photographic essay to *Christmas in Purgatory* published 13 years later. In these excerpts we see the evolution of Burt's thinking about institutions. Although Burt was one of the first vocal advocates, along with Gunnar Dybwad and Seymour Sarason, for the creation of community services as an alternative to institutions in the 1960s, he also believed that the institutions could be reformed to be humane places for at least some people with mental retardation. By the 1970s, he had abandoned this belief and called for the evacuation of all institutions. In Burt's words: "imprisonment and segregation can be made more comfortable, but they can never be made into freedom or participation."

Enter, now, the gates of purgatory.

Christmas in Purgatory[2]

> "They cover a dung hill with a piece of tapestry when a procession goes by."
>
> *Miguel de Cervantes*

There is a hell on earth, and in America there is a special inferno. We were visitors there during Christmas, 1965.

During the early fall of that year, United States Sen. Robert Kennedy visited several of his state's institutions for the mentally retarded. His reactions to these visits were widely published in our news media. These disclosures shocked millions of Americans and infuriated scores of public office holders and professional persons responsible for the care and treatment of the mentally retarded.

A segment of the general public was numbed because it is difficult for "uninvolved" people to believe that in our country, today, human beings are being treated less humanely, with less care, and under more deplorable conditions than animals. A number of the "involved" citizenry—i.e., those who legislate and budget for institutions for the mentally retarded and those who administer them—were infuriated because the senator reacted to only the worst of what he had seen, not to the worthwhile programs that he might have. Further, this latter group was severely critical of the senator for taking "whirlwind" tours and, in the light of just a few hours of observation, damning entire institutions and philosophies.

During the time of these visits I was a participant in a research project at The Seaside, a State of Connecticut regional center for the mentally retarded. The superintendent of The Seaside, Fred Finn, and I spent a considerable amount of time discussing the debate between Senator Kennedy and his governor, Nelson Rockefeller. We concluded the following. It does not require a scientific background or a great deal of observation to determine that one has entered the "land of living dead." It does not require too imaginative a mind or too sensitive a proboscis to realize that one has stumbled into a dung hill, regardless of how it is camouflaged. It is quite irrelevant how well the rest of an institution's program is being fulfilled if one is concerned about that part of it which is terrifying. No amount of rationalization can mitigate that which, to many of us, is cruel and inhuman treatment.

It is true that a short visit to the back wards of an institution for the mentally retarded will not provide, even for the most astute observer, any clear notion of the antecedents of the problems observed, the complexities of dealing with them, or ways to correct them. We can believe that the senator did not fully comprehend the subtleties, the tenuous relationships, the grossness of budgetary inequities, the long history of political machinations, the extraordinary difficulty in providing care for severely mentally retarded patients, the unavailability of highly trained professional leaders, and the near-impossibility in recruiting dedicated attendants and ward personnel. But, we know, as well as do thousands of others who have been associated with institutions for the mentally retarded, that what Senator Kennedy claimed to have seen he did see. In fact, we know personally of few institutions for the mentally retarded in the United States completely free of dirt, filth, odors, naked patients groveling in their own feces, children locked in cells, horribly crowded dormitories, and understaffed and wrongly staffed facilities. After a good deal of thought, I decided to follow through on a seemingly bizarre venture. One of my close friends, Fred Kaplan, is a freelance photographer who has worked for many national publications. The following plan was presented to him. We were to arrange to meet with each of several key administrative persons in a variety of public institutions for the mentally retarded. If we gained an individual's cooperation, in spite of the obvious great risk he would be assuming with respect to his institutional status and possible job security, we would be taken on a "tour" of the back wards and those parts of the institution that he was *most* ashamed of. On the "tour" Fred Kaplan would take pictures of what we observed, utilizing a hidden camera attached to his belt. During the month of December 1965, we visited—at our own expense—five state institutions for the mentally retarded in four eastern states. Through the efforts of courageous and humanitarian colleagues, including two superintendents who put their reputations and professional positions in jeopardy, we were able to visit the darkest corridors and vestibules that humanity provides for its journey to purgatory and, without being detected by ward personnel and professional staff, Fred Kaplan was able to take hundreds of photographs.

The latter point deserves some comment. Our photographs are not always the clearest and, probably, Fred Kaplan is not proud of the technical qualities of every one published in this book. On the other hand, it required a truly creative and skilled photographer to take these pictures, "from the hip" so to speak, unable to use special lighting, not permitted to focus or set shutter speeds, with a small camera concealed in multitudes of clothing and surrounded by innumerable "eyes" of patients as well as of staff. Although our pictures could not even begin to capture the total and overwhelming

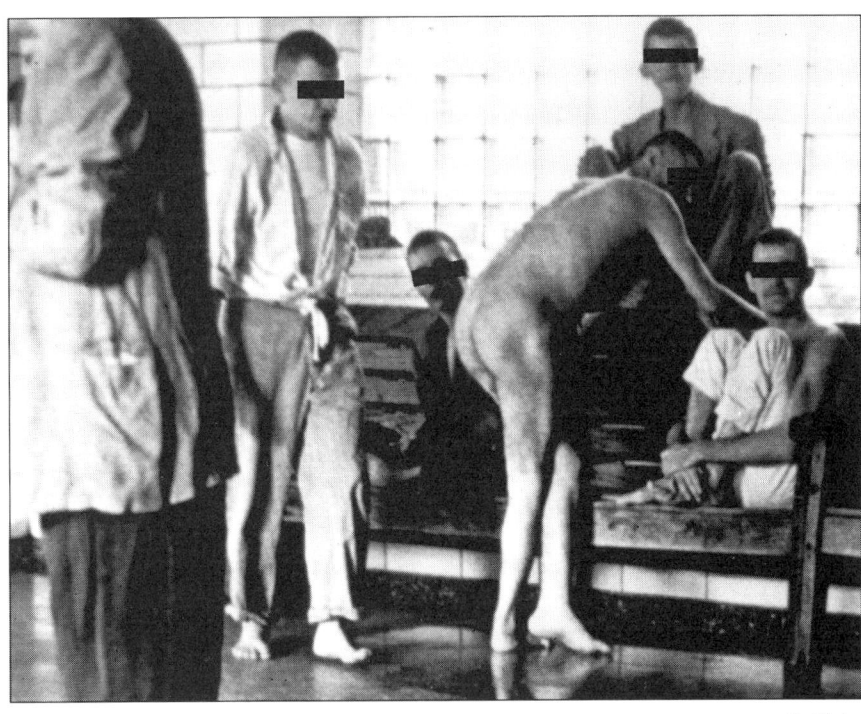

Fred Kaplan

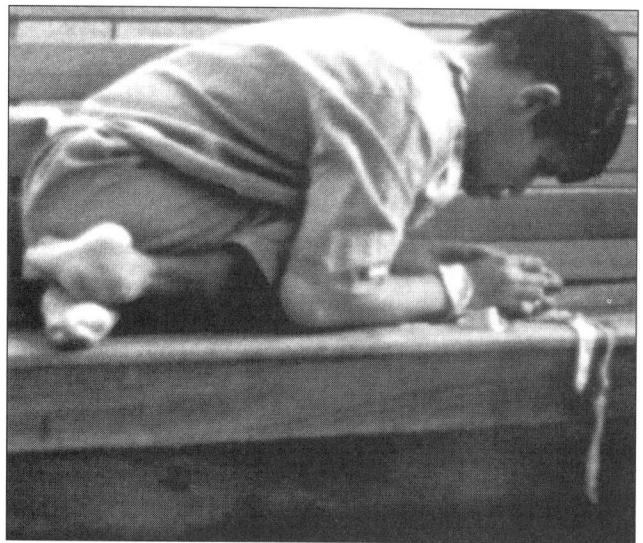

Fred Kaplan

horror we saw, smelled, and felt, they represent a side of America that has rarely been shown to the general public and is little understood by most of us.

We do not believe it is necessary to disclose the names of the institutions we visited. First, we have a deep debt of gratitude to those who permitted us to photograph that which *they* are most ashamed of. To reveal the names of the places we visited is, assuredly, an invitation to invite their instant dismissal. However, we have a much more forceful reason for not admitting to where we have been. These pictures are a challenge to all institutions for the mentally retarded in the United States. We are firmly convinced that in many other institutions in America we could have taken the same pictures—some, we are sure, even more frightening.

Our "Christmas in Purgatory" brought us to the depths of despair. We now have a deep sorrow, one that will not abate until the American people are aware of—and do something about—the treatment of the severely mentally retarded in our state institutions. We have again been caused to realize that "Man's inhumanity to man makes countless thousands mourn."

It is fitting that this book—our purgatory in black and white—was written on the 700th anniversary of the birth of Dante.

"I Sometimes Wish That God Were Back…"

"I sometimes wish that God were back
In this dark world and wide;
For though some virtues he might lack,
He had his pleasant side."

Gamaliel Bradford

In each of the dormitories for severely retarded residents, there is what is euphemistically called a day room or recreation room. The odor in each of these rooms is overpowering. After a visit to a day room we had to send our clothes to the dry cleaners to have the stench removed. The facilities often contribute to the horror. Floors are sometimes wooden and excretions are rubbed into the cracks, leaving permanent stench. Most day rooms have a series of bleacher benches, on which sit unclad residents, jammed together, without purposeful activity, communication, or any interaction. In each day room is an attendant or two, whose main function seems to be to "stand around" and, on occasion, hose down the floor "driving" excretions into a sewer conveniently located in the center of the room.

We were invited into female as well as male day rooms, in spite of the supervisor's knowledge that we, male visitors, would be observing naked females. In one such dormitory, with an overwhelming odor, we noticed feces on the wooden ceilings, and on the patients as well as the floors.

The question one might ask is, Is it possible to prevent these conditions? Although we are convinced that to teach severely retarded adults to wear clothes one must invest time and patience, we believe it possible to do so—given adequate staff. There is one more requirement. The staff has to be convinced that residents *can* be taught to wear clothes, that they *can* be engaged in purposeful activities, and that they *can* learn to control their bladders. The staff has to believe that their "boys and girls" are human beings who can learn. Obviously, the money and the additional staff are vitally important. However, even more important is the fundamental belief that each of these residents is a human being.

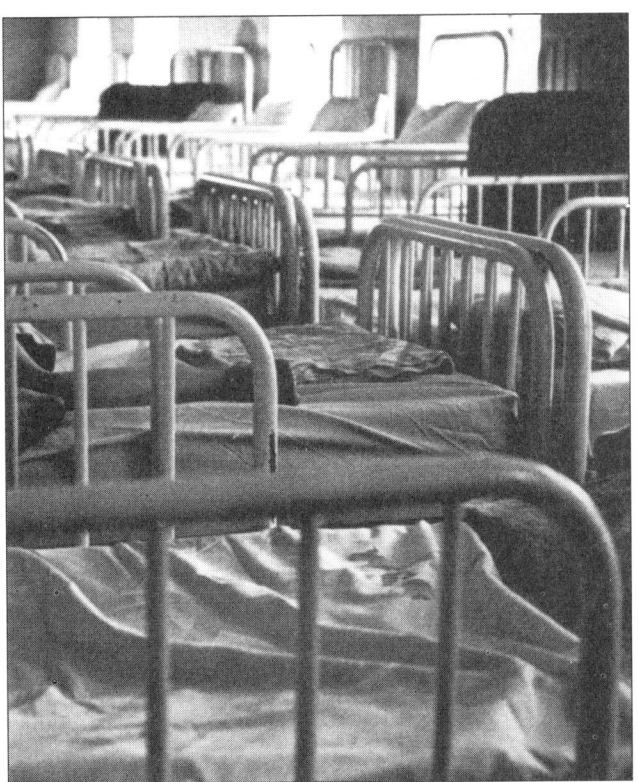

Fred Kaplan

"Suffer the Little Children…"

The infant dormitories depressed us the most. Here, cribs were placed—as in the other dormitories—side by side and head to head. Very young children, 1 and 2 years of age, were lying in cribs, without interaction with any adult, without playthings, without any apparent stimulation. In one dormitory, that had more than 100 infants and was connected to nine other dormitories that totalled 1,000 infants, we experienced a heart-breaking encounter. As we entered, we heard a muffled sound emanating from the "blind" side of a doorway. A young child seemed to be calling, "Come. Come play with me. Touch me." We walked to the door. On the other side 40 or more unkempt infants crawling around a bare floor in a bare room. One of the children had managed to squeeze his hand under the doorway and push his face through the side of the latched door. His moan was the clearest representations we have ever heard of the lonely, hopeless man. In other day rooms, we saw groups of 20 and 30 very young children lying, rocking, sleeping, sitting—alone. Each of these rooms was without toys or adult human contact, although each had desperate-looking adult attendants "standing by."

In another dormitory, we were taken on a tour by the chief physician who was anxious to show us a child who had a very rare medical condition. The doctor explained to us that, aside from the child's dwarfism and misshapen body, one of the primary methods for diagnosing this condition is the deep guttural voice. In order to demonstrate this, he pinched the child. The child did not make any sound. He pinched her again, and again—harder, and still harder. Finally, as if in desperation, he insured her response with a pinch that turned into a gouge and caused the child to scream in obvious pain. In some of the children's dormitories we observed "nursery programs." What surprised us most was their scarcity and

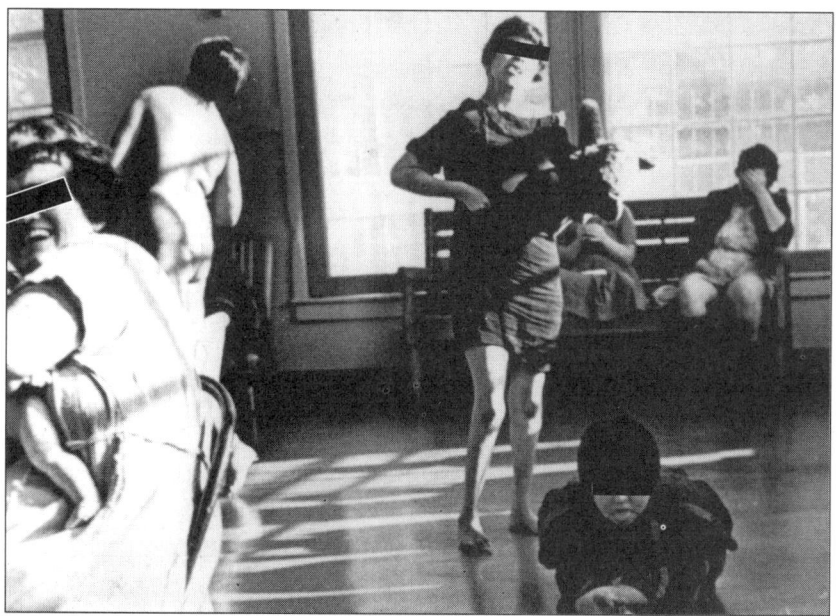

Fred Kaplan

the primitiveness of those in operation. Therefore, we were not unprepared to see several children with severe head lacerations. We were told those were "head bangers." Head banging is another condition that some people think is inevitable when confronted with young severely mentally retarded children. We challenge this. We have reason to believe that head banging can be drastically reduced in an environment where children have other things to do.

The "Special Education" we observed in the dormitories for young children was certainly not education. But it was special. It was among the most especially frightening and depressing encounters with human beings we have ever experienced.

Postscript[3]

It is not necessary here to discuss the flood of extraordinary encouraging mail and calls that I have received in response to the first edition of *Christmas in Purgatory*. It may be instructive to mention some of the negative, or otherwise puzzling, comments and hectoring that came to me.

One well-intentioned clergyman believes that I exhibited bad taste in reproducing photographs of nude men and women. An acquaintance in our field thinks our use of concealed camera immoral and he believes our work to be fake, comparing the atypical worst I had seen with "posed pictures" theatrically staged at The Seaside. A wise and beloved commissioner of mental health asked me if these conditions exist in his state's institutions. (How can I tell him about something he, as the principal responsible officer, should be aware of—and doing something about?) In another state that I have deep feeling for, a legislator who has championed mental health legislation circulated copies of *Christmas in Purgatory* in the vain hope that it would help in the passage of social welfare legislation. He received scant support from his own party which did not want the "opposition governor" to gain stature through such legislation in, this, an election year. The bill appeared doomed for many weeks, but subsequently passed, due, I have been informed, in some part to the influence of our book.

Albert Camus wrote, "Again and again there comes a time in history when the man who dares to say that two and two make four is punished with death." I have written the truth, as plainly and as simply as I see it—not for power or for fame, for there has been precious little of either connected with this assignment and there has been a good deal of grief. I would be surprised if this work changes radically the nature of institutions. My current depression will not permit such grand thoughts. On the other hand, Camus wrote further, "Perhaps we can't stop the world from being one in which children are tortured but we can reduce the number of tortured children."

In spite of those who protest this presentation, there will be no turning back; the truth can no longer be concealed. Some good must come from all this pain and anguish to so many institutionalized residents and their families. Once seeds are sown, one only has to wait for the crop to harvest. It has also been said that, when the bellman is dead, the wind will not toll the bell.

So hurry wind! Or revive yourselves noble bellringers.

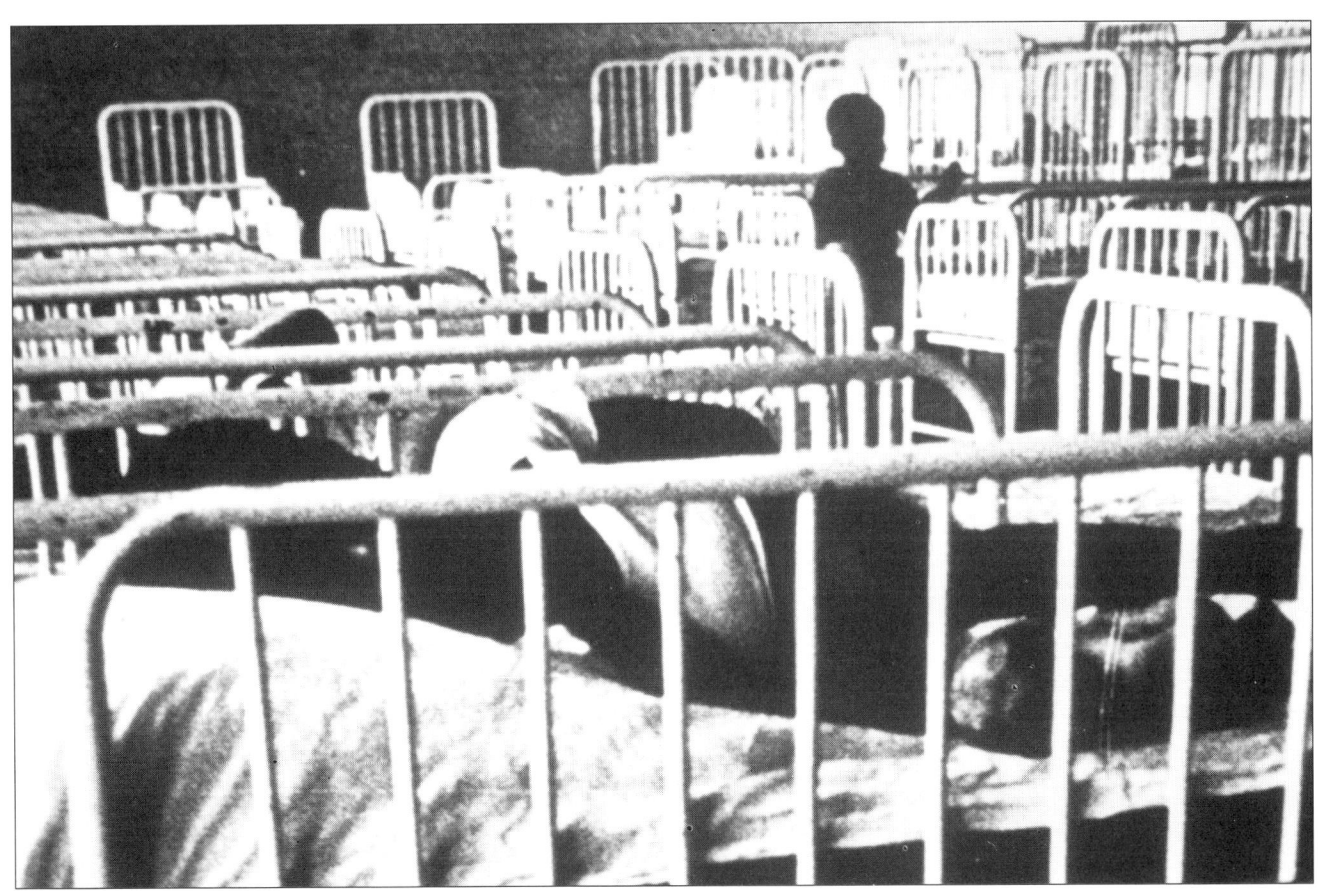

Fred Kaplan

Reprinted by permission of Steven D. Blatt and the Blatt family.

THE DARK SIDE OF THE MIRROR[4]

In 1949 I started a teaching career and serious study with the mentally retarded. In the subsequent years, I learned some valuable lessons concerning this human condition. Notably, from the inspiration and clinical acumen of three great teachers and one institutional administrator, I began to understand and appreciate several major concepts concerning behavior, concepts that have been verified repeatedly during interactions with those generous children and families who welcomed my intrusions into their lives. I learned, or do not disbelieve, that:

1. Man traditionally underestimates his potentials for changing or, to use a more common term, for learning.

2. Man's pessimism concerning the conditions of change becomes a self-fulfilling prophecy. We don't learn when we become convinced that we can't or when we become convinced that we shouldn't.

3. Given proper conditions, it can be demonstrated that intelligence is a function of practice and training. That we have not been able to guarantee such behavioral modification is, I believe, less a defect of our theory than it is of our practice.

4. I believe in a design of things, I believe there is some spiritual workmanship about. And, I believe, the design for all of us holds nothing but good.

But there is a dark side of every mirror, a side beyond inspection because it is without thought. And while the optimism and pride—the light—of our lives is for the gains made in civil rights, for our achievements in mental health, for the concept of the Declaration of Independence and the Constitution, surely a dark side in the evolution of our civilization in this mid-20th century must be reserved for the deep unremitting, unrewarding lives of drudgery and pain we inflict upon our institutionalized brothers who are called severely mentally retarded.

As some of you may know, I have recently completed a study of children and adults in state institutions for the mentally retarded *(Christmas in Purgatory: A Photographic Essay on Mental Retardation)*. It was my purpose to describe in words and pictures the treatment of the retarded in these institutions, point out some of the more serious imperfections of their programs, and suggest ways to prevent or ameliorate problems. I expected that men of goodwill from all walks of life and all professions would then sit down at the planning table and seek viable solutions to the issues uncovered. It is not necessary here to discuss my findings, my recommendations, or the flood of extraordinary encouraging mail and calls I received in response to this study. However, it may be instructive to mention that some of the reactions to the project were negative. I was subjected to mild direct hectoring and a good deal of indirect and second-hand pejorative assaults. I had undertaken the study of institutions and written the truth, as plainly and as simply as I saw it. As some of you may know, there is little reward in exposing the ugliness (or beauty) of certain truths. It can be a dangerous business.

The view I am about to share with you today is no less to me than our photographic essay—in spite of its impressionism, its vagueness, its distorted textures and freely associated constructions. This is the stuff of which nightmares are made and, if you will permit me, I will share mine with you. I have been to many state institutions for the mentally retarded, before and subsequent to the just-mentioned study. It is fitting that we concern ourselves today with one local state school. I accede to this reasonable decision. On the other hand, my remarks have a much more general applicability.

I have been to the depths, believing all the time that I would awaken, as I always had before, from this most terrifying of all nightmares. And, as I always had before, I did awaken—to the mawkish horror and degradation of N. and W. Buildings. I have walked beside their soiled waters where, floating gently by their day room shores, were the human flotsam and jetsam, the wasted and unfulfilled programs, hopes and plans of countless generations of discouraged failures who were once known in these buildings as patients, attendants, and professional staff. I have filled my nostrils and inflated my lungs in N. Building until every pore of my body felt the nauseating zing of 70 years of cankered rot that will continue to generate *ad infinitum* until the seams of N.'s construction burst at the top and at the bottom and at its sides, until its cup of human refuse and despair runs over and drowns us all or causes us to realize, in time, what grief we perpetrate there. I have sat in its day room, surrounded by desperately lonely patients huddled together in their nakedness of body and spirit, defenseless against the elements, defenseless against assaults to their persons, to their souls, and to their consciousness. I have seen a hand reach out for human contact—if not for ennobling friendship—only to see it struck down by the fear and confusion of its intended recipient, as he was struck down by the fear and confusion of another recipient, as he was struck down, as he was struck down—*ad nauseam*.

If these remarks this day communicate any of my deepest thoughts and hopes, it should become very clear that I do not believe we can correct the blight of an N. Building and the plight of its residents with a new set of curtains, or a new paint job, or modern plumbing, or increased attendant staff there, or new words and slogans. In the past, to one degree or another, all of these shibboleths and gestures were implemented and found wanting. All were enveloped by the mire of that totally oppressive environment. We do not suffer so much the lack of structural architects and interior designers as we do the absence of ideational architects and moral interventionists.

It is not that the amenities and courtesies are not appreciated. They are, for they demonstrate that, essentially, the conditions at N. Building are *not* due to evil people. They are *not* due to more incompetent or mendacious people than one finds in any large sociopolitical organization, such as are found in your insufficient capital budgets and ludicrous per capita operating costs. Obviously, a more appropriate financial structure, a more tangible and pervasive method to encourage the considerable number of dedicated and enlightened individuals who are employed at the school, and better ways to cashier those who are incompetent, will reduce many of the problems you observe here and will make life habitable for those whose lives are now intolerable.

However, significant change, meaningful change, change all of us can be truly proud of, change that will result in objectively superior residential treatment—not subjectively relative improvement—will not obtain until we alter our conceptions of human potential and our methodologies implementing those conceptions. In addition to a far greater share of the public treasure; in addition to more competent, more numerous and more available staff; in addition to much smaller living and training units, we must develop more optimistic convictions concerning the abilities and potentials of those we call mentally retarded, however severe that retardation may be. The prophecy of incompetency and vegetation associated with the mentally retarded is self-fulfilling. Equally self-fulfilling can be the prophecy of competency and achievement.

I have irrefutable evidence, from 18 years of clinical experience in the field of mental retardation, that NO RESIDENT needs to live in a denuded state, needs to be a head banger, or needs to be locked in solitary confinement. I have irrefutable evidence that practically every resident can be taught to eat meals independently, can be taught to live among his fellows without being in danger to himself or others and without the use of physical restraints. I have irrefutable evidence that *all* building odors can be eliminated without the need for even more powerfully repugnant chemical treatments or electronic gadgetry that masks the sources of these odors but does not eliminate the causes: filth and neglect. I have very substantive evidence that intelligence is educable, that is, people can change—learn—and that this concept applies both to the retarded and those who minister to their needs. It applies to us too. We can change in our conception of human potential and, thus, we can promote change in others. The lives of Anne Sullivan and Helen Keller speak volumes about this concept, as do the lives of Jean Itard and Victor, the Wild Boy of Aveyron.

It is my hope that our governor, our legislature, and commissioners who have faith in these immodest claims will encourage us to develop a network of small community-centered residential facilities, interrelated with a total community program of pre-service and in-service training and research, collaborating with our best universities where students in medicine, nursing, social work, education, and psychology may be employed during the course of their training, and may devote to our common need and common good their idealism, service, and professional skills. From such endeavors, we will develop new pathways and new models and new and vigorous ideas and ideals to better comprehend and confront that complex devastation, mental retardation. Without such approaches, we will continue to divert overwhelming problems with flimsy thoughtless plans. We will continue to fertilize huge deserts with watering cans. Without such approaches, for every N. Building we demolish we will participate in the procreation of a new—equally large—residency which will be little more than the portrait of N. Building as a child.

This address need not be necessary to convince you of the imperative need to—*at least*—destroy forever the physical structures and the symbolic disease represented by N. and W. Buildings at our state school. Some men dedicate their lives to build edifices. Before *we* can build, we must first dedicate ourselves to systematic annihilation. That these buildings continue to exist is either a massive indictment of our collective intelligence and relatedness or a colossal testament to human inertia or our incompetence. All that would be necessary to convince you that the danger point was reached many generations ago, that the point of no return—the time for physical and conceptual demolition—was passed before the oldest in this assembly was born…all that would be necessary would be to lead you now to these buildings.

"The triumph of evil requires only that good men do nothing." Good men do something; do not turn away from these blights we call N. and W.! Do not rest until you can guarantee to all of our citizens that these buildings, wherever they exist in our Commonwealth, no longer serve the gods of pain, sorrow, and chronic hopelessness. And do not rest until, across the land, the hundreds of these buildings—and the philosophies they breed—are laid to their unholy eternal damnation.

A little child we knew and loved was buried a few days ago and my wife and I, in shocked awe, pondered the senselessness of a life taken almost before it was lived. However, Michael did not live and, as all of us must, he died. Although his life was too brief, Michael lived a good life. We rejoiced in his life and now mourn his death. But the funerals for those in N. and W. Buildings come not with death but in life. For them, it is life that is the terrible avenger; it is life we mourn. And as we are part of this grand design, we mourn for ourselves and for our helplessness.

Believe that you are more than your brother's keeper. Believe that, while on this earth, you are his savior and he is yours.

Reprinted by permission of Steven D. Blatt and the Blatt family.

Leaves From a European Diary[5]

August 27, 1968; 2:00 A.M., Natick, Massachusetts

One year ago today, Edward (then age 13), Steven (10), Michael (7), my wife, Ethel, and I, boarded a plane for return home to Natick, Massachusetts. Our trip had begun on June 11, and during the ensuing 11 weeks we visited the Scandinavian countries, the British Isles, Luxembourg, France, Austria and, for 7 weeks, West Germany. Of all the places on Earth, why should we set foot in that dread land, that inspired Dachau, Auschwitz, Treblinka, and *100 others?*

Several years ago, Boston University developed overseas graduate programs in a few selected fields, primarily for servicemen and teachers assigned to American dependent schools in the European theater. One such program is in the field of education, and I had been asked to teach my course "Nature and Needs of the Mentally Retarded" during one of the summer sessions sponsored in Germany. After considerable family discussion, over a period of several months, we agreed to participate in this program. The plan was for all of us to travel to Munich for a briefing period early in June, drive to Heidelberg for participation in the graduation ceremonies for the preceding year's students, teach a 3-week intensive course in Stuttgart, and return to Munich for a repeat of the Stuttgart course. At the conclusion of that assignment, we would have one full month remaining for travel through Scandinavia and the British Isles.

What were the advantages, as we envisioned them then, and what were the liabilities of such a plan? The opportunity presented would permit our family to spend 3 months together, much of this time free to explore, to visit the museums, to enjoy the scenery and countryside. This opportunity would permit a retreat, albeit temporary, from what had been a very rigorous year and what was expected to be a continuation of work pressure and personal demands once the new academic calendar and schedule dominated the fall season.

Why did we hold back, have reservations about this trip, refuse an identical invitation of the previous year? It was Germany! Why couldn't we be asked to teach in France, or England, or—better yet—Israel? That which at first had made us hesitant about going to Germany later made me resolute, determined to live for a period of time in that land. I must admit that my determination to go to Germany, once I had made up my mind, was a minority position in our household, as well as a selfish one. Further, my reasons for this determination did not fully crystallize until we were firmly ensconced in that country. From the time when the possibility of a summer in Germany first presented itself until our plane landed in Munich, I had been slowly—but increasingly—developing the notion that it would be important for me to observe and study the German people, in light of the Holocaust of the 30s and 40s, a period in history to which I had become morbidly attached. It was not until several weeks after our arrival that I began to think seriously, in fact regularly, about the striking correlates of Nazi Germany and its concentration camps and American mental health and its institutions for the retarded. That summer in Europe gave me a perspective of things that increases in importance as I review them.

It is hoped that this presentation of selected passages from that summer's diary—impressions recorded not with any thought for eventual publication but in keeping with the roles we were assuming as travelers and tourists—will contribute something toward comprehending mankind's capabilities for destruction, and the conditions that appear to be present during these periodic barbarisms in which human beings participate. I had already spent considerable time observing attendants in some of our most wretched back wards. I have spoken to these men and women, calmly and rationally, eye to eye. Now, I wanted to observe the German citizen, speak to him calmly and rationally, eye to eye. I wanted to visit Dachau and try to understand what was then—and now—an incomprehensible and fiendish period of inhuman history. Certainly, these excerpts can make no pretension insofar as unraveling the puzzle of the Third Reich or understanding the German culture as it is known today. Far more sophisticated and erudite attempts toward these kinds of understandings are available to the reader. However, these impressions may be useful within the context of a book on human abuse. There is no doubt in my mind, after reading too many histories and personal accounts of the German death camps, that the Germany of our generations will be recorded as the most savage, inhuman, ungodlike tribe ever to inhabit this Earth, the likes of which we pray will never be seen again. For one interested in the foundations of human abuse, in retrospect, it seems clear that the German people should be studied from every angle possible, with even an *ex post facto* analysis likely to prove valuable.

June 17, 1967: 6:15 P.M., Bayrischer Hauf, Heidelberg

Most aspiring Germans carry briefcases. I am told these are used to store lunch and other necessities. Usually, middle class workers—both male and female—carry these briefcases, although some blue collar workers also find them valuable accessories. Those blue collar workers who do not carry briefcases, oftentimes an "old time factory hand" or "laborer," generally wear what we in American call "laboratory coats." Some workers wear boots and knickerbockers. All bellhops wear green aprons and bus and street car conductors have uniforms identical to my stereotyped conception of a German military officer. It must be an overreaction, but my impressions lead to the conclusion that there is some design to all of this.

June 20, 1967: 3:45 P.M., Robinson Kaserne, Stuttgart

From a few discussions and observations, it is clear that the Germans build private homes to last at least a hundred years. It isn't unusual for a family to buy a modest home, which is terribly expensive, after many years of saving. Unfortunately, the family cannot possibly keep up the mortgage payments with their family income. So they buy the house to rent it, using income from the rental to meet mortgage payments. During these many years of mortgage obligations, the family that owns the home lives in a small apartment elsewhere or in a small section of the house, oftentimes the basement. The plan is to complete the mortgage payments sometime before the retirement of the head of the household when, at that time, the family moves into their "new home."

One may ask why this is necessary in order, eventually, to own a home. And why is housing so expensive? One would think that the Germans—especially the Germans—would have the affluence to be able to afford to purchase, and live in, homes in the same way that Americans do. I don't have the depth to understand the so-called German mentality, if there is such a special mentality. However, I do know that their homes are built to last many generations. The walls are very thick, aplastic, sensible, dark, and functional. Don't make it fragile, elegant, or graceful. What that country might need is a Levitt and a Levittown. It seems to me that, especially in Germany, less permanent-type homes would be an appealing economy. There doesn't seem to be much point in building a home to last a hundred years, while, at the same time, preparing for or waging wars that destroy the homes every 30 years.

June 23, 1967: 1:15 A.M., 77 Lembach Strasse, Stuttgart

We spent the best part of a beautiful day in Killesberg Park, a short walk from our house. This park is dedicated to the millions of Jews killed in German concentration camps and, ironically, it must be the most beautiful park we have ever been in. The Germans enjoy and take care of their parks, which are very safe and comforting. Everywhere around us is kindness, consideration, dignity, and contentment. The Germans are not arrogant about their language. Unlike the French (so we've been told) they will try to understand you and help you if you make an attempt to speak their language. They have no false pride, so it seems, when confronted with a fumbling tourist who is trying to communicate while relying on long-forgotten high school German and faint remembrances of a grandmother's Yiddish. How could these kind, thrifty, and bright people have participated in such horror? Killesberg Park, and the people we encountered there, do not make sense in the light of history.

July 8, 1967: 7:00 P.M., The Grand Hotel, Nuremberg

In this city where the Trials were held, I compared my daily observations of Black GIs with the riots and troubles in the States that are reported here daily. I have noticed—possibly wrongly—that the Black GI in Germany is less alienated, less alone, more integrated in the army than in Boston, Massachusetts, or anywhere else in civilian life with which I am acquainted. I have noticed no special groups of Black GIs, but rather, Blacks and Whites together. I don't want this reaction to appear to be something it shouldn't. However, compared to what I have seen in the United States, Black GIs in Germany seem to have a better deal than Black civilians in New Jersey.

Why do we have prejudice? This diary, now to the point of embarrassment, continues to disclaim any special insights or depth concerning the questions raised. However, I have noticed that most of the poverty, misery, and suffering in the world is in the Southern Hemisphere. So-called "civilization" is in the Northern Hemisphere. Color seems to be less important as a determiner of either income or racial bias than is place of residence. Men of color populate the Northern Hemisphere and are not viewed—because of their color—in pejorative ways, e.g., the Chinese and Japanese. It almost seems as if color isn't inferior; the South is or the heat is. White isn't superior; the cold is. What might be needed is not more civil rights legislation but a good cold wave in the Southern Hemisphere or continent-to-continent air-conditioning.

What are the trappings of the favored? Geographically, living in the temperate zone is tremendously important, probably necessary. We must also include such items as: a religion, preferably Christianity; whiteness; cleanliness; the written work, monogram; and taking the past seriously (e.g., museums, antiques, catalogues, tours). Symptoms of the favored are ties, briefcases, symbolic expressions of wealth, Culture. Most of the favored can be located in Western Europe, the British Isles, and North America (with the possible exception of Mexico), and Japan, which is becoming White in attitude. The USSR will soon be favored as any nation and is now, practically "White." China is "Red." Soon they will be colored "White." Find a little "Blue" and you have Old Glory, McCarran Act and all.

July 11, 1967: 5:15 P.M., McGraw Kaserne Munich

We went to Dachau today. It's a short, pleasant drive on the autobahn from Munich to Dachau, really just a few kilometers before reaching the autobahn exit sign "Dachau." After a drive of about 4 kilometers through level farmland, you arrive in the middle of the town. We stopped a passing pedestrian, asking, "Pardon, wo ist der koncentrazion kamp?" in our best school German and pidgin Yiddish-English-gesture. No response! Possibly, the pedestrian was a stranger in Dachau or didn't understand you. So, you ask again, and again, and again. You don't give up. You ask, in a German dialect that has been very well understood until now. "Where is the concentration camp where 200,000 Jews, French, and clergymen from many nations were tortured during the years 1933-1945?" You ask, "Where in your town are the crematorium and mass graves?" Finally there is an answer from a man you were able to intimidate sufficiently to respond to your, by now, enraged questions, "Ah! Sie gehen zudem Americana kamp!" You don't understand the answer, but you get the directions and, within a kilometer or two, you are standing at the entrance to the infamous Dachau KZ.

Certain things must be cleared up. Is this Kamp so unknown to the local population or is our German so poor that our inability to locate the camp was the result of unintentional roadblocks—nonfeasance rather than malfeasance? What did my informer mean by "the Americana kamp"? I'll try to answer those questions, and hopefully unravel a number of puzzles that confronted us this morning in Dachau. First, anyone who lives in Dachau must know exactly where the concentration camp is and how to get there. Literally, one can see the camp from parts of the town. Secondly, to date, more than 300,000 people from 30 different countries have visited the camp. Since the camp has been developed as a memorial and museum, it appeared impossible that any citizen of this small town had not been asked directions to the camp on innumerable occasions. The most frequent answer I received to my question for directions to the Kamp was, "Es gibt kein koncentration kamp heir in Dachua" ("There is no camp…"). Lastly, the Kamp is called the "Americana Kamp" by the townspeople because, after the World War II, our army occupied Germany and, to this date, we have not returned this camp to the German Republic. That is, in a legal and technical sense, the Dachau Concentration Camp is an American camp. This is one instance where changing the label cannot remove the history or the stench of the product.

July 12, 1967: 10:35 A.M., 17 Badelschwingh Strasse, Munich

More on Dachau. The first German concentration camp was opened here on March 22, 1933. During the ensuing 12 years, 13 million defenseless human beings were slaughtered by the flower of Germany. There is little I can say that hasn't already been much more eloquently said. What struck us, really hit us hard, was the list in the museum of all the concentration camps and the destruction each had wrought. Imagine, more than 100 such hells strategically placed both in Germany and conquered nations! As you visit the crematorium, the grave sites, and the memorials—as you examine the documents on display in the museum—over and over is the reminder, "Remember us. Do not forget." You see a warning to the living, for all time to come or until there are no longer any people, "Help us to testify of the past. Help us to protect the future." And as you see pictures that, two generations later, can torture, you ask, "How can anyone have participated in such barbarism?" And when you look across the bucolic splendor of Bavaria, passing idle moments in pleasant conversation with a good man, a decent and honest German, answers don't come easily.

How can these good Germans continue to live in the town of Dachau, with a constant reminder of their inhuman past? How can a young family move into a new garden apartment, a couple hundred yards from the entrance to the concentration camp? How can the townspeople claim ignorance of what transpired in a camp located on Route 471 that existed for a dozen years, almost in the middle of a town? How can they plead ignorance and why do we believe them? It's too frightening to remember the terror they participated in and it's too frightening for us to disclaim their innocence. Human beings can understand—even tolerate—pathology or sickness among some of our less fortunate. However, it is probably too terrible to contemplate an evil such as Germany perpetrated. A conspiracy of the sick and degenerate and psychopathic is unpleasant but manageable. We must remove these sick ones from the mass, the healthy, the group that can be called human beings. A conspiracy of this kind led by the cream of the nation, the harvest of its years of toil and drudgery, is an affront to all mankind. It is an assault on our personal eminence as human beings and it demonstrates what man is capable of, given certain conditions and opportunities.

To understand Nazi Germany—to comprehend what drove them to their terrible misdeeds—will lead to our understanding the treatment of Blacks in the United States, our past treatment of the American Indians, and the care we provide for the mentally retarded in the back wards of our state institutions. To understand Nazi Germany, or to understand the background to any of the evils mentioned, is to help unravel what I consider the most important and basic problem known to man. What are the conditions required before a man can abuse another man? I cannot believe that the abuse of individuals, or, for that matter, the abuse of groups proceeds in a random or haphazard manner. I believe that the proper study of human abuse will reveal a theory leading to understanding the factors that give rise to it. The results of this study may, some day, provide us with ways to prevent human abuse or—at the very least—sublimate or mitigate mankind's apparent need to inflict pain and cruelty.

July 17, 1967: 9:20 A.M., Bachelor Officers' Quarters, Garmish

We were invited to the Casa Carioca International Ice Review last night by two friends we had met in the States. After what really was a most enjoyable ice show, all of us went to a local restaurant for coffee. We talked about many things, including responsibility, even had a mild argument. The husband is an unusual man who has remained a classroom teacher for many years despite strong pressures from government school authorities to promote him to one or another administrative post. I understand completely his decision in this matter, and both congratulate him and agree with his logic. However, the point I made to him was that if part of his decision were dictated by an absence of any personal ambition, then I should understand with reluctance and regret. People who have little personal ambition may be as dangerous to society, possibly more so, as those who have driving personal ambition. People without ambition, but with talent, abrogate the positions they should have taken (or sought) to those with the ambition (but not always with the talent). One shouldn't overstate the line of this logic but, in these troubled times, one must at least raise the question as to how much individual freedom a man has in accepting or rejecting responsibility. There may be a kind of collective concern that each individual must respect with whatever insight he has to bring to bear on the decision.

We discussed Dachau with them; the husband had visited there, and his German wife had lived in Munich during the war. His wife, who is a wonderful woman, doesn't appear to feel any more personal guilt about such places as Dachau than most Americans would feel about institutions in the States where atrocities have been known to occur. I believe she feels a kind of responsibility as a citizen of the Third Reich. However, I don't believe she feels any individual responsibility for Hitler, the KZ, or the 13 million humans slaughtered. Who can fault her? The ambivalence and vacillation between the horror I saw at Dachau and the horrors I am acquainted with in the United States trouble me and, at the same time, permit me to understand something about how abusive situations are allowed to arise and to continue unchecked by "civilized" people. Don't most of us in the United States deny any individual responsibility for the "Black problem," the "migrant worker problem," and the problem of back wards in state institutions?

July 20, 1967: 11:30 A.M., 17 Badelschwingh Strasse, Munich

We had a marvelous day yesterday visiting the great Munich art museum, Alte Pinakotheck, with George and Julie Tsiramokes. George is a major in the air force, stationed with the American consulate in Munich. Some random thoughts: (1) Why are we surprised with reports of brutality, murder, and terror coming from the emerging African countries? After spending a day at the incredible Alte Pinakothek, one must become convinced that the relationship between Culture and Decency is a very obscure one, if it exists at all. It is probably true that the Germans weren't cannibals. Their industrial inventiveness led them to manufacture lamp shades. (2) Toilets in public places are sometimes free to the user, but more often there is a charge of 10 to 20 pfennigs. At such public toilets where there is a charge, the attendant, from 70 to 80 years old, lurches about the foul smelling men's room, placing the fees collected in nondescript, grubby-looking folds of clothing. It seems to be an affront to the dignity of old age to permit someone (anyone) to work at this occupation. First, the smell is horrid (which questions the tradition of German cleanliness). Second, it desexualizes this woman who, by the very nature of her work, is either a disinterested observer of male genitalia or a female voyeur (a neat trick at 80). On the other hand, after occasional visits to nursing homes in the United States, it is difficult to decide which of the two would be the more appealing existence. (3) Every day, I have been reading reports of riots in Newark and Detroit and New York. Today, suburbia is good; the city is not good. It hasn't always been that way. Most of us can remember when the "poor" countryman left the farm for the luxury and richness of the city. When he came in sufficient numbers to the city, the wealthy cityman (whom the countryman came to emulate) moved to the country. Now certain urbanologists are suggesting that we take undeveloped suburban areas and plan housing for the poor. If this succeeds too well, it will only drive the middle and upper classes back to the city. The favored land is where the favored are, not necessarily where the birds are.

July 25, 1967: 3:00 P.M., Badelschwingh Strasse, Munich

We will be leaving Germany in less than 48 hours for Scandinavia and, then, on to the British Isles. What has it been like to spend 7 weeks in Germany? Our daily existence forgives the Germans for what they have done. Our hearts and our minds—even our so-called logic—can't forgive. We play the part as they, in another way, play theirs. We are civilized to them, engage them in pleasant conversations, feel—for the moment—very warmly toward them. They have been the most polite of all the Europeans during our limited experience here. Surprisingly, we have been most comfortable with them. They are not arrogant about their language and customs, easily forgive the frequent mistakes that tourists are wont to make, and are honest and reliable people.

But we must never forget what they did. We may forgive individuals but we must never forgive the Third Reich. We must be remorseless and relentless. No one can give us a "testament" to insure remembrance, as others have been given testaments to insure other thoughts and deeds for all the ages. Our individual zeal to remember and to pass on what transpired here must be in our "mortal to mortal" and, thus, "immortal" insurance.

August 30, 1968, Natick, Massachusetts

I have just completed the preparation of this chapter taken from my diary of last summer in Europe. One particular thought keeps returning through my mind, a thought I heard chanted continuously two nights ago. "The whole world is watching, the whole world is watching." Those brave words, chanted by the demonstrators on the Chicago streets as the television cameras recorded it all, did not stop the policemen's clubs, the gas, and the strong-armed forces of Mayor Daley's order, if not law. Now that the whole world has observed, what will we do? History has taught me that the chances are excellent we will do nothing. Good German citizens did nothing. The Northern White liberal did nothing. The humanitarian Chicagoan will do nothing. I am fearful that the administrator of the back wards will do nothing.

The more I study the problem of human abuse, the more convinced I become that the ancient Chinese proverb, "Virtue is not knowing, but doing," is as profound as any words put together by man. Further, I am persuaded that unless we find better ways to convince the man-who-knows that knowing isn't enough, our children's children will pay homage to memorials yet to be conceived, protesting horrors yet to be imagined. For too long, the good people have sought solace from human outrage in their religions or have told their troubles to the wall. Possibly, this is the time we might convince ourselves that our protection and salvation on Earth is with each other. We must tell each other and must act on behalf of each other.

Reprinted by permission of Steven D. Blatt and the Blatt family.

THE FAMILY PAPERS: A RETURN TO PURGATORY[6]

This book is an indiscretion, and there are many who will be angry with us for committing it because no family likes its sordid side brought into public view. The sordid side of ordinary families can remain hidden—to reveal it is often even more sordid. But with other kinds of families, it can become not just permissible, but necessary, to reveal their secrets. Such a family is the large group of men and women who have protected the hidden world of mental retardation from public scrutiny. It is a family which has—whether wittingly or unwittingly, by deception or self-deception—prevented thousands of mentally retarded people from participating in the sort of life to which Americans are entitled.

The Family knows things we haven't been telling the world about. Important things, more important than the Pentagon Papers, which were about senseless war and unnatural deaths. But the Family Papers are about senseless and unnatural lives, lives disfigured by a society which lays claim to the Declaration of Independence and the guarantee of justice for all people. War is terrible, but explainable. What we do in the names of mental health, human services, and education is unexplainable because we do it to ourselves and not to the "enemy," and it's even more terrible because we do it to babies and don't quit our dirty work until dirt covers the evidence.

And who is this Family? It consists of all those who work, or say they work, with the problems of retarded people in institutionalized settings. It is the supervisors and superintendents and commissioners. It is the professional societies such as the American Association on Mental Deficiency and the Council for Exceptional Children. The Family includes government agencies such as the National Institute on Mental Health and the Office of Education, even groups like the Associations for Retarded Citizens. From the attendants who show up for an impossible job every day, to prestigious professionals who often don't show up at all, the Family consists of

everyone who should know better than to permit that hidden world to continue. And the academic community, which legitimates it all by issuing so-called credentials and generating so-called expertise, is also part of the Family. Many of you, our readers, are probably members, as are two of the three of us who worked on this study. In spite of professed intentions, and ideals and commitments to reform, we in the Family have acted to preserve the most abhorrent abuse of human beings.

To some extent, the Family still protects itself through concealment and secrecy. Ten years ago, to bring the horrors of institutions for mentally retarded people to public awareness, the only photographs we could get had to be taken with a concealed camera. The secrecy was strict and one could visit institutions only by stealth or arm twisting or string pulling. Today, the barricades of rules and restrictions are less formidable, but they still exist. The institutions are still hard to get into, and taking photographs remains very difficult for anyone and next to impossible for most people. Some of today's institutions refused us access altogether for this study; one admitted us for a tour, but demanded that our cameras remain locked in the superintendent's office. The change from a decade ago is that in five of the big traditional institutions our pictures were taken openly. The cameras caused a lot of nervous suspicion, we were often admonished not to take pictures of people's faces (why?), but we were able to finish our work and leave with the film.

Only later did we discover that the institutions had yet another way of preserving secrecy: by controlling permission to publish the photographs. The permission, of course, is not theirs to give; the recognition of human rights of retarded people has advanced far enough that only they or their legal guardians can authorize publication. But the institutions can—and do—obstruct the process of asking for permission. They can "judge" that a person is not competent to give permission; they can have records so confused or out-dated that family or guardians cannot be located; they can judge the request as "not in the best interests of the client" and refuse to approach the relevant person with it; they can put the matter off indefinitely by insisting that it be considered at various meetings and then referred to still other meetings. These obstructions are the most reprehensible because we know they are not necessary even in the bureaucratic nature of institutions. We know this because one institution—and not the "best" one—chose to be cooperative and obtained most of our permission forms promptly. But most institutions remain secretive and, almost instinctively, it seems, move to hide what goes on within their walls. The Family secrets continue to be well guarded from public sights. With reluctance, we decided to black out the eyes of people in some photographs which we consider important to show. They are photographs not of people who refused us permission to publish their pictures—in such cases we happily respected their wishes. Rather, they are pictures of people whom the Family denied the opportunity to refuse permission.

But more impenetrable and sinister than overt secrecy is the misleading publicity with which the Family defends its dominions. The first thing one discovers in these places is that the official description of what goes on gives no clue to what one sees actually happening. The hypnotic language of humanitarian concern encapsulates the victims of institutionalization and seals their world off from examination or understanding or even hope. An elaborate camouflage of benign vocabulary—rehabilitation, treatment program, normalization, therapy, modularized privacy…—is thrown over the reality of idleness, segregation, neglect.

We are used to condemning this kind of practice when we discover it somewhere else. If the Soviet Union locks up political dissidents in psychiatric hospitals on the pretext of looking after their mental health, we are quick enough to protest. Yet in our own institutions for retarded people, thousands of Americans continue to be locked up on the pretext of receiving care, training, and education, and we continue to speak as though the pretext were reality. We call for money and resources to implement the pretext rather than confess it was all a terrible mistake.

In seeking understanding of human rights in the Soviet Union today, we ask the victims, not the victimizers, for their analyses. We take the reports of the dissidents seriously and dismiss as propaganda the versions told by state officials and state psychiatrists. But in examining institutions around us, we dismiss the opinions of the incarcerated. We turn instead to the Family—the psychiatrist, social workers, educators, all the professionals—to tell us what is happening, and we accept what they say as true even when it contradicts the reports of their victims. The Family tells us about innovative, new treatments and the need for more research in situations where even a minimal human sympathy is enough to discover that the treatments are brutal or heartless; it tells us that each resident is served by an individualized program in a place where countless residents can be seen aimlessly sitting or standing or lying around; it tells us that an institution is in compliance with all sorts of federal standards, though we see barren environments and wasted lives everywhere. The Family discourages taking photographs and tells us that it is protecting the privacy of the residents, though the residents must live in environments in which there can be no such thing as privacy. The Family talks piously about healing the wounds of the mentally retarded but has not yet stopped inflicting those wounds.

Our indiscretion is that we are making public what the Family does, not what it says. We believe with our hearts

and our minds that these Family Papers are as vital for us to see as any that have been hidden during the last 200 years in this government. While they do not speak as to how our society was created, they raise the more crucial contemporary question of how it should endure. The malaise in our culture stems not from doubts about what our forefathers did, but from doubts about what we do.

There is little challenge here to the idea of America. But there are grave concerns about what we have made of America. And of ourselves.

If there is hope in what we have learned in our examination of institutionalization, it is not in any improvement of institutional life—imprisonment and segregation can be made more comfortable, but they can never be made into freedom or participation. The only hopeful sign is that while 10 years ago and for generations before, those institutions were run by one happy Family, today they are run by one unhappy Family. If it must become unhappier still before it changes its ways, then we are willing to contribute to the Family's unhappiness with our report.

As we did 10 years ago, we have revealed some of America's papers, a Family's papers. We feel no guilt, because we show you papers from the guardians of a closed society which professes that any decent society should be open. As you will see, everything has changed during the last decade. As you will see, nothing has changed.

Years ago, but long after the horrors ceased, I forced myself to visit the Dachau Concentration Camp, now a memorial park bordered by attractive garden apartments and other common scenes. But within that still dreaded death camp, remnants of the Holocaust linger. On hundreds of pictures, in dozens of languages, imbedded in every grain of dirt, written even on the shiny walls of the new facsimile barracks, there is a message: do not forget, remember what happened here, remember us, remember, I once lived. But the Jews were the People of the Book. They expressed their anguish and their pleas the ways all literate people express themselves, through their language. And because they knew that voices are eventually silenced, and theirs especially would be, they scrawled their message on the walls of the barracks: do not forget us.

Today, in the United States, one can see scrawlings of the anguished. Today, in the institutions across the land, one can find what remains of an American shame, but the words here are not in Yiddish or Polish or Russian. Because the inmates couldn't talk, because there was no one willing to listen, because there was no one wanting to understand, these institutional inmates used fingers instead of pens, and feces were their ink. But whether it was the fine hand of a former professor at the University of Heidelberg or the ugly smear of a drooling mute, the message is constant: why are we forsaken?

Conclusion

A decade or so ago, we went to five state institutions for the mentally retarded, the purpose then not as clear as the purpose for our return last year. Then, we found little to give us hope, but we were reluctant to admit that the concept of "institutions" is hopeless. Today, we find much to give us hope, but we are now unable to see a way to save the institutions. Ten years ago, with the exception of The Seaside Regional Center, every institution we saw was terrible. We convinced ourselves that by making them smaller, providing more resources, developing ways to insure proper inspection and accountability, by working at improving things, we could make good institutions out of bad institutions. The subsequent years and this most recent round of visits convince us that those were foolish ideas.

We must evacuate the institutions for the mentally retarded. There is no time any more for new task forces and new evaluation teams. The time is long past for such nonsense. Joint accreditation commissions do no good. We need to empty the institutions. The quicker we accomplish that goal, the quicker we will be able to repair the damage done to generations of innocent inmates. The quicker we get about converting our ideologies and resources to a community model, the quicker we will learn how to forget what we perpetrated in the name of humanity.

Those who fear that community placements will cause problems are quite right. To live with our retarded children, our handicapped friends, our aging parents does place burdens on us. What we must learn from the nightmare of institutions is that these are burdens which cannot be avoided or delegated: to have a decent society we must behave as decent individuals. Ultimately our society will discover that it is actually easier to meet than to avoid the responsibilities we have as human beings.

Thus, we demand that every institution for the mentally retarded in the United States be closed. We insist that a society which claims to be civilized can find the proper ways and means to include the people who have been institutional inmates in decent community environments. The inmates have suffered enough. Society has done enough damage.

And what about the Family? The Family is dying. Though they continue to cling to what remains of their dominions, they no longer even defend their position because they are so busy agreeing with their enemy's position. They have lost their pride, their status and every purpose they once had. All they have are their institutions and their inmates—which is a lot if you are an inmate but not much if you are a member of the Family.

The Family is dying, but theirs is a lingering terminal illness. Although we are impatient to be rid of them and to free the 200,000 inmates, although it is so terribly sad that those inmates must continue to suffer even though everyone knows their suffering is unnecessary, although so many would do almost anything to put this American horror behind us, we should feel glad that it will soon be over. We not only demand that those institutions close, every sign predicts they will close in your lifetimes.

Reprinted by permission of Steven D. Blatt and the Blatt family.

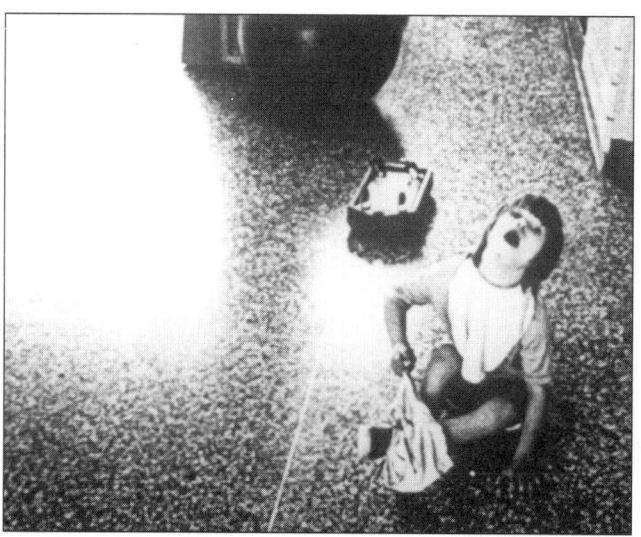

Part 2

In and Out of Poetry

Fred Kaplan

Editors' Introduction to Part 2

Burton Blatt loved—and lived—to write. The form in which he wrote seemed to be less important to him than getting his ideas and feelings down on paper. His writings include not only academic articles and essays, but novels and poetry as well.

Part 2 contains selections of poems and aphorisms written by Burt. In his poetry we see some of his most personal reflections. These poems were published in his books *Exodus From Pandemonium* (1970) and *Souls in Extremis* (1973). Pandemonium was the capital of hell in Milton's *Paradise Lost*. The archaic meaning of the root of the word *extremis* is "the end of life; dying."

No more interpretation of his poetry is warranted here.

Poems and Aphorisms[7]

Verse

    The most personal, the words that cut and sting,
are the words men call "poetry."
    These words are little more than the accumulated
pain and reason of each man who denudes his mind and his
soul and his heart—for himself.
    For to himself he will be true, as he knows there
is no truth
    As he knows that truth eludes him and he is incapable.
    But less incapable than others who have tried,
and have failed.
    As he has failed.

Reformation of Pandemonium

Pandemonium is the capital of hell. It is the fantasy of Milton, yet, to many, it is the reality of being. One does not describe Pandemonium but reacts to it. Let us examine the mentally retarded in Pandemonium and the reformation that is attempting to return them from the brutality of institutional back wards to the realm of human awareness, compassion, and interrelatedness.

    In Pandemonium, there are many aliases: solitary
        confinement is therapeutic isolation; restraint is protection;
            punishment is negative feedback; and indifference to all of these is
                thoughtfulness.
    In Pandemonium, a girl has seven healthy teeth extracted to prevent her
        from eating threads of the day-room rug.

> In Pandemonium, the physically handicapped become more disabled as each day passes each identical day and as each old contracture is the cause of new contractures, and as both old and new are the effects of indifference and ineptitude.
> In Pandemonium, we appropriate such progressive terms as "comprehensive," "community," "regional," and "prevention," but nothing changes, or we wouldn't be in Pandemonium.

In Pandemonium, there is little drug addiction, but there is pervasive, more destructive, environmental addiction with its accompanying withdrawal syndrome and sickness.
In Pandemonium, the cry of the anguished is, "I am here!"

> In Pandemonium, children are locked and forgotten in solitary confinement cells for such crimes as breaking a window or speaking disrespectfully to an attendant.
> In Pandemonium, the tunnel is endless, the darkness unendurable, the light extinguished.

In Pandemonium, weakness is strength and strength is weakness.
In Pandemonium, causing nothing to change is Power.
In Pandemonium, trivial questions are answered erroneously while meaningful ones are never asked.

> In Pandemonium, Utopia is anywhere else.
> In Pandemonium, humanists dislike people.
> In Pandemonium, both labor and management are represented by one collective negotiator, the devil.
> In Pandemonium, we find new ways to express horror and debasement.
> In Pandemonium, to embrace life is to kiss death.
> In Pandemonium, the humanists are inhuman, the theists are atheists, the lovers are haters.

In Pandemonium, you die before you live; the end precedes a beginning.
In Pandemonium, the luxury of life is death.

In Pandemonium, labeling someone or something makes it fact.
In Pandemonium you are in the eye of the eye of that mischief named hell.

> Pandemonium is the sophist's paradise.
> Pandemonium disguises inertia as reasonableness.
> Pandemonium demonstrates the tautology of the "evil of massive institutions" and the non sequitur in "excellent large institutions."
> Pandemonium is entranced with medical curiosities rather than concerned with human necessities.
> Pandemonium is a phantasmagoria which is real.
> Pandemonium proves the gnostics' thesis that man is wicked and the world is an evil place.

Pandemonians hope for their nightmares to end while knowing their terror is permanent, for the floods to subside while expecting the deluge.
Pandemonians have learned that the meaninglessness of one's question is only exceeded by the valuelessness of its answer.
Pandemonians respect an equality that understands no difference between "he" and "it."
Pandemonians have learned that the next hour will be a greater catastrophe than the last.
Pandemonians who are deaf never speak, who are palsied never walk, who are retarded never think; in Pandemonium, the blind have no eyes and the lame no feet.
Pandemonians know that life is war.

> Good works are inherited from evil deeds in Pandemonium.
> We are trapped because the priest does practice what he preaches in Pandemonium.
> There is no need to talk through one's problem as there is no shade of difference, just an omnipotent MAN who proclaims what is in Pandemonium.

Artists distort reality to present reality; distortion is the reality in Pandemonium.
Naivete and innocence cannot survive in Pandemonium.

Subterfuge is the shortest distance between two
        conspirators in Pandemonium.
One man lives in the future, another in the past, while
        no one has either in Pandemonium.
Nothing changes, yet there is an illusion of
        change, for things do not change differently, now,
        from the way they have not changed before in
        Pandemonium.
There are many liberals but few equalitarians
        in Pandemonium.
No one is dehumanized because he is a man, but many
        are dehumanized because they are residents
        in Pandemonium.
Sick people live in a healthy culture and healthy
        people live in a sick culture; the mix is Pandemonium.
Today is Doomsday in Pandemonium.

        The law of Pandemonium is to know right and do
                wrong, think well and behave poorly.
        The law of Pandemonium is to believe that nothing can
                be done so nothing need be attempted; the
                system is wrong while we are right.
        The law of Pandemonium is to treat other humans as if
                they weren't, then treat ourselves as if we were.
        The law of Pandemonium is to promote the
                administrator's pseudo-giftedness while he promotes
                the patients' pseudo-custodialness.
        The law of Pandemonium is not to believe in the
                fulfillment of every human being.
        The law of Pandemonium relates more to ahumantia
                than to amentia.
        The law of Pandemonium is to present a public image
                that disguises closed systems as open systems.

The law of Pandemonium unfolds the animal
        ethos leading the human spirit.

The law of Pandemonium is to build ideational and
      physical tunnels to deny man the sensation
      of natural light and experience.
The law of Pandemonium is to learn geography while
      neglecting etiology.
The law of Pandemonium relies on the truth of its deceit,
      the courage of its cowardice, and the love of hate.
The law of Pandemonium is for the state to give
      the patient everything but he gets nothing.

Pandemoniacs destroy relationships.
Pandemoniacs respect chaos.
Pandemoniacs build evil.
Pandemoniacs exude unforgiveness.
Pandemoniacs induce pain.
Pandemoniacs cause mental retardation.
Pandemoniacs revolt against competence.

      What will the reformation of Pandemonium bring?
      We will agree that mere intention is meaningless; mere
      speech is noise; behavior is character. We are what
      we do! And, we will question not only truth but value!

In our relationship with humanity, we have learned that:
Love penetrates hate.
The heart moves mountains while the mind moves only
      the heart.
And the soul is man's ultimate triumph.

      The saga of humanity has its glory in the human value.
      The glory of humanity is its saga of humanhood.

In the cause for humanity, we must agree that:
All men are human beings.
All human beings are valuable.
And all the rest is commentary.

APHORISMS OF A BURNED-OUT PESSIMIST

  I have confronted the foul,
and we are all people.
  I have been to the bottom,
and it is part of the human continuum.
  When appearances tell you that nothing remains,
you either die or become an optimist.
  Optimism is not in believing that
things will turn out well, objectively,
  But in believing that one can face things,
subjectively, however they turn out.
  Optimism is not in feeling good,
  But in feeling that good has a chance to survive.

  Optimism flows not from defeats
and bitterness or victories and joys of the past,
  But in being here now, knowing that
the past has strengthened you.
  Optimism is in believing there is a grand design
that holds eventual Good—for each of us.
  All optimists are lucky people.
As all lucky people are optimists.

  The lucky man neither works to live,
nor does he live to work.
  His work is a necessary one part of his life.
  He has difficulty deciding what is work
and what is pleasure, not because he
cannot recognize joy in leisure but because
he does not encounter drudgery in work.

  The lucky man knows that the language
of computers will not replace the language of
humans,

    The hardware of technocrats will not
decelerate the thinking of thoughtful people,
    The technological process will not obscure
the humanitarian ethos.
    And the Group will not overwhelm the
person.

    The lucky man is rarely asked to
climb a mountain of Moriah,
    He is rarely forced to choose between
love and duty,
    Between compassion and justice,
    Between humanity and integrity,
Or between friend and friend.
    When he is required to choose, he makes his
own decision.

    The lucky man is judged for those things he did,
not for those things others believe he should have done—
or his accomplishments as well as for his failures—
For that which he attempted as well as for that in
which he succeeded—
For his lovely defeats as well as for his glorious victories—
For his intentions as well as for his credits—
For his credits in spite of his intentions—
And for the style and process as well as for
the content and achievements of his life.

    The lucky man walks with the belief
that his friends are steadfast, in spite of
his defects, not because of his virtues—
In spite of his thoughtlessness,
not because of his generosity—
    Not because of what he may give to them,
    but because of what they must do for him—
    Because they need him as he needs them.

The lucky man has been taught to
love, because he has been loved.
    He has learned to care, because he
has known those who care.
    He can give something he values,
because he has been given all that is priceless,
    He has learned that there is never shame
in true emotion, never embarrassment
in true feeling, and never fear in truth.

    The lucky man has a wife who believes
he is a lucky man.
    He has children who, in their maturity, continue to
believe he is a good man.
    He has parents who respect as well
as love him.
    And he has brothers and sisters,
and uncles and aunts who do not envy his luck.
    He has everything,
and he has this time to reflect and to understand.

Primary Connections

Scientists turn eventually to philosophy,
    As theologians turn to Man,
    As men turn to God,
    As those who seek faith bring it,
    As each man returns to the beginning,
    As he turns inward to cope with the universe,
    As he seeks to discover his being,
    As he learns how the self reveals and illuminates.

On Institutions

In the special world of institutions,
One learns the rules only by breaking them,
And is happy if he's not depressed,
With full control when not unhinged,
For he's alive just because he's not dead,
But dead while he lives.

Humanness

Secretiveness is the handmaiden of anxiety
Anxiety is the enforcer of repression
Repression is the progenitor of violence
Violence is the catharsis of madness
Madness is the escape from reason
Reason is the revolt from chaos
Chaos is the sperm of control
Control is the harbinger of abuse
Abuse is the device of totalization
Totalization is the process of evil
Evil is the flight from humanism
Humanism is the hope for mankind
Mankind is the center of the being
Being is the life of the physical
Physical is the shell of the soul
Soul is the essence of the humanness
Humanness is the universal truth.

POINT-COUNTERPOINT

There is virtue in sin and sin in virtue.
There is good in evil and evil in good.
There is right in wrong and wrong in right.
And black is white.

The just are unjust and the strong are weak.
The foolish are wise and the hateful are loving.
The honest man lies, the cheat fulfills.
And the cowardly braves.

Laws are good, and to obey them is virtuous,
And to obey some is sinful.
Laws that permit a man to:
      devalue another man
      hold him in contempt
      remove his liberties
      lay bare his defenses
Or to:
      destroy his humanness
Are sinful, and those who believe in them are sinful.

Traitors may be evil, and to follow them is folly,
And to follow some is wise.
Traitors who are traitorous to the ideals of:
      War
      Murder
      Genocide
      Enslavement
      And humiliation
Are virtuous, and those who support them have virtue,
And we, who turn from their deeds, are less virtuous.

Philanthropy is piety, and to give is loving,
And to give can be prideful and self-serving.
Those who give to:
> Degenerates
> Institutional cases
> the Slothful
> the Putrid
> and the Tainted

Give neither to humanity nor to man,
Give not to human beings but to piousness.

They give to save themselves, not to serve their brothers.
They give to live at the expense of others who perish.
They give to become better as others are made worse.
Their virtue is sinful as their goodness is greedy.
> Each point has a counterpoint,
> As the wisest man alone knows his infinite foolishness,
> As the just man understands his capacity for injustice,
> As the thief never loses conviction he will walk somehow,
> With the righteous.

Each point is its own counterpoint.

STRANGE ALLIES

The man who suffers with his institutionalized brothers and the man who hardly knows they exist
> Both seek alternatives to commitment—
> The former to save humanity,
> The latter to conserve prosperity.

> One educator finds little comfort in new school laws, modern buildings, and fashionable slogans,
> While another expects few improvements with increased school support, greater attention to individual needs, and community participation;
> The former, who has learned that laws, and architecture, and words do not guarantee progress,
> And are not harbingers of greater wisdom and behavior;
> The latter, who wishes only to return to the halcyon days of memory so dimmed,
> That he no longer sees the pinched faces, the pained expressions, the empty school desks, and the totally controlled environment,
> In his mind's eye.

> One citizen votes not to tear down the old and build a new state institution,
> As another votes not to build a new rehabilitation center.
> The former, who is resolved to witness the destruction of all institutions.
> The latter, who is committed to a philosophy of individual responsibility and governmental passivity in these matters.

> A mental health professional seeks support for a community-based program, while another for an institutional program,
> Both being against the construction of a new community mental health center.

The former, because he visualizes those plans as the portrait of a mental institution at conception.
The latter, because he visualizes those plans as the enemy of his institution's justified share of the public treasure.

We ask ourselves if there is any profit for men to ally themselves with one another when their destinies differ,
But they share common tactics and immediate goals.

We must ask if a cause is violated as allies are recruited who are not allies,
And as enemies are identified who are not enemies.
Essentially we need to review our fateful journeys; those who have joined us, and why they remain; and those who have left us, and why they departed.

This is but another way of asking for an audit of means and ends,
And of reminding each other that—in our struggles—the means must be the ends.

Benchmarks of Civilization

Mutism, nudity, and fetters are the enemies of the civilized.
And language, clothing, and freedom are the benchmarks of civilization.
Language prompts a man to engage symbolically with other men.
Language prompts him to communicate that which he cannot demonstrate,
To demonstrate that which he must communicate.
Clothing permits a man to walk among other men.
Clothing permits him to seek out the larger society,
To physically and spiritually go beyond his room and his pallet.

Freedom persuades a man that he is a man.
Freedom persuades him that there is dignity on earth, that man's civilization is for all men.

What are the benchmarks of civilization?
Noise and talk, and laughter,
And crying, and sighing, and responding,
Giving answers, asking questions, prompting,
And seeking out to touch, to hold, to caress.
A cover, a dress, a robe,
A cover to hide the flesh, and free the body,
A cover to soothe the wounds, to conceal man's trembling uncertainty,
Man's unshakable humility and unquenchable vanity.
And freedom!
Freedom to walk, to talk, to think.
Freedom to contemplate one's destiny and contrive one's future.
To leave, to stay,
To wait, to flee.
Freedom to disdain that which another man loves dearly.
And freedom to cherish that which all other men disdain.
Mankind, if you yet have one,
Return all the incarcerated to civilization.

ANTECEDENTS AND CONSEQUENCES OF EVIL[8]

The public has conquered, and the danger is gone.
The burden is lifted, and our souls have won.
In Boston, little old ladies will lay aside their tennis shoes.
While in Syracuse, men will breathe easier,
And women will return to household chores with stronger spines and softer smiles
The seals will live and long live the seals.

The baby, cuddly, snow-white seals will live until—
They live a month,
And until they turn brown,
And until they weigh 80 pounds,
And until they leave their mothers,
And until they are no longer as cute as they were.
Then their time comes, the once-baby cuddly, snow-white seals will not be—
Clubbed to death
    or
Skinned alive
    or
Garroted
When their time comes, these 2- or 3-month-old brown animals will be
Shot:
With a modern clean rifle,
    or
With sleek and swift arrows.

And when their time comes, heed
Prime Minister Trudeau's admonition:
"Those who protect won't be shown the same photograph of baby seals with their big blue or brown eyes."

And when their time comes, protect your government,
Complained Minister of Fisheries Davis, for:
"A lot of young people in distant
Countries now think of Canada only in terms of
Seals."

A lot of young people in distant countries now
Think of the USA only in terms of
Vietnam, Chicago, and Selma.

And legions of people in all lands have thought:
Of Germany, only in terms of Nazis,
Of Rome, only in terms of lion pits,
Of USSR, only in terms of cancer wards,
Of Russia, only in terms of czars,
Of Chamberlain, only in terms of "Peace for Our Times,"
Of King John, only in terms of murder and deceit,
And of evil, only in terms of its ability to flood out
Goodness.

And the baby seals will lead mankind out of the wilderness.
And we will learn from them:
That evil thrives as the being is devalued,
That evil flourishes as it is rationalized,
That evil is Man's unique gift to the universe.

And that man will learn that he, and all men
are judged and judge by that which makes us less than men,
By that which we hate, not that which we love,
By that which shames us, not that which gladdens us.
By that which is in our hands, not that which is in our
hearts.
By that which makes Man the animal, not that which makes
the animal Man.
The antecedents of evil require a disregard for life,
As he who is selected for debasement *must* be judged
A less equal being—
As consequently, he who so judges *must* be known
For that judgment.

THE SMELLS OF HELL

Urine, trickling down naked flesh,
Running on smooth terrazzo,
Streams of hot piss inching toward the center,
As gravity pulls the wicked, sticky yellow,
From one hole to another,
Leaving its markers here and there,
Straight lines of dried piss,
Amid islands of old, old shit,
As attendants in gleaming white,
Step daintily to avoid the inmates,
While bravely they navigate through the oozing slime,
Gleaming white and untouched by human hands.

VICTIMS AND VICTIMIZERS

In the back ward, who is the victim, and who is the victimizer?
Each is; all are.

Who is dehumanized, who are the cruel, and what is cruelty?
Each is; all are; everything!

In any institution, if there is a back ward, can there be anything but back wards?
In that institution, as the back ward continues to exist, are all people chronic victims and pervasive victimizers?
In that institution, is not the term "back ward" a synonym for "institution"?

He who victimizes others is the victim
of his inevitable dehumanization,
  As he who is dehumanized must contribute
to the dehumanization of others.
  All men—willing or unwilling, knowing
  or unknowing—are victimized during the
  trials of living as their debasements and
  agonies victimize other men.
  Our way of living tests each man's
humanity, assaults it, and sometimes is its conqueror,
  As each man contributes
  to our way of living, to his
  own dehumanization, to the dehumanization
  of all others,
  As each man is his own victim and victimizer.

HUMAN ABUSE AND PERSONAL RESPONSIBILITY

  The most beautiful words in our testament admonish us
not to wrong a stranger,
  For we were strangers in the Land of Egypt.
  These words are beautiful, not in the morphological sense—
for alone they are no more than ordinary words—
  But in their pristine elemental truth concerning man,
  His needs,
  And his anxieties.

  Each man must live alone, must be consumed or learn to deal
with his being,
  And his mortality.
  Each man must find his way to:
    Fight the perils,
    Ignore the demons,
    Sustain a personal meaning of the Cosmos and his share
and place in it.

In the intimate sense, each man is a stranger to all mankind.
In the social sense, too many men are total strangers,
Are globally estranged.
In the intimate sense, each man must face the omnipotent alone and resourceless.
In the social sense, some men find their brothers and, thus, find their strength and their contentment.

What responsibility do I have for you,
And you for me?
Am I my brother's keeper, and are all men my brothers?
If all men are my brothers, is there meaning to the word "brother"?
What are the links between us, between your life and mine, your past and my future?
What are our ties from:
    The genetic pool,
    The metaphysical relationship,
    The human reality and mutuality?
Is each man a responsibility of all men, and is each man responsible for all men?
Am I my brother's keeper, and are all men my brothers?

I am and they are.
We are intertwined as one.
And, as one, each man must pursue his individuality and unique destiny.
And, as one, when my brother suffers, I suffer.
And, as one, until the world is righted for all people,
No one is safe,
Neither you, nor I, nor our progeny.
And, as one, each man is part of all men, as all mankind is the sum and effects of each man.
My issue, my brothers, and I are all mankind.

FAITH

Professing on evil may be personally therapeutic and cleansing to the soul. Oftentimes, it obtains a great deal of benefit for those who have been violated against. However, in spite of whatever good such professions provide, they become mere empty words—hypocritical words—when the professor doesn't commit himself directly to the eradication of the evil.

It is claimed that few "truths" are known to Man.
Are there any?
But, Man is expected to be true…
    to his family.
    to his faith.
    to his country.
    to his profession.
Isn't it difficult to be true to something when you must be in doubt from where (or if) that truth obtains?

People who engage themselves in the research of an issue have a more humble view of the illumination they can bring to the issue than those who are "working at it" in the clinics, the schools or whatever. On the other hand, I have found that the researchers are much more optimistic than the latter group that the issue eventually will be resolved or brought under scientific control. It isn't, I believe, that the researchers are more humble people; many I have known are rather arrogant. Nor do I believe that they are *intrinsically* more optimistic concerning human nature and the ability to modify it.

The advantage enjoyed by researchers, and difficult for others to attain, is their ability to take distance and form an ideological detachment from an issue, its consequences in general, and its influence on their personal lives. It is very difficult to be dispassionate and disinterested in the face of certain issues—even for the very best researchers. However, both their training and the way they must go about their business makes such objectivism possible, if not certain, for them where it is almost impossible for others to achieve.

It is the objectivism that permits researchers to better understand the hidden variables that many of us never appreciate. It is this comprehension of the complexity of an issue that causes the researcher to be humble in the light of his ignorance and optimistic and faithful to his scholarly creed and the eventual triumph of science.

>   You have conviction if
>   you know you are right
>   When you do something
>   others know is wrong
>   Or, when you do something
>   you know is less wrong
>   than anything else you can do.

Horror

I have been told that, in times past, families of institutionalized mentally retarded were advised to publish obituaries for such persons. Given the *current* circumstances in many state schools for too many inmates there, my common sense—despair notwithstanding—does not permit me to take exception to such advice *today*.

> From the elegant view of the sensitive
> The saving virtue of the institutionalized retarded
> Is their inability to communicate agony.

More people than buildings need renovations in our
    state schools.

    If, in the logical order of affairs, philosophers inhabit
        universities and theophists churches, then—surely—
        thanatosophists rule institutions for the retarded.
    Poor institutions are responsible for good decisions.
        They completely discourage certain parents from
        institutionalizing their children, some of whom
        should best remain at home.

A Parable: Milling Rot.

    What is Utopia?
    It is the remembrance of things that
        never were,
    And the embellishment and the improvement
        of these for a future
        that will never be.
    What is Pandemonium?
    K. Building.

Thanatos, gorge yourself in the gore of K. Building!

    This is neither an exercise in sophistry
        nor is it a non sequitur;
    It is a circumstance that confuses
        and misleads otherwise skilled professionals:
    It should not be an unexpected condition
        among severely mentally retarded residents
        of state schools—
    Many of whom are both chronic patients
        and acutely ill.
Is the behavior of people similar to the behavior of
    apples? Curious question, but we sometimes act as
    if it were so. Even stranger is, at times I think we should.

For example, consider a barrel of apples. What do we
    do when we find a rotten apple? We remove it, not
    add a healthy one to mitigate the effects of the
    diseased one.
At the institution, we segregate the "rotten" people
    into back wards. At the institution, we add healthy
    staff to rectify the abuses perpetrated by our sick or
    recalcitrant colleagues.
I think it may be helpful for us—at least once in a
    while—to think of the patients as people and the staff
    as apples, not vice versa as is presently the case.

Styles of Behavior

The Realist: tells it the way it is.
The Historian: tells it the way it was.
The Idealist: tells it the way it should have been.
The Humanist; tells it the way Man must make it
    become.

        Some believe that Man is innately good.
        Others believe that Man is innately bad.
        Wouldn't the human race be more
            predictable if Man was either
            innately good or bad—not both
            good and bad, as he probably is?

To some colleagues, a dedication to the field of mental
    retardation is impossible.
To others, it is unthinkable.
Whatever their flaws, frailties, and professional naivete,
    we must entrust our energies and resources with the
    remaining minority—and not dissipate these in
    courting the reluctant, however talented and potentially
    useful they may be to the cause.

The door always must be open, but people must choose
 to enter and not be chosen, they must be encouraged
 but not forced or seduced, we must offer them a
 philosophy and not our federal gold or promises we
 may never keep.

For better or worse, we have only each other. Our
 mission must not be to convert the disaffected
 professionals. We have much more important and
 fruitful responsibilities with the mentally retarded
 and their families.

In every movement for human betterment, at least
 three generations have been involved concurrently:
 the oppressed generation, disinterested onlookers,
 and leaders of the movement committed to rectify
 errors of past and present.

Unfortunately, until today, our leaders have been one-
 generation jaded and two-generations removed. They
 have been too feeble to remember real passions
 connected with the issue and they have, more
 recently, remained on the sidelines when something
 better might have been done.

Only today, when youth are led and lead—when youth-
 fulness and involvement extend to the later years,
 when middle age may be 60—is there the possibility
 that leadership will emerge from the ranks of the
 afflicted, not from the afflicting or the condescending.

The hippie has a point!
He looks you right in the eye
 and through your head.
He doesn't answer your, "How are
you?" unless he believes you
care about how he Is.

It isn't the bureaucracy of our democracy that offends
> the young. They believe our unforgivable sin was the
> creation of a "gerontocracy," a government by and
> for old men.

Law

I have read the chiseled rocks of all ages, proclaiming,
> at the courthouse entrance, that a commonwealth
> must have a government of laws, not of men. I can't
> agree. Our government may be of laws *for* men or,
> better yet, *of* men *with* laws, but in the ultimate
> dimension, of men *not* laws.

>> With the law, too many civil servants settle for the comfort of atomistic
>> literalness and find it their, and our, prison—not a vehicle to
>> freedom. I, as one, would rather have a cabala. A mystical
>> interpretation of the law has the virtue of unpredictability and,
>> hence, there is a chance for good to obtain. A literal
>> understanding offers but little opportunity to move ahead, to affirm
>> positively. Its seemingly singular ambition is to deny, to reject, to
>> stay within the letter—never understanding the word and the idea,
>> which are man's only special gifts.

Order and truth are not always compatible bedfellows.
Law is not morality.
Intelligence is not thoughtfulness.
The able do more than know.
The evil do more than believe.
And the good must do more than curse them.

>> If a state repeals the death penalty for acts which were
>> previously capital crimes, the attorney general
>> should require it to desist from assigning its death-
>> in-life penalty—sentence to a back ward—for
>> "mental" crimes.

Oftentimes, the punishment of wrongdoing is, itself,
    wrongdoing.
Consequently, there are situations when wrongdoing is
    punishment and punishment is wrongdoing.
That is, it is impossible to distinguish one from the
    other.

    The *Rouse v. Cameron* decision, written by Chief Judge
        David Bazelon for the majority of the United States
        Court of Appeals for the District of Columbia, the
        Nason v. the Superintendent of Bridgewater State
        Hospital decision in Massachusetts, the *Whitree v.*
        the State of New York finding, and others certain to
        be made before publication of this book advocate
        the *legal* right of a patient in a public mental hospital
        to *adequate treatment*.

It appears as if the day will be fast upon us when our
    reluctant civilization will be required to serve as our
    brother's treaters.
We are beginning to appreciate, now, that morality
    can't be trained satisfactorily into people; nor, so it
    appears, can reason be modified easily.
Possibly, we have learned that it is almost futile to attempt to reason
    unreasonableness out of people, to deal logically with the illogical.
Possibly, these are legislative, more than moralistic, matters.
Possibly, during the years, our major advocates should
    have been jurists and lawmakers rather than
    theologians and philosophers.

Love

When one speaks out for "humane treatment"—and if
>he has thought much about his choice of words—he
realizes that the "humane" refers to the humans
giving the treatment not to those receiving it. Animals,
as well as people, can—and do—receive humane or
inhumane treatment. What animals can't do is
dispense humane treatment.
The standards for "humane treatment" are: (1) it be
>developed and given by human beings; and (2) it
meets humanity's wish and expectation for treatment
of man or beast.

>People who love well have difficulty understanding
>>and reacting constructively to hate and,
>People who hate often have similar difficulty
>>with love.
>It's the rare man who comprehends and appreciates
>>one and deals well with the other.
>Such a man is necessary to help solve our problems.

A true interface requires:
>interfaith
>intertrust
>interinterest
>>and
>inner intercommitment

>Concerning my friends and the things we value in our
>>relationship, we mention such matters as: idealism,
>>honesty, trust, *and* the novelty that each of us brings
>>to the other's experience.
>This last characteristic, novelty, is little appreciated,
>>less understood, and terribly important. It adds
>>color, zest, anticipation, and a feeling of being alive.

The "we-they" syndrome requires the "we" be right
        and "they" be wrong.
Insofar as we are concerned, that's the way it really is.

      There are two kinds of people I try to avoid:
          Those whom I must be untruthful with,
          Those who have been untruthful with me.

There doesn't appear to be a right way or a wrong way
        to interact with another human being, other than to
        know that the wrong way always involves thoughtlessness,
        a mechanistic approach—or ennui—that is
        determined irrespective of that human being, what he
        wants, or what he is.

CIVILIZATION

The malaise of this civilization is that truth relates so
        precariously to justice, and law not at all to order.
Our strength for the coming generations is our knowledge
        of this and our compassion for those who do not
        view this unhappy condition unhappily.

      Boredom is the marasmus of the masses.

All too often, our battles in mental retardation are good
and vigorous; unfortunately, our opponents well might
        have been our friends; unfortunately, our causes
        often are forgotten before they are realized.
Our battles are true but too many victories are
        defeats.

There are senators and there are congressmen. In
    mental retardation, there are too many senators and
    not enough congressmen. There are too many friends
    of the mentally retarded who are willing to take
    responsibility for all mentally retarded but not for
    one mentally retarded, who have a commitment to a
    cause but not to a person, who represent everyone
    but not someone.

The world is changing more quickly than our comprehension
    of not only what a change means, but if it
    has occurred.

    The outspoken personality may be one whose public
        and private views are not discrepant, while the
        submissive personality may be one whose public
        and private views are discrepant.
    There is a great deal both to admire and abhor in
        either personality.

I've noticed that our society is enamored with old
    buildings, old crockery, old books, almost anything
    old—excepting old people.
Strange that it's chic to have regard for old furniture but
    not for people older than the end table.
Is the creation of humanity so much less interesting
    than that of an overstuffed Victorian love seat?

    In the history of mankind, two unique races have been
        excused from the legal and moral protections
        afforded all others. The Jew and Negro have been
        lynched and burned, partly because one was
        believed to be intellectually and the other sexually
        superior.
    There is danger from a new source. Some claim the
        mentally retarded are morally superior.

The Jews of the Nazi nightmare and the mentally
    retarded, in our own time, share a common heritage.
They evoked feelings not of blind hate but of deep
    repugnance, not of vengeance but of annoyance, not
    of wrath but of necessity, not of subjectivity but of objectivity, not of "you" and
    "I" but of "the" and "it."

    What was 1968 really like? Or 1969/1970/2000/
        2,000,000? We might have begun counting these
        things a thousand years later; it would now be 968.
        Better yet, next year could be year one. But most
        people don't appreciate the insignificance of dates.
        For a few, it is the people and places that signify real
        meaning. But for most, it's Columbus Day, New
        Year's Day, and Memorial Day, not Columbus,
        renewal, and peace.

The report of incompetence's death has been greatly
    exaggerated. So too has the reputed influence
    of intellectual power to hasten the interment. Quite
    the contrary: the activity of the mind appears
    to be almost indifferent to the accomplishment of the
    person—indifferent to and independent of!

    To implement any conceptualization requires an
        incredible array of planners, technicians, clinicians,
        and willing manpower. For this, among other
        reasons, a poor conceptualizer does the work of the
        devil.

All too often, the practice bears little relationship to the
    theory. At such times, we must judge whether
    to change the practice or throw out the theory. To
    err here is to compound our waywardness.

All too often, our personalities—irrespective of the
    merits of a particular circumstance—prejudge
    our course of behavior. Therefore, our personalities
    must be taken very seriously during such
    deliberations—for our personalities are true to the
    issue even when they cause wrong decisions
    to be made.

    The collar, the yoke, the posey belt and the
        straitjacket are the merchandise, the soft and
        hardware of restraint and punishment.
    The pessimistic evaluation and the negative prognosis
        may be more hurtful ideational restraints and
        punishments.

Language is the expression of civilization.

    There are two kinds of questions, one that seeks an
        answer and one that gives an answer.
    And, further, there is a third kind of question, a question
        that both seeks and gives, a question that's both
        cynical and hopeful, both not caring and eager
        for new evidence and a way to retreat from dead
        center.

Am I a Tautologist?

1. Do children with low IQs read poorly or do children who read poorly have low IQs?
2. Do nongainers not learn or do nonlearners not gain?
3. Do good teachers have good methods and bad teachers have bad methods, or do good methods and bad methods depend upon good teachers and bad teachers?
4. Is something tautological something in the eye of the beholder?

    We sometimes forget that the word is a deed
    And, possibly, the deed.

Xenogenic Yahoo Yahoo

The word is a deed and the label is the deed. For
    example, eventually a label must be invented for
    Daniel Hugon, Richard Speck, and other XYY
    "criminally insane."
Shouldn't we label them:
    Xenogenic Yahoo Yahoos?
The definition of XYY would be:
    Brutish, degraded, vicious men,
    Completely different from either of their parents.
It's so much easier to understand Richard Speck
    when we know he's a Yahoo.

    What is emotion?
    The sounds of words, not the words,
    The way one moves, not the distance he
        has travelled,
    The look of the eye, not the vision
        in the eye,
    The silence, not the quiet.

    Sin is to crime,
    What cruel is to hurt,
    What deliberate is to consequence,
    What societal will is to individual action, and
    What victimizer is to victim-victimizer.

Institutions, much more than individuals, are responsible
    for the earth's good and evil. Yet when we attempt
    to comprehend and cope with good or evil,
    we persist in studying individuals and individual
    actions.
We hardly recognize institutional and group influence.

I have observed two problems interfering with orderly
 and fruitful developments in the Science and Art
 of behavior. What seems to be more and more
 common during the conduct and reporting
 of a "scientific" program is the conclusion (my
 interpretation) of the "scientist" that it
 hardly matters what one does as long as he does it
 with style.
On the other hand, the "art of teaching" and the "art of
 clinical interaction" seem acceptable, to both
 scientists and practitioners, only to the degree
 that there are things scientific about these
 involvements.
In life, contradictions are necessary, because life is a
 contradiction.

GLORY

Greatness is not the goodness of a man
But the goodness he inspires in others.

Honesty is as beautiful a technique as it is a virtue.

Reprinted by permission of Steven D. Blatt and the Blatt family.

Part 3
In and Out of Human Policy

Fred Kaplan

Editors' Introduction to Part 3

Burton Blatt was deeply concerned with public policy. Although he would certainly have condemned individual acts of abuse or neglect against human beings, it was systematic, legally sanctioned abuse—whether in institutions or in Nazi Germany—that most troubled him and commanded his attention. In contrast to many others who have been concerned about abuse and neglect, Burt forced us to examine how people in authority and society itself contributed to inhuman treatment.

Part 3 contains excerpts from some of Burt's writings on public policy. For Burt, public policy had to have a solid foundation in human values and humanitarian concern. Hence, the title to part 3 is "In and Out of Human Policy." "Human Policy" was the name he gave to the policy center he founded at Syracuse University. The title of the proposal he wrote that helped to establish this center, "A Proposal for an Institute on Human Treatment and Public Policy," lends insight into what he thought was important in the formulation of policy toward people with mental retardation and other disabilities.

Man Through a Turned Lens[9]

It has been said that artists distort reality to present reality. Most of us must distort reality to preserve it. For things aren't what they are, but how they appear to a man. He views his world in his own way, and each perception is a special perception. If, in this chapter, you believe my lens has taken a wrong turn, please attempt to adjust your focus, not my vision. In this special way permit me to behave as though things are how I see them.

My thesis is that society will not eradicate institutional back wards, will not guarantee human rights, and will not eliminate hunger by tearing down back wards or "guaranteeing" human rights or feeding hungry people. Mankind must change if we are to reduce inhumanity, if humanity is to survive.

You and I have experienced too much. We observe and record the devastation and consequences of mankind's mad excesses and, in bewilderment, we grope to comprehend this sickness infecting normal people. In despair, we must conclude that, while humanity is imperiled, life continues to flourish heedlessly. In anger, we realize that, as man perseveres, his soul dies. In frustration, we observe that, during our evolution, we have camouflaged the body but accomplished little on behalf of the spirit. We have smoothed the skin but not the conscience, brought dignity to the carriage, but scant any to the carrier.

In humility, and with knowledge that I am no better qualified as accuser than those to whom I speak, I seek redress for certain acts committed by and against mankind.

I am a collector of injustices. Is there a profession as vilified, held more in contempt? I appear as a modern-day Pharisee, and enjoy my role less than those upon whom I intrude. I cringe with embarrassment, presuming to tell you what you must become. Yet I abandon caution, not to save my brothers, but to preserve myself. And, to preserve myself, I ask you to please hear this review of a small segment of human history.

Have you been to Dachau? Can you add all of the Dachaus to all of the Siberias? Is there a man willing to catalogue our own Southern history, life in demented mental hospitals, Vietnam, and the world of man-made subhumans some call state institutions? In his own manner, each man thinks about evil. And, in his curious mind, there are times and situations where he is comforted by its presence. But is there a man who will tolerate a flood that is endless and fathomless and senseless?

In his own manner, each man dreams about clean, happy, laughing people. And, watching a lively girl stroll the avenue on a clear morning, a day that is perfect for mankind, is there a soul who can think about beaten and made-ugly humanity? Yet I am driven to remind you that the moon does have its dark side; the human spirit does entice the inhuman act; man does not always please. Without credentials for these responsibilities, I seek to preserve the precarious thread between each of us and the humanness that we are fast losing. Without credentials, I make demands—yet prefer to follow. I am forced to enjoin my betters, for you have rejected the wisdom of your betters. While the time is long past when mankind ceased its climb upward, there is yet a chance to revive that destined goal and divert ourselves from this faithless journey to nowhere. And, today at least, I believe our one chance lies not in extolling the glories and virtues of that dreamed-of ascendancy, but in describing, dissecting, and comprehending our debasements and agonies. We may save ourselves, not with promises of a new good life to goad us, but with plain accounts of the real-unreal world we have fashioned for ourselves and now must either change or eternally wallow in its slime.

What must we change? Where shall we do battle? Who are the people responsible for Dachau and Song My, for Hitler and Stalin, for some now nameless forgotten German officer and for our own, for the Cancer Ward and the State School, for bloated starving Biafran children, and too many of our children, for wars and killings and hunger and slavery and avarice and dehumanization and inhumanity? Who are the people responsible? You are the only person and I am the only person responsible and accountable. If you do not change, all is lost, and if I do not change, nothing will change. If I blame an evil world, a stupid system, blind leaders, or man's obvious imperfections, I may be right. But if it means I do not have to change, I contribute to the evil.

You and I are all that is needed to change the world. Our necessary confrontation is not social. It is personal. The battle is not against society but with oneself. It is not political, but psychological; not within the group, but in the mind; not to safeguard one's civilization, but oneself, not legal, but moral. The final confrontation will not be among groups of men such as those seated at the United Nations, but within the depths and images and mazes that comprise and consume the substance of each man. The race to eternity will be between a civilization moving toward its infamy and each man weighing his belief in its glory or his worship of its obscenity. In whatever way the race concludes—win or lose, the survival of humanhood or the triumph of savagery—individual man will determine the outcome.

My thesis is, and must be, expressed with repeated use of such terms as *I* and *my*. This cannot be an objective discourse concerning ambiguous Man. It must be the subjective revelation of someone who is forced to flee the safety and comfort of dispassionate exchange. Both this report and whatever you and I do in reaction to it must be personal—in the profound sense—not social.

During my travels through Germany, I had
    often wondered,
"Was he guilty? Was she involved?"
Having never encountered one who was guilty
    or involved,
I realized that I had been asking the wrong
    questions.
Can a man be guilty just because he is not
    involved?
Where were those 50 million uninvolved
    Germans?
Where are the 150 million (175 million?)
    unbigoted Americans?
Were the good Germans innocent?
Is liberal America racist?
They were guilty.
We are racists,
not because we abuse and destroy,
but because our voices are silent.
The silent Americans are guilty!

The racist tells the coon joke and the kike joke and
The racist listens without rancor.
The racist does not rent to Blacks and
The racist does not protest.

Every German who lived unharmed was guilty.
Every American—white and black—who is
   comfortable in his society is racist.
All who have experienced or know of Purgatory,
   asylums, and totalization—and are un-
   troubled—
Dehumanize their brothers.

To observe sorrow untouched is to cause it to
   continue.

I ask you to change humanity by changing yourself, to solve the riddle before you attempt to solve the human puzzle, to commit yourself before you commit mankind. I ask you to think of yourself, not society, and how you must evolve, not what civilization must endure. And for he who concludes that I ask the chicken to change the egg when I say that the individual must change himself first, and then society, does he still doubt that man one day will change his genes?

It is clear that, ultimately, each man must account for his personal behavior and the behavior of those he influences. And it is clear that each point has its counterpoint. For each deed there is another deed or a misdeed. And all these fulfill a grand design for man to alter and improve. As man comprehends his mission and destiny, the design for each of us will reveal as much as he wishes. Man is able to judge and determine his future, and the condition in which he will achieve it. Man is capable of understanding *how* the human world is the complex parts, the sum, and the substance of infinite points and counterpoints.

As each point has its counterpoint, each paradox can unfold understanding. To study human behavior is to study apparent paradoxes—as it is to seek truth. If to know all is to accept all, to know people is to bring one closer to understanding and accepting them—and their weaknesses as well as that which makes them unique and marvelous. In the profound sense, there is no paradox to:

   the thief who is honest,
   the harlot who is virtuous,
   the noble man who is ignoble,
   the wait for Godot that is the wait for God.
   And knowing that to be comfortable in a mad
      universe one must operate in a state of discomfort.

In the profound sense, it may not be paradoxical that, as we grope toward an understanding of dehumanization, we may be led to accept the puzzle of humanity. In the process, we may learn that, while living is a paradox, life is a simple and self-revealing truth.

Since time immemorial, man has heard—and done little—about starving and tortured children. However, even the cleverest among us is unable to conceal or justify mankind's historical denial of fundamental human rights to some among his brothers. There is a difference between truth and fantasy, and he who doesn't appreciate this difference can be dangerous. Such a person finds his truth as it conveniences him and as it fits his behavior. To that man truth is operational belief, a kind of functionalism; if I do it or believe it, by my definition of the infinite it is the correct thing to do or to believe. Even such a person is unable to conceal or justify our sorrowful heritage.

Despite my belief that we in America no more—or less—than other nations sanction human indignities, what I have to report draws its reference from the historical antecedents and the contemporary character of life in America. For we must admit that the *Zeitgeist* of our obese society is menacing:

> Fat, indolent, oppressive
> America, America
> God shed thee of your waste
> Plunder and spoil
> You destroy
> And that which you destroy
> Destroys
> And much that you conserve
> Destroys

> Busy ingenious, submissive
> America, America
> Your crown has thorns
> With paradoxes that have paradoxes
> Our days are better
> As they grow worse
> We become more affluent
> As we sink
> Lower

> Our obese and hungry together average where
>   we should be
> Not where we were or what we are
> All of our wars have been righteous and we fight
>   mental illness
> As we continue to kill and be killed
> In foreign lands and at home
> We are confused and inept with the Blacks
> The Reds, the Yellow, (not Yellows?)

> No not Yellows, never Yellows
> Always the Yellow Menace, the Yellow Horde

> And in our crises with the Blacks
> And the Yellow Horde
> We lose what we know of ourselves
> And what man can make of himself.
> While bright young Ph.D.s and other D.s
>   engage themselves
> And prove to us
> That ants are elephants
> That the world is a marvel
> That society brings me happiness

> That I cannot change the world
> That I am not responsible

Our pioneering forefathers carved out a great and mighty civilization from an indomitable wilderness that required billions of years to form and but a mere hundred or so to conquer. And the price of that wondrous achievement was destroyed Indian civilizations, exploited and brutalized Oriental field workers, victimized Italian railroad laborers, hollow-eyed children working in Manhattan sweat shops, and probably the longest and most continuous and most systematic dehumanization program known to mankind—American slavery. Through some quirk, we are as careful to record for posterity our sicknesses as well as our spiritual victories. There has never been a scarcity of injustice collectors, and in view of our behavior through the years they should have been kept quite busy. It would benefit each of us to review recorded descriptions of the auction block. Read about men, fighting and crying, begging not to be separated from wives and children; a girl, no more than 15, her dress torn away to show that she has no whiplash scars, to demonstrate she isn't a "mean nigger." Slaves branded on the thigh, head, breasts, or back—chained together and marched from one state to another—and those too old or too tired or not caring to live anymore, left by the wayside to die. Generations of Blacks, engulfed and mired in a culture so inhumane that only now can some appreciate the myth of their inferiority and natural subservience. And although there will always be the rebel leader and heroic freedom fighter, America's humanscape will long bear the scars of a system that taught human beings to believe they were not human while they were taught to pray to, and believe in, a merciful God. From the beginning, our history is not unspoiled.

In New York, recently, the papers reported the arrest of a man and his wife for murdering the woman's daughter. The child was starved and beaten and eventually thrown into a river and anchored to 45 pounds of rocks. However, it is not child beaters, insane killers, pathological rapists, and humanity gone berserk that I seek to write about here. Horrifying and painful as those situations are, for thousands and thousands of years civilization has upheld the illegality of such behavior, and thus society has recognized and accepted its responsibility to exact an "eye for an eye" or to impose whatever punishment or retribution it finds necessary to protect itself. Rather, I ask you here to consider our legal or quasi-legal, sanctioned policies and practices that lead to and encourage the denial of human rights to human beings. I ask you to consider the public's will, not the criminal's code; society's ethics, not its prohibitions.

I ask you to reflect upon the consequences of our unique American slave system, injustice in our schools, and the evil perpetrated within our mental hospitals and state schools for the mentally retarded. I ask you to view contemporary American life and your personal activities and convictions with the same diligence and remorselessness we in America judged Hitler's policies in the Warsaw ghetto, Stalin's at Lubyanka, and Mussolini's. As—to our misfortune—the American list is not unlike most other nations', this review will focus particularly on children and their treatment in institutions.

As I exhort you to change, and as I remind myself that reform will not come unless I change, I am compelled again to seek a form more personal than prose to communicate beliefs concerning man and his interrelatedness.

For mankind must believe that:
Each man's life means everything,
Or it means nothing.
He is the only man,
Or no man exists.
Each life and each death
Is a profound event,
Or no life—not a single life ever—
Was of any consequence.
Everything matters or nothing has mattered.

But to account for oneself as one accounts for his brother, to speak of personal anguish so as to deal better with the anguish of others, is a severe test. To do this and to be optimistic in the face of reality—in spite of reality—is the test of poets.

For who can describe beauty in institutions
Who can pay honest tributes to their bucolic scenes
of lush fields and clear streams
Who can so reduce the terror inside
to permit its physical appreciation outside
Who can view the scatological in relation to its
tautological—not its villainy

Who will attempt to discuss the humanitarian
   ethos in terms of:
      asylums
      custody
      totalization

Who is so capable that he may bring dignity to
   such words as:
      inmate
      patient
      material

Who is so sensitive, and insensitive, as to drive
   from his mind:
      the back ward
      the day room
      the nonschool school

Is there a poet—has there ever been one—so
   brave or wise that he dared:
         to squeeze out the truth until it appeared as
            a lie
         to be so objective as to be beyond reality
         to stare down evil and find goodness

Are there men—is there a human being—who
   can detach themselves from passion and
   prejudice
Who can write a true account of life in the
   institution
   who can write about:
      the good as well as the evil
      the beauty with the horror
      the profound asylum and the vivid confinement

Is there one person not of the establishment—
   and not of the reformists—whose axes are
   ground and whose battles are won:
   who can take distance and yet have compassion
   who is neither frightened of evil nor awed by
      goodness
   who can forgive everything and nothing

Is there a poet with words so true, with a mind
   so clear and soul so deep that:
   he comprehends the incomprehensibility of
      asylums
   his language permits new understandings
   we accept his words as deeds

If there is such a poet
   he would appear

Some day, a man will be known
   Who will teach us of life, of beauty, and evil
   Who will help us unfold the meanings of
      things
   And will cause us to learn that there is a design

He will teach us that:
   in spite of the back wards
   in spite of the inmates
   in spite of the evil

 The design for each of us holds nothing but good

 In Paris, on December 10, 1948, the United Nations
General Assembly adopted a Universal Declaration of
Human Rights. Its preamble spoke of dignity and
equality and freedom, once revered concepts that—
in recent years—have fallen upon evil days. I am com-

pelled today, more than two decades after adoption of the Universal Declaration, to review some of the Articles—thereby assessing the state of humanity as I have experienced it and as I judge it to be.

If "All human beings are born free and equal in dignity and rights," then why have I seen, in dormitories for the severely mentally retarded, solitary confinement cells that are continuously filled and with waiting lists for their use?

If "Everyone has the right to life, liberty and security of person," then why have I seen a female resident at the state school for the mentally retarded who has been in a solitary cell for 5 years, never leaving—not for food or toileting or sleep?

If "No one shall be held in slavery or servitude," then why have I seen men who have been held in state school custody for 20 or 30 years, neither having been granted a review of their cases nor genuine consideration of the possibility that they may be capable of discharge and community placement?

If "No one shall be subjected to torture or to cruel, inhuman, or degrading treatment or punishment," then why have I seen two young women in one solitary cell at the state school, lying nude in a corner, their feces smeared on the walls, ceiling, and floor—two bodies huddled in the darkness, without understanding the wrongs they have committed or those committed against them?

If "Everyone has the right to recognition everywhere as a person before the law," then why have I seen another young woman, in solitary confinement, day after day and year after year, nude and assaultive, incontinent and nonverbal—except for 1 day each month when her parents call for her, and when she is washed and dressed and then taken home or for a ride in the country—except for 1 day each month when her clothes remain on her, when she communicates, when she is a human being?

If "No one shall be subjected to arbitrary arrest, detention or exile," then why have I seen men and women—residents of state schools for half a century—never knowing why they were placed originally, no longer caring to experience the outside world, and with no possibility that anyone outside is either interested in them or knows that they exist as human beings?

If "Everyone is entitled in full equality to a fair and public hearing by an independent and impartial tribunal in the determination of his rights and obligations and of any criminal charge against him," then why have I seen a boy at a state school, in continuous seclusion 24 hours a day, described by the dormitory physician as a "monster"?

If "No one shall be subjected to arbitrary interference with his privacy, family, home or correspondence, nor to attacks upon his honor and reputation," then why have I seen incoming mail to state school residents, and their outgoing mail, read and censored by institutional supervisors?

If "Everyone has the right to freedom of movement and residence within the borders of each state. [If] Everyone has the right to leave any country, including his own, and to return to his country," then why have I seen human beings who have never—in 10 or 20 or 30 or 70 years—left the 100 or 200 or a 1000 acres of the state school—they who were delivered there at birth, whose souls only will leave?

If "Men and women of full age, without any limitation due to race, nationality or religion, have the right to marry and to found a family," then why have I seen the mentally retarded, the epileptic, and others denied such rights by state statutes; why have I seen young women sterilized as a condition for their release from the state school?

If "Everyone has the right to own property alone as well as in association with others. [If] No one shall be arbitrarily deprived of his property," then why have I seen residents of the state school deprived of their personal possessions and their entitlements under public assistance?

If "Everyone has the right to freedom of thought, conscience and religion," then why have I seen some residents at the state school required to attend church services and other residents prohibited from such attendance?

If "Everyone has the right to freedom of opinion and expression," then why have I seen a child berated by his state school teacher because of the opinions he expressed and why did I hear her tell him how ungrateful, how wicked he was, in light of the bountiful state that had given this unwanted child everything and expected only loyalty and gratitude in return?

If "Everyone, as a member of society, has the right to social security," then why have I seen more securing than security, more solitary than social, more indignity than dignity, more enchainment than freedom?

If "Everyone has the right to work, to free choice of employment, to just and favorable conditions of work and to protection against unemployment," then why have I seen residents of state schools in custody long beyond that time when they merited community placement, in custody because they were performing essential and unpaid work at the institutions.

If "Everyone has the right to education," then why have I seen children at state schools for the mentally retarded permanently denied any semblance of education, treatment, or training?

If "Nothing in this Declaration may be interpreted as implying for any state, group or person any right to engage in any activity or to perform any act aimed at the destruction of any of the rights and freedoms set forth herein," then why have I seen human beings who have been given nothing, who have nothing, and who, tomorrow, will have less?

Why have I seen a state school superintendent who did not call for a postmortem, an inquiry, or even a staff conference to determine the possibility of negligence or other unusual circumstances surrounding the death of a severely retarded child who choked when an attendant fed her a whole hard-boiled egg?

Why have I seen a state school director of nursing leave suddenly for a 3-day vacation, without assigning additional staff or someone to succeed him in his absence, during the midst of a hepatitis epidemic where in one building alone 27 of 71 patients were diagnosed as having this dreaded disease?

Why have I seen a severely retarded ambulatory resident, stabbed in the testicles by an unknown assailant while he slept, who almost died because the night attendant bandaged him as best she could, with no one doing anything else for the wound until 10 hours later?

Why have I seen children at the state school go to bed each night wearing dungarees instead of pajamas, on mattresses without sheets, without pillows, and not one child "owning" even a single article of clothing?

Why have I seen children nude and bruised, sitting, sleeping, and eating with moist or dried feces covering them and their surroundings?

Why have I seen children lying on filthy beds, uncovered, flies crawling all over them?

Why have I seen children playing in and eating garbage?

Why have I been forced to view my brothers, and the world in which they live, as if I were standing in garbage, as if it were to consume me?

Form in your mind's eye this scene, this continuation, this last vulgar ounce of value squeezed from those least valued. Visualize this short true story.[10]

Fine grains of snow fall gently on the roughly hewn gray stone fort. Inside, amid the harsh lives and broken thoughts, a procession silently and fleetingly mourns. Those who comprehend learn that one has passed and they mourn, not for him, but for themselves and for each other.

They mourn for lives lived without hope, that end without meaning.

They mourn for a soul used in his lifetime as material, whose bones and meat continue to serve science.

They mourn for those deadly years and now this restless death, swirling in gleaming vats in Boston and Syracuse, waiting for bright lively boys in white to perform one final necessary obscenity.

They mourn for their wasted lives that shall end as this one ends, not cleanly, neither in sympathy for the living survivors nor with respect for the immortal spirit.

But they mourn more for the creations of God and obstetricians than the final indignities imposed by chairmen of medical school cadaver committees.

For the law requires that their bloated, mutilated, and sewn flesh must be scooped together, someday, and returned to the earth they long for, the earth that will treat them more gently than the world that spawned them.

For is there a law, is there an authority that can do for one—in life—what all beings achieve in death?

Is there a mundane justice that, however infinitesimally, compares with the equality and brotherhood of the ground?

Dare we believe that there is a faithful conclusion, even for one whose life is as faithless as his mortal mission is senseless, as it is a violation of his right to be faithful?

Dare we hope that dead people bear no grudges, even as the living remorselessly pursue the unforgiven, unblessed departed?

I have brought up the past and now the deceased. What of the living and how may we predict the future? For the living confound as we are drawn to them. Can there be a better world for the mentally retarded? Asking the question implied that, indeed, there can be a better world, that, in retrospect, this is a better world. Asking the question denies the inevitable answer.

Some among you may conclude that an insuperable chasm lies between this discourse and evidence. Some may claim that I bring the softest data to support these words. In truth, I need no data, for everything reported here is well known to those who know about such matters; and anyone who requires data is unlikely to put such evidence to useful purposes. We need no data to conclude that there never was, there isn't now, there will not be a better world for the mentally retarded.

There cannot be a better world for the mentally retarded, or a poorer world, or any world. Worlds and futures are for the living, not for labels and nomenclatures and retards or defectives. Worlds are for lives, not for things or prejudices or administrative configurations. The mentally retarded are no more people than is the photograph a person. To understand this permits one to appreciate the beauty of a Helen Keller and to realize that—while she was not mentally retarded—before she was not mentally retarded, and before Anne Sullivan, she was mentally retarded.

We are trapped. Now that man has created the "mentally retarded" (and the "mentally ill") he must label and categorize him, not only as he seeks to help him—irony of ironies—even as he struggles to wipe away the effects of his evil taxonomy, even as he strives to erase forever the taxonomy itself. As I entreat you to destroy the concept "mental retardation," I find myself using the term as you use it, adding to the layers of inhumanity heaped upon those souls so foully designated. As I tell you there is no future for the mentally retarded, there will not be any until they are returned to their brothers as men and women; as I tell you these things, I meander about human beings as "mentally retarded." We are trapped by civilization's penchant for creating insane problems. And our brothers and we will not be rescued by psychologists or sociologists or special educators—and, although they will better describe and teach us about the benchmarks of civilization, not even by poets or historians. We have a modest chance to permit the now-retarded, the now-disturbed, the now-abused to enter our world—albeit an imperfect world—and, I believe, that chance depends upon a decision society must take, but only insofar as each man must make his personal decision.

Men can no longer hide their faith and their souls in the United Nations or with any other group. What we have done to each other no nation and no group can rectify. What I have done to you, only I can repay and correct. Before each man seeks to change the world, he must change. Before these words become more than just words, I must become more than I am now. As I lament on the plight of mankind, I must account for my own plight:

> For, who can tell a man, "We will make up to you for the lost years"?
> Who can return to a man the sweet pleasures of a summer day,
> His wife and carefree children at his side—
> To a man destroyed before his marriage,
> With children never to be conceived?
> Who can describe the fragrant sensation of a pine-covered hill in May,
> Backdropping a neat farmhouse overlooking fields and streams,
> And living things—
> To one who had hardly lived and had barely been given time to stop,
> And gather in these wonders?
> Is there a man who can claim, "I have seen these times restored,
> I have been given back the years that were taken,
> The flesh that was ravaged,
> The being that once ceased to be"?
> Who will unfold the years that are gone,
> The times that are past,
> The moments that are wasted,
> This instant that will never again be?
> When a man thinks about these questions, he cries.
> He doesn't cry for mankind, nor for you.
> He cries for himself and for the wasted times in a
> Desolate and plundered
> Cosmos.

Man is a wise fool and a sentimental sadist. Is this his natural manner? The fundamental question is whether man is able—and if, as I believe, he is able, is he willing—to change. Both fearfully and hopefully I conclude that if he doesn't change, nothing will matter. And if he doesn't, all of our past could not have mattered. If he doesn't, he will have become an example of the rabbis' ancient saying that God gives wisdom only to those who have wisdom.

Further, I believe that what each man does—and how his every act causes and effects—is more than a reflection of his selfhood. It is a recreation of it. But what has he fashioned?

Man differentiates himself from other beings.

He has speech.
He can protect himself from the elements.
He can leave the old and adapt to a new environment.

Man's speech, his clothing, and the ingenious ways he travels and migrates,
Allow him to be freer than:
    The Eagle
    The Jungle Beast and
    Even
    The Wind.

Man is capable of controlling the forces of nature more than they are capable of controlling him.
But man has not demonstrated his capability to control himself.
And that which permits him to fly, to build, to shape his destiny,
Causes him to impede and destroy other men.
That which gives some men their freedom, gives enslavement to others.
That which makes man uniquely free,
Makes him uniquely harassed.

Our gifts are our demons.
Never having spoken, the lion rules with a roar.
Hardly moving, the snail endures.
In his pond, the fish is free.

But man, prideful and eloquent man!
He disdains the matter and struggles against a relationship with them.
He binds the crippled and increases their spasticity.
He restrains the weak and incompetent and guarantees their infirmity.

He envelopes the old and feeble and ensures their loneliness.
He segregates the ill and re-creates their mental and spiritual disabilities.

Man enforces his retribution on those who do not speak by incarcerating them.
On those who do not think by enchaining them.
On those who do not conform by denuding them.
On those who will not be broken by breaking them.

The animals have fewer gifts than man but
    fewer imperatives
    fewer options but
    fewer requirements
    fewer accomplishments but
    fewer needs.

Animals are less civilized than man but have more civilization.
Animals have less freedom.
But the animal world has more freedom.

Mankind has enslaved his brothers and himself.

Some may wonder why I wrote this paper. There is a compelling Israeli dialogue wherein a visitor asks, "Why did you come here?"

The Israeli replies, "I came to Israel to forget."

"To forget what?"

"I forgot."

I wrote this paper to remind those who have forgotten and to help instruct those who claim not to know. For there are other compelling words, born and nurtured and forevermore carved in the soil of Dachau:

"Remember us. Do not forget."

Our Jerusalem will be the back ward. And we must not forget its existence—and all of mankind's ideological back wards—until civilization makes it unnecessary for us to remember.

Most of all, I wrote this paper to remind myself. I must not forget.

Reprinted by permission of Steven D. Blatt and the Blatt family.

How to Destroy Lives by Telling Stories[11]

> Someone once told Rabbi Mendel that a certain person was greater than another whom he also mentioned by name. Rabbi Mendel replied: "If I am I because I am I, and you are you because you are you, then I am I and you are you. But if I am I because you are you, and you are you because I am I, then I am not I, and you are not you."
>
> *Author Unknown*

God and Popeye

Perhaps there is no more human activity than the telling of stories. Perhaps nothing better characterizes the human being than his ability to tell stories. The rational person exhibits his humanity by telling rational stories, while the religious person explains and guides his life by stories from the Scriptures. And where our ancestors sought to understand the world by telling stories of giants on the backs of turtles, scientists today tell stories of a Big Bang and relentless entropy. People seem driven to capture or construct their reality through stories. Each of us has a memory filled with stories which explain the world and ourselves, stories of Santa Claus and storks delivering babies, stories of our origins and hopes, stories of misplaced ambitions and good and bad excuses. When a child is born, no developmental milestone is as eagerly awaited or as crucial to attain as the miracle of language. And what is so astonishing is that, soon after birth, almost every child is on the way to being a teller of stories. In a fashion and with a suddenness which even the experts don't fully understand, only the truly exceptional baby fails to develop an elaborate system for communicating. Hence, almost all people participate in the human drama of storytelling.

It is a drama, of course! It is the drama which binds people to a common cause, as it is the drama which separates others and leads to conflict. Our stories not only stir people to want to live together but also to want to live apart—to make war, to kill. While there are people who live by the word, and while there are still some who would die for it, too many of us are eager to kill if the right words are spoken, if proper orders are given. Consequently, those few people who do not have stories have, instead, grave troubles. It's probable that, more than anything else, their inefficient language causes trouble for people who are mentally retarded. And it is certain that the language the rest of us employ so effortlessly deepens those troubles. We tell stories about people who can't tell stories, people who can't stop us from telling our stories about them. Our stories have been known to kill the mentally retarded.

Because language has such power and importance, and because not to have it is to be in such serious trouble, I want to spend some time thinking not so much about retarded people as about the stories we tell, what kinds of consequences stories have, and what guidelines there might be to steer us through the inescapable dilemmas of human language and life. Because their inability to use language defines and causes trouble for people who are mentally retarded, because we live in a world constructed of stories and the mentally retarded cannot tell their own stories, and they cannot stop us from telling destructive stories about them, I want to concentrate here on stories as both antecedent to abuse as well as reflection of concern. In this way, I intend to build a case for stories as the context in which to understand the harm we cause other people, even those whom we profess to regard as brothers.

When God says, "I am," and when Popeye says, "I am what I am," both are affirmations that everyone—that even God—has and tells stories which define us. When God says, "I am," He warns us of course that there is nothing more to be said, that He is everything. But when the sailor says, "I am what I am," he, too, announces that nothing more need be said—imperfections notwithstanding—that you could take him or leave him, but if you take him, you must take the total person, the coarseness as well as the good nature, the spinach with the muscles. You can't have one without the other. That's why, while "I am" is the most serious story, "I am what I am" is the most serious individual's story. A person is defined by the stories he tells about himself as well as the stories that are told about him. But sometimes, one's definition of oneself is challenged, and this signals the beginnings of abuse.

Language is such a miracle! It begins with the infant, who very soon after birth achieves a sophisticated system for communicating. Language stirs people to make love, to initiate wars, to lay their lives down for their country, or their God, or their youth, or their excesses. Language drives away boredom, enriches our lives, makes life worth living. Language also hurts, may make one's life unbearable. Language can kill! Nothing is more certain than that there are inescapable consequences of language. That is, one can rarely if ever say "I'm sorry" and, thus, patch things up as if nothing had occurred after announcing to a lover that the relationship had ended. One can't simply say "I didn't mean it" and get away with it after telling someone something for his "own good." One can't always say "I made a mistake" after declaring that so-and-so is mentally ill or he or she is mentally retarded. Writers live to produce language, others have died to rid themselves of mischievous language. Is it any wonder that telling false stories about people can destroy their lives? Is it any wonder that the process of abuse is initiated at the invention of a disease assigned to a person? By merely telling a story, the scene is set for abuse.

Once upon a time, there was an old woman who lived alone in a very old house which had been her father's house, which had been his father's house. Everyone in the town said that she had a mattress full of money. One night while she slept, three young men stole into the house, killed the old woman, and tore open the mattress. They found old feathers.

Once upon a time, an old man and an old woman lived together in the same house for 60 years. When the old man died, the couple's children decided that the old woman couldn't take care of herself any longer. She needed "care." They placed her in a nursing home, although she didn't need "care" until after she was placed there.

In the first of these stories, the intention was to do harm. In the other, good. But both stories about these old people had evil consequences. Intentions aside, stories which are not true usually have evil consequences.

Abuse is to be expected from stories about mattresses filled with money. The most benign consequence of such a story is that it is made false, that the thieves and murderers find out after invading her privacy that the old woman doesn't have any money hidden in a mattress. The most benign consequence of doing something for someone's "good," in spite of that person's objections, is that the "busybody" doesn't get away with it. When Socrates said that you can't have good ends from bad means, he must also have meant that you can't do people good if you lie to them or about them, if you invent stories about their lives.

Centuries ago in this country, there were stories about women who were witches, women who cast spells or who gave birth to calves. Such women were hanged, not because they broke any laws, not because they weren't church-going or honest, and not because they didn't watch over their families. The women were hanged because they were witches, and witches were hanged. That was surely not history's first example, but murdering witches illustrates what can occur when abuses are invented to deal with invented diseases. In many quarters, a "67" means "educable mentally retarded," and stories are told about the "educable mentally retarded." And a "44" means "trainable mentally retarded," and stories are told about those people. In 1969, 200,000 people lived in state institutions for the mentally retarded, and one of the stories about virtually all of those people was that they were not able to take care of themselves out of the institution. And while there are fewer people in such institutions today, that same story persists for those who remain there. Indeed, by definition, most people in institutions are there today because they are presumably unable to manage their affairs competently, if at all, in the larger society. *We* wrote that story, presumably on their behalf.

When God says, "I am," He tells us to hear in our hearts what He says, and see with our souls what He does. He informs us that He is everywhere, that He is everything, and that we should know Him from the stories which are told about Him, all the stories, even those which mortal man can't yet fathom. And Popeye? Popeye isn't merely the spinach-eating strong man. He's also what he thinks about Olive, and what she thinks about him. And not only is he defined by his friends, but by Bluto, too, and by Popeye's other enemies. The stories about us, true and untrue, those we tell and those which are told about us, represent the substance of the human dictionary. That's why it has been said that to know all is to understand all and, thus, to forgive all. That's why it can be said that no one ever has the complete story. Hence, we had better be careful about what incomplete stories we tell.

Invented Abuses for Invented Diseases

Stories based on false premises are almost necessarily abusive. Of course, not every abuse is of this kind. Old women are murdered in their beds by people who neither know them nor the stories about them. My point is that invented stories often cause a lot of harm, and rarely if ever do any good. And the other point is that invented stories—i.e., invented diseases—lead to invented treatments, which never do anyone good and often do them a great deal of harm. Virtually any treatment designed to deal with an invented disease is abusive because it is based on a story which isn't true. Even when we invent a story that compliments a man, that announces his wisdom or courage, it will cause him to suffer eventually. If we try to convince our child that he plays the fiddle like Heifetz or the piano like Rubenstein, it's all very nice until reality inescapably reveals itself. Sometimes in our eagerness to be "nice" to people, we impose burdens upon them which are as hurtful as if we wanted to hurt. *We must be true to people.* And, consequently, our stories about them must be true. Of course, there are dilemmas, which I will get to but not deal with well.

Mental retardation is an invented disease, an untrue and unnecessary story about a large group of people. In some families, old age is an invented disease, while in other families it is an honored state of being. In some families, manual work is an invented disease, while in other families it is an honored occupation. But *always,* mental retardation is an invented disease. That is, to understand the disease of "mental retardation," one needn't be a neurologist, a psychologist, a social worker, or a teacher. Of course, to do something about neurological impairment, it's good to have a neurologist handy, as it's good to have a teacher available if a child is waiting to be taught. But mental retardation, itself, can't be appreciated by a study of marbles and holes or neurons and dendrites. Mental retardation, *itself,* requires the study of our prejudiced inventions about certain people who have wires loose or who read poorly. Illiteracy is real. Blindness is real. However nonrevealing and misinforming it may be, the 50 IQ is real. The chronological age of 80 is the truth about the octogenarian. But mental retardation is an invention, an untrue story. And as nothing good obtains from such untrue stories, the treatments for mental retardation are necessary inventions and, consequently, are always abuses.

What Practitioners Should Know

I cling to the conception of practitioners who are determined to benefit society, who are less interested in finding out whether a person can or can't be helped. The role of the school psychologist should be more to find a way for the child to profit from the regular class than to find the law or the reason to place the child in a special class. The role of the teacher is to find a way to help teach the child rather than to find a reason for excluding the child, physically or psychologically. I cling to the belief that practitioners should develop optimistic stories concerning their clients. But I say that every person is entitled to have only true stories told about him! Yes, but I also admit that there are dilemmas here. For example, parents should never tell trivial stories about their own children. Indeed, their stories about their children should be more on the grand side, if not so grand as to mislead or burden the child. Parents should tell stories for their children to live up to and not stories to shame them and to live down. And that's what professionals should do, tell stories that their clients will want to live up to. Quite literally, the intention of therapy is to get people to change their stories, to rescript their lives, *to learn,* which is merely another way of saying *to change.* But what does a therapist do when the man in the bughouse proclaims, "I'm Napoleon"? Is the only goal of therapy to correct a false story? And if so, how is it accomplished? Do we shock it out of him? Or condition it out of him? Or drug it out of him? Or beat it out of him? Possibly, the man is entitled to his fantasies. Maybe he is Napoleon, even if not the same Napoleon who fought the battle of Waterloo. Maybe the therapist deals with Napoleon well only when he remembers the Golden Rule: "You should believe and tell stories which, if you were in that person's shoes, you would be willing to have told about you." That is, telling someone's story is also believing your story. And so the question is, "Could there be an institutional story, a Willowbrook or Pennhurst story, that someone—client, staff, someone who knows—would want to live up to, or own up to?"

Many of our books and discussions in the field of mental retardation seem to concentrate on what can be done to our subjects. But ironically, the most important research question we have is what can be done to help those who aren't retarded to live more compatibly with those who are retarded. The obsessive commitment of professionals to remain outsiders is a logical and absolute barrier to our ever becoming important in the lives of our clients. For example, what can we tell the couple whose marriage is troubled by the presence of a severely retarded child? Is there a curriculum for marital happiness? Not really, yet we think it is important to have our students learn about the "Impact of Mental Retardation on the Home."

Retarded people have problems of mobility, perception, articulation, reading, and arithmetic. But these are not the problems that students of mental retardation need to address. Mobility problems of the mentally retarded will be solved by the architects and by the application of the sort of technology that makes travel on the moon possible. In a sense, that is a trivial problem, not that a child or "anyone" can solve such a problem, but that we have sound methodologies for tackling such problems in the same way that the cure of some cancers is trivial. The serious problems we have in the field of mental retardation are the ones related to the cultivation of moral attitudes and to securing respect for the rights of others, and not merely in complying with the laws guaranteeing such rights.

Our scholarship in the field of mental retardation hardly touches upon these serious problems, except to the extent that it "proves" what *doesn't* help, how administrative strategies *break down,* and what *not* to try. Of course, there are "intuitive" understandings we have of what it is to be intelligent and what it is to be retarded. Not only professionals but *all* people think of *something* when they hear the word "retarded." That's the point! While ranging widely in quality and frequency of such thoughts, there are common understandings which transcend occupational level and even personal involvement. And although these thoughts can dominate and blind us unless we attend to them very carefully, they also help to keep us honest, because they give us a sense of what we actually think in contrast to the modish words we usually employ.

At times, science and scholarship curiously muddle our comprehension. That is, science and scholarship make it easy for us to compose and tell nonrevealing, unrelated, or erroneous stories ostensibly connected with mental retardation. Of course, science deepens understanding and increases knowledge, but there is also a sense in which science may have nothing to do with ordinary experience, such as what it means to be a person labeled mentally retarded. We must be careful lest science leads us away to its own lofty but irrelevant domains. For example, science tells us that black is not a color, but the absence of color. What are we to make of this? Sensible people entirely disregard such information. The thing to realize is that neither science nor sensible people are wrong. Science has discovered something important about the portion of the electromagnetic spectrum which is detectable by human eyes. However, science makes no contribution to the ordinary person's deliberations in choosing new clothes or cars because those are deliberations which, by their nature, can't be facilitated by increased knowledge of the properties of light. A harmonious wardrobe is not based on a knowledge of optics. But this is not to say that we would want the lenses for our eyeglasses to be designed by fashion experts based on their knowledge of colors. The scientist teaches that matter is "mostly empty space." Then, if I go to the refrigerator after stocking it with groceries, what should I expect to find? "Mostly empty space" in refrigerators means "no food," even though that's not what the scientist means. While saying something true, the scientist obviously isn't speaking about refrigerators.

Science can illuminate the universe as well as muddle our tiny portion of it. Consequently, we have to remind ourselves of our subject, *mental retardation,* and make sure that it is being illuminated rather than distorted or obscured. In mental retardation, the problems to be addressed must be problems which arise in *life,* not in the laboratory. Neurologists have much to learn from studying mental retardation, but mental retardation must not be confused with neurology. Certainly, there are inquiries which can be most satisfactorily addressed in the laboratory. If not exclusively, we may profitably study intelligence and learning in the laboratory. But such research questions are no more about retarded people than they are about any other people. Consequently, when we call upon the laboratory sciences, we must understand that the questions we ask, however important they may be, are removed from the direct study of mental retardation. Scientists curing mental retardation is the quintessential science fiction story in our field.

Preventing Abuses

There may be some truth to a story which nevertheless leads to abuse; the old woman indeed had a mattress, never mind the lies about what was in it. Then the question is, "How can we make sure that we tell 'true' true stories about people?" Any intervention based on the premise that a person can't learn anything is a story almost certain to destroy that person. The story that a person's condition is hopeless, or that mental retardation is incurable, or that mental retardation is genetic (i.e., in the same way that Tay-Sachs disease is genetic) are either not at all or not sufficiently true and, thus, can destroy people. Practitioners, administrators, and policy makers need to be guided by the conviction that human capability is educable, that there are procedures and conditions and stimulations which can bring out an individual's capabilities for changing. And abuses are prevented when individuals are given opportunities to contribute to and not merely to cope with society. Abuses are prevented when more of us behave as if people can learn, but even more so when we vigorously support each person's right to his fullest development possible, irrespective of the course of his life or his actual contributions to society. It is with that belief in human educability as well as in our common relatedness and natural rights as human beings that people find ways to prevent abuses. Such stories truly prevent abuse.

Rediscovering the 19th Century

The story I heard was that Indonesia has but one inconsequential residential facility for a few mentally retarded children, located near Jakarta, its largest city. The story I heard was that the institution, as the country itself, was very poor and scientifically backward, and that I should not expect to see much there. There was truth to that story but, as I learned, even more that was untrue. Here again was a story which was not only descriptive but diagnostic; while the facts about this Indonesian institution were true, what I was led to believe was untrue. Constructed from my notes from that visit several months ago, this is the "true" story, or as much of a true story as somebody could give who hardly knows the country, its history, or what it thinks about itself.

Indonesia is the fifth largest country in the world. Then how could it be that this place we were about to visit was the only institution for multiply handicapped children in the entire country? How could it be that an ordinary looking house for 16 children is the country's institution for multiply handicapped children? They also told us that this was our lucky day: the Rupiah is devalued approximately a third and we're sitting on a hotel bill which, therefore, will be reduced a third. But if we're so lucky, why don't we feel lucky sitting in the back seat of a car that is propelling us back in time to an institution, the likes of which were more commonly seen in rural America 100 years ago? And as we ride on that bumpy and dust-generating road, with windows closed in order to keep out the choking pollution which hangs heavy everywhere and remains until the car is far out of the city, we sit frozen, hoping that our faces do not betray the anxieties which we're trying to keep in check. We don't want to insult Julie, our volunteer guide. So, with eyes darting here, then there, we fill ourselves with exotic scenes of lush vegetation pushing against homes made of paper and sticks. And everywhere there are milling people; everywhere there are teeming mobs. And the amazing thing is that everyone seems to be doing something; everyone seems busy. The car moves too quickly to figure out what is going on, so we hardly have time to notice that it's midday; yet the children too are on the streets. We hardly have time to think about why the children don't appear to go to school and why the adults aren't working someplace. But don't misunderstand, this is not like a scene in New York's or Detroit's ghetto. In America's ghettos, no one seems to be moving, everyone stands still, seems frozen except when something bad is happening, then chaos is boss.

We've been driving approximately 40 minutes. There are more open spaces here. We see people who must be farmers working what must be their fields. The air smells cleaner. Some of our anxiousness is submerged, possibly because the fresh air and real countryside cause us to forget for the moment how many people are needed to support one of us in the style to which Americans have become accustomed. We've forgotten for the moment how many people here seem to live by the narrowest of margins, without any support from industry, government, or even the elements. And as we're thinking about these matters, the car slows down, makes a sharp right, and stops. We're here. We had to travel 13,000 miles to learn again what our forefathers knew, what the Amish know, and what we know in our souls. But while everyone knows what we're about to say, it seems that only those whose religions require them to believe it actually believe it. That's why the Amish don't need to read this, and that's why we don't expect many of you to buy this story.

The institution was built about 8 years ago. Before that, nothing of a group residential nature was provided for such children. What happens to the thousands of others in this country who are born very delicate and very handicapped is anybody's guess. You don't rule out the possibility that some of those children do survive and are cared for by family or others, and I won't rule out the possibility that thousands of children die needlessly because there is no one to care for them or to fix their broken spines or misfunctioning enzymes.

We're met at the door by the nurse in charge. She's an old woman, recently retired from a position in a general hospital. She's assisted by 8 or 10 young women who are also called nurses, but who probably don't have any formal nursing training. There's also an old man who serves as some sort of caretaker for the facility.

The main floor consists of a couple of small dormitories, a staff dining room, some sort of a reception room, possibly another small room or two. The cribs are lined up side by side. And that's it.

In some respects, this institution is exactly like Willowbrook, Belchertown, Fernald, and the others. Of course, it's much smaller; there's hardly anything to this place. Of course, there's also nothing here for the residents to do. It's a typical institution. But to conclude that is to miss the point, to construct an erroneous story.

We go from crib to crib. One blind child is trying to get about. He's the only child who seems to have the freedom of the dormitory. We ask if he is being taught anything. No, there's no itinerant teacher of the blind to come to teach him. There's no Anne Sullivan for this child. We move on. In the next crib is a child with hydrocephalus. His enormous head tells us that there may be little hope here. Through Julie, our interpreter, we ask the head nurse whether a shunt operation was attempted. We are told that it was not only not attempted but is unknown. We move on to a child with beautiful eyes who lies in his crib staring. He seems to want to say something to us, but we don't understand Indonesian. We move on to the next crib, and the next, and then to the next room, and on to the next crib, and the next. We ask about the rest of the institution. But this is it. There is a second floor, which is a dormitory for the nurses. We chat for a few more minutes, thanking each other for the same reason: our visit. We are grateful, but they too seem grateful.

The ride back to Jakarta is quicker, quieter. Each of us is thinking about what we've just seen. We have been to an institution whose entire operating budget is 10,000 American dollars a year, less than $700 a resident. And we're soon going back to a land where yearly institutional budgets for 3,000 residents often run higher than $75 million, $30,000 a resident, sometimes higher than $90,000 a resident. Of course, we know that the average Indonesian doesn't earn $700 a year, and if he did, so what; one cannot compare Indonesia to the United States in this regard. And we know that, in America, children with hydrocephalus are afforded shunt operations to sometimes prevent the devastating effects of this malady. And while we know that even 75 years ago in America, there was an Anne Sullivan for a Helen Keller, we know some other things too. We know that in our multibillion dollar mental retardation system, children lie in beds unattended. We know that what happened between Helen Keller and Anne Sullivan was an official miracle. We know that institutions which spend $50,000 a year per resident still send their clients to bed without proper food, still can't find ways to provide their clients with clothes which they would own, still have dormitories which stink. We know that everything is supposed to be better in the United States, and lots of things are better in the United States, but not so many things are better in the United States for severely and multiply handicapped children.

How could it be that this country, which hasn't yet discovered shunt operations, a country that spends only $700 per year per child in an institution, a country whose capital city has open sewers, could have created an institution whose dormitories smelled sweet? How could it be that a country whose money was devalued a third during the few days we were there, whose average citizen doesn't read, whose institutional superintendent doesn't have a college degree, who doesn't know about Braille, who doesn't know about perinatology, who doesn't know about all the things which make life beautiful in the United States, can run a cleaner and more decent institution than we in New York State run? There might be a howl about the assertions here—a howl not only from commissioners of mental retardation but even from some of my friends who will point out all of the flaws in this argument. But I wonder if there would have been a howl from Jean Marc Gaspard Itard, Edward Seguin, Maria Montessori, Samuel Gridley Howe, or Albert Schweitzer. Was it really as bad as we'd like to say it was before the dawn of science? Are we as good as we like to think we are, as we marvel at the wonders created during this modern era? Or is it that while science does a lot of good, it does good in such a narrow way that only a very few or only a small part of each of us profit from it? Is the magic bullet of science miraculous for only the few with PKU, Rh, and the handful of others with specific and controllable conditions, while it ignores the throngs?

Other Stories and Other Dilemmas

Stories about our people today are more important than ever before. In the 19th century, the diagnosis that someone was an incurable idiot would be known to the few who treated him, to his family, to possibly a handful of others. Today, in Western society that information is stored by computers, can be transmitted anywhere, is retrieved instantaneously, and need never be destroyed or discarded. What happens in an Indonesian institution is learned by few of that nation's millions, which is a useful definition of the nontechnological culture. What happens at Willowbrook or Partlow is known by anyone who owns a television set and wants to listen to Geraldo Rivera. Stories are increasing at an exponential rate. Computers, telecommunications systems, direct dialing across the world, airplanes, the other modern wonders quickly spread untrue stories. Worse, whoever notices, much less believes, retractions? And it is the handicapped and other fragile people who are the likeliest and easiest victims of untrue stories in this age when everybody has "the right to know" and demands to know everything about anything. Of course, anyone—you or I—can be hurt. A teacher's notation about a clumsy first grader is filed to haunt an adult decades later. A computer fouls up then refuses to desist spewing forth its erroneous information, thus causing one's credit to be impaired. How many untrue stories has the FBI filed? How many have been filed by the elementary school you attended?

Stories are told about women with big breasts, others about women with small breasts. Stories are told about male nurses, others about people whose parents were immigrants, or Jews, or alcoholics, or Anglo-Saxons. One man's story is his poison but, to another man, that same story is the antidote. One doctor's treatment is to cut the leg off, while another doctor tries to talk that same patient out of his neurosis. In King Farouk's mind, each of his issue was born with a birth defect, the female gender. He didn't want to hear about chromosomes, only male heirs to succeed him. Kings and pawns, every one of us has a story. Or better, each of us has many stories which comprise "the story." Here are a few from among the countless stories about how the mentally retarded are treated. But these together, even these and many more, do not tell "the story" about any one person, much less about the mentally retarded.

Recently, in a northeastern state, the deputy commissioner of mental retardation and developmental disabilities visited with a group of home owners in an affluent community. His purpose was to explain to those "good and substantial citizens" why the state had intentions to invite other citizens—mentally retarded people—to live in a particular home. The deputy commissioner felt the meeting had gone well, that the discussion was reasonable and the local citizens understood the state's point of view in the matter. He certainly never expected what happened only a few hours after he left the community. A torch was put to the home. What horrible stories had these "good and substantial citizens" contrived to drive them to arson?

This letter sent by a state official responsible for "quality of care" to another official responsible for "employee relations" tells another story:

Dear _____,

I am writing to call to your attention a significant problem in the current contract between the State and the _____ Employees Association which adversely effects [sic] the ability of a facility director to take actions which he deems essential for assuring quality patient care.

Recently, an employee at _____ Children's Psychiatric Center was charged with patient abuse as result of an assault upon a fourteen-year-old child which necessitated several stitches in the child's face. The employee was found guilty and a penalty of two months suspension was imposed. When the employee returned to work, the Director of the facility, Dr. _____, decided to reassign him, at the same salary, to a function that did not involve direct patient contact. The employee has challenged the director's decision and litigation has ensued, since the contract does not recognize the director's right to make such a reassignment without the employee's consent. In the judgment of the employee relations and legal staff of the Office of Mental Health, it appears that the employee will very likely succeed in his lawsuit and that the director will have no choice but to assign such an employee to his old job which involved direct patient contact.

At _____ Psychiatric Center, an employee was disciplined for ripping a patient's face with a can opener. The arbitrator permitted a **temporary** reassignment of unspecified duration of this employee as part of the penalty awarded. The director of _____ Psychiatric Center will confront the same dilemma that the Director of _____ Children's Psychiatric Center has already confronted.

While denying a director the right to keep employees with patient abuse convictions from direct patient contact may be protective of the employee's interests, it is a measure that seriously erodes the director's ability to be responsible for quality care within the mental hygiene facility.

The Commission on Quality of Care strongly recommends that a better balance be struck between the employee's right to continued employment and the patient's right to be saved from forseeable [sic] harm. Where an employee has been found guilty of patient abuse after all the due process safeguards provided by the disciplinary procedure, it appears to us that the facility director ought to have reasonable latitude in reassigning such an employee, at no loss of pay or other benefits, to functions that do not involve direct patient contact.

Sincerely,

_____

Chairman

Recently, in a large state institution for the mentally retarded in a northeastern state, a nonambulatory client was fastened to a hoist in order to transport him from a swimming pool to his wheelchair. In the process, the hoist snapped. The client crashed to the tile floor, breaking his neck and dying instantly. The next day, the State Department of Mental Retardation issued orders to have every such hoist inspected in every institution under its jurisdiction. What stories are created in attempts to humanize systems that must function in a manner similar to how the airlines function when a motor falls off a plane? Is there a story to normalize the "DC10 syndrome"?

A teacher whom I work with has a child in her class with many problems, a fragile, handicapped, and neglected child. Because we live in a small community, and people who run things in the human services tend to know each other rather well, we were able to piece this story together about that child's family. This little girl and her brothers and sisters are on foster placement in the care of their maternal grandparents. Meanwhile, the children's actual parents are caring for five unrelated foster children. At the time of this account, those parents are enlarging their home in order to expand their foster care business. Everything is legal, or at least allowable. Of course, there are uplifting stories written and told about foster children and foster parents, but there are indecent stories, too, for situations such as the aforementioned to be enacted. Much of the interest in "child abuse" these days centers around what I call "unintentional abuse," the abuse which a parent usually inflicts upon a child, sometimes deliberately so, but even then without intent to abuse. However, every now and then, especially when the state or the county gets involved, parents behave like workers for the state, and then the abuse is indeed intentional. The difference between institutional abuse and parental abuse is usually the difference between intentional and accidental abuse. And while related, these are very different problems. They are similar, on the one hand, when the parent acts as a disinterested party might act, either for profit or to do harm. They are similar, on the other hand, when officials act as parents would, out of love or frustration, worry and concern, stupidity or madness. In either case, parents rarely act like state officials and state officials rarely act like parents. Rarely do parents and state officials abuse children for the same reasons. But in both types of situations, wrong stories about the children are the underlying culprits.

Quite recently, I was asked by the attorney general of a New England state to serve as an expert witness on behalf of that state, which was defendant in one of the now-common deinstitutionalization cases. Not a week later, I was asked by the United States Justice Department, representing the plaintiffs, to be their expert on the same matter. I proceeded to point out to attorneys for both defendant and plaintiff that, as both had independently agreed that I was indeed an expert, wouldn't it be simpler, least expensive, and most logical for me to serve as a "true" friend of the court, an expert for *both* parties. No! Apparently, a person can be an expert only if he curses one house while blessing the other. I don't like such stories. A pox on both their houses. And besides, all of this litigation is becoming tiresome and doesn't seem to lead to much in the way of improved programs for plaintiffs. And also besides, the story is getting around that every decent gesture and act must be witnessed in court. If that's what we've become, nothing can save us. Then we're doomed.

I serve as president of the Board of Visitors of our region's developmental center. As part of their orientation and inservice training, employees there are required to enroll in a course on "the gentle art of self defense." And from the looks of my mail, such courses are now the rage. For example, one such 30-hour program, advertised as "nonabusive physical intervention," is designed "to teach control of aggressive outbursts of behavior." It was created primarily for "direct care mental health and retardation workers, as well as psychiatric nurses, with quick and nonviolent solutions to such client behavior as biting, punching, kicking, choking, and the resistance of transport." The reader is informed that the course "will be thoroughly grounded in the principles of crisis intervention and team leadership." How ingenious! Who could have envisioned during one's innocence that combat training could be couched in such professionally appealing language? And for those who don't want or need the full dose offered by the 30-hour course, there is a 16-hour option, "designed to give the direct care force the ability to intervene effectively in an occasional problem situation." The last words of the program's originator insisted that, upon completion of the full program, each graduate will be able to protect himself and others from the following aggressive behaviors: punching, kicking, biting, choking, hair pulling, being pinned on the floor, being choked on the floor, ankle and clothing grabs, flailing, and resisting transport. I'm not new to this work, and I don't get my kicks taking cheap shots at people who, for the most part, are as dedicated and decent as I aspire to be. Work with severely and multiply handicapped people is arduous. Work with aggressive and acting out clients is very difficult. But why do we have so many aggressive and acting out clients? And whatever the reasons for the inappropriate behaviors of severely handicapped people, what kinds of stories must we teach ourselves in order to prepare in such fiendish ways to deal with not only psychologically but, *by state definition,* physically defenseless human beings? And does a state teach its employees about mental retardation when it inflicts such a course, such a story, on its hundreds or thousands of employees? Even when such courses "work," they tell untrue stories about the people connected with them.

From the period between July 1978 and June 1979 at that institution which I serve, there were a total of 2,391 reported incidents involving the approximately 500 residents. An incident ranges in seriousness from a death to a scratch, a resident argument to the abuse of a client. By far, the most prevalent incidents were "accidental injury" (647) and "assault" (423). When, during the course of a year, there is one reported accidental injury per client, and when during the course of a year, the average client is assaulted, would you say that clients at this facility are abused? Not according to the state's recordkeepers. During 1978-79 only 13 abuse incidents were reported at our facility. The story at our developmental center, which in my view is a good facility compared to most others, is that residents fight a lot with one another or with staff, that they fall down and hurt themselves, and that they are fragile and need lots of drugs, lots of protection from each other and the outside world, and lots of doctors around to mend their wounds and their spirits. So far, that story is more or less true. It becomes a lie when we say, "Yes, there are too many accidents, too many assaults, too many medication errors, too many other errors, but there is hardly any abuse here."

Is this abuse, as reported by my colleague, Wolf Wolfensberger, in a manuscript-in-progress:

> During the 1960's, Dr. _____, a pediatrician, distinguished hepatitis researcher, and chairman of the Vaccine Board of the U.S. Food and Drug Administration's Bureau of Biologics, had operated a research program at the _____ State School for the Retarded. In this project, retarded children between the ages of three and ten were experimentally infected with live hepatitis B. Despite all of the exposes of the atrocities committed at _____, Dr. _____ proposed as late as 1979 that retarded children should continue to be used as subjects in experiments designed to test out vaccines made from the diseased blood of hepatitis victims. A major rationale he advanced in support of this proposal was that because of crowding, unsanitary conditions, and poor personal hygiene, retarded institution residents would get hepatitis anyway.
>
> On top of the fact that German physicians were pronounced guilty at the WW II medical war crime trials for experiments of this nature, the ideology of rejection and destruction embodied in such a stance were further underlined by 1979 actions of the _____ Board of Education. In _____ state, governmental structures at various levels have waged systematic warfare against retarded people for decades, and tried virtually every ruse to exclude them from services

other than institutions, and especially from education. The latest strategy, after all previous strategies had been ruled illegal, was to exclude those retarded pupils from the schools who had been ascertained as being carriers of hepatitis B—the very same condition with which Dr. _____ had infected the children at _____. The school board declared that these pupils posed a significant health risk to other children in the schools. After efforts to exclude these pupils from the schools were blocked by the courts, the board fell back on the next typical line of defense: segregation in separate programs. As far as the facts of the school board claims go, hepatitis B is generally thought to be communicated only through blood-to-blood contact, and the judge ruled that there was no documentation of even one actual transmission from a retarded pupil to another child. The profound irony in all this is that most of the pupils in question had contracted the disease as guinea pigs in Dr._____'s researches. This kind of event illustrated the "blaming the victim" strategy: victimize someone, then use the inflicted affliction as an excuse for inflicting even further affliction.

There are more stories which I could tell. But a book would not be big enough to contain them all. Neither would a lifetime. I've written books, possibly too many, and papers, certainly too many, and I haven't been able to tell all of the stories I know which treat the problem of intentional and unintentional abuse, of sanctioned institutional abuse as well as unsanctioned child abuse. Those I told here are "merely" some which I recently learned about and which I haven't told before.

How to Reduce Human Abuse

Mental retardation is an invented disease. The only treatments possible for invented diseases are those which are themselves invented. And in that sense, all treatments for mental retardation are abusive. To be sure, lots of people have problems which can be treated, which a caring society will want to treat. And probably people who don't read well, specifically, or don't think well, generally, would benefit from treatments to ameliorate their disabilities. But in each such instance, the "disease" is not mental retardation, but something else. One way to reduce abuse is to better control our cravings for inventing diseases and, then, treatments to cure them. The best way to cure an invented disease is to forget it. The best way to reduce abuses of those people unlucky enough to have "caught" invented diseases is to offer no treatment, because abuse is the only treatment for an invented disease.

Another way we can reduce human abuse is to be very careful about the stories we tell about people. Invented stories are like plays. In very good plays, believable characters and situations are invented so brilliantly that even the actors believe the truth of the fiction they portray. In very good plays, not only for the audience but for the cast as well, invention replaces fact and, thus, becomes truth. So, too, with ingeniously invented stories concerning mentally retarded or fat people. Being fat today is an invented disease. Of course, Hitler's inventions became "true." So convincing was he that the Jews were monsters, that they became monsters to the citizens of the Third Reich. Hitler's response to the "Jewish Problem" was the correct response if he told a true story. Obviously, a sufficient number of people believed the story. And there are people today in our own country who yet believe that very story. And just as surely as Hitler tried, they would eradicate the Jews.

I assume that, since the first woman, there has always been a menopause. But today, the story is surely different from that first story. What was once a natural expected consequence in life is now treated medically as a disease.

The illiterate's story has changed from a person not being able to read to one not being able to think, from being a common man to being mentally retarded. Before we became so affluent, what we didn't know wouldn't kill us. Today, we worry to death about what we don't know, even though we often don't know what to do now that we know what we didn't know. Thirty years ago, there had to be a fairly serious reason for a patient to be subjected to an electroencephalogram. There are so many people given such tests today that it is estimated that 15% of the total population have abnormal electroencephalograms. But our doctors don't know what to make of the enormous number of people with abnormal EEGs who are in every respect perfectly normal. Consequently, through the widespread usage of electroencephalograms, electrocardiograms, x-rays, and blood tests of almost infinite variety, we have uncovered more and more abnormal, *but irrelevant,* characteristics in people. Maybe we ought to go back to the idea that what we don't know won't hurt us. But if you won't buy that radical suggestion, maybe you will consider the possibility that what we do know can hurt us, especially if it encourages us to invent stories about ourselves. Maybe overall, Alfred Binet's test was good for civilization. But maybe also, it did and does mischief.

While we are attempting to reduce human abuse, we may keep our spirits up by remembering that people change very slowly. Of course, that's both good news and bad news. The bad news is of the kind which led Chrysler to announce that it was going under. That is, people change so slowly—even big-boss industry people—that with all the evidence and expertise available to them, Chrysler refused to believe that we didn't any longer want their big cars, that not only were the people worried that a big car would cost us 30 or 40 cents more a day to run but that, for any amount of money, we might not continue to get gas for our cars without a lot of waiting and struggle. Further bad news is that the principles of normalization, least restrictive environment, zero reject, and mainstreaming will not easily be implemented because other competing principles must first die. The good news is that people inevitably change!

In this chapter, I have attempted to uncover the rules of storytelling.

A. Those about whom stories are told have:
   1. The right to tell their *own* story. A man has the right to claim he is Napoleon. Children have the right to "explain" themselves with whatever fantasies they find useful. Even "madmen" have that right.
   2. The right to have *true* stories told. Every human being is entitled to the story that he is educable.
   3. The right to *good* stories. I am valuable. You are entitled to stories that confirm your value. Even criminals are entitled to stories which do not deny their value as human beings.
   4. The right to withhold participation in another's story about them and, thus, the right to stick to their own story. *I am what I am!*
   5. The obligation to live up to good stories. Parents try to live up to their stature as parents as children attempt to live up to parents' expectations.

B. Those who would tell stories about others must respect these rights. They have the obligation to:
   1. Listen to the stories of those about whom they tell stories. Professionals must be especially vigilant, because they *always* have their own versions to "sell."

2. Tell good and helpful stories. Of course, there is always the question, "Help whom? And how?"
3. Tell true stories. We must be vigilant because professional truths tend to be irrelevant and are usually sterile. More often than not, the injuries we inflict are by neglect and not by design.
4. Take responsibility for the stories they tell. Professionals don't enjoy such responsibility. We blame "syndromes" or our victims.

C. Those who hear stories by or about others must:
1. Distrust bad or destructive stories.
2. Seek to *know* the truth of stories, and to *understand* the *good* of stories. Knowing and understanding can be entirely different matters.
3. Remember that they become (we become) the sum total of stories they (we) believe. It becomes their (our) story.
4. Dismiss any story presented as finished. Even dead peoples' stories are not ended. There are stories that need to be told about Hitler, about Sacco and Vanzetti, about Moses, and about the billions of all the "ordinary" people who left legacies and lessons to be learned.

Of course, most of the above rules are at odds with each other. Sometimes, we must fabricate a good story and *make* it true. That's why I said earlier that there are dilemmas which I cannot adequately deal with. That's why stories about a Hitler or an Idi Amin must be told, but must also be regarded as "over" if not "finished." Consequently, these are rules which are safe to have only accompanied by judgment, concern, friendship, and respect for all life and our common mortality.

There are other dilemmas. Not everything that is true about people belongs in the stories we should tell. It was true that Sacco and Vanzetti were Italian, but it did not belong in the story of what happened at Braintree that day. Of course, there shouldn't be harm in gratuitously throwing into a story a few extra facts, but the reality of human nature is that it can and does cause confusion and mischief. Consequently, good stories have to stick to the story; the "red herring" is never part of a good mystery. There should be enough complications in such a story to sustain interest without it, as in real life there always are enough complications to sustain interest without "red herrings." And that's why there are many things true about mentally retarded people which do not belong in the stories we tell about them, things such as IQs, head circumferences, distance between eyes, shoe sizes, national origin, and educational prognosis. As scientists and professionals we can only be helpful by putting our clients in a position to have stories in which head circumference is only relevant in a hat store, shoe size is only relevant in a shoe store, and national origin is perhaps relevant in choosing a church or bowling club. And we will only be helpful when IQ is hardly ever relevant. As for educational prognosis, our job is not to predict such futures but to start enacting a story in which they unfold naturally and compellingly, as in a good story. And of course, it is no crime when a good story ends happily.

The good news is that in between catastrophies, ideological wars, real wars, true stories and invented stories, ordinary life goes on. There is hope, even in the most fragile human being. And there is sustenance and stability because there is hope, but also because everyone knows that state management is horribly inefficient and, consequently, not much changes unless the masses want things to change. That is, when 100 years ago the "menace of the mentally retarded" was once proclaimed as the state's story, the people didn't believe that invention. The people don't easily believe lies any more than they believe true stories. Yes, the bad news is that things change slowly, but that's also the good news. The bad news is that ordinary life proceeds while people suffer horribly. But the good news is that ordinary life proceeds in spite of wars, lies, and other catastrophes.

In this chapter, I have attempted to indicate how words and language are important. I have attempted to show why stories must be true, why false stories—for bad *or* good—cause harm, how false premises lead to false conclusions, false treatments. I also tried to speak to the dilemmas which will not go away, but which can be understood better. That is, while what we say should be true, the laws of life are not like the laws of physics. The laws of life are rules of thumb, not rules of science; stories about people must be true but also deeper than the merely factual. To be decent, all human truths—truths about one's children, one's country, one's friends—require judgment and magnanimity.

Somewhere I once wrote that while illnesses are man's curse, handicaps (stigmas attached to illnesses) are his invention. I wondered then when we will learn the difference between what we must endure and what we bring upon ourselves. I complained that while we still have lots to learn about illnesses, we seem to have everything to learn about handicaps, that while not all illnesses have effective treatments, all handicaps are preventable and curable. Handicaps are conditions of the soul. Therefore abuse won't be "cured" by scientists, for the same reason that mental retardation won't be conquered by science; abuse is a disease of the spirit.

Reprinted by permission of Steven D. Blatt and the Blatt family.

Aspirations and Values[12]

In this chapter, I continue to explore the dilemmas and paradoxes in the field of mental retardation. Because they are rarely discussed does not necessarily mean that they are unimportant. I assert that a first responsibility of the community is to ensure that *everyone* has useful work to do—even if a *modern* farm must have the cows milked by hand, just to make jobs. Yes, that *would* offend some persons' sense of rationality, especially since American society has not, for the most part, been willing to "make work" for healthy unemployed persons. I discuss technology, how it helps, and how it can interfere not only with purposeful work but also with human interactions. I share some of my worries about a relatively recent trend in our society—the bureaucratization of values—using Ralph Nader as a case example; he has both performed a remarkable public service and also fostered the new "disease" of overregulation. And lastly, I return to the "life and death" issues—killing babies, euthanasia, the value of a human life. All of these issues are related to the question of values in the field of mental retardation. It is critical that such values be carefully considered in order to understand their fundamental contribution to the shaping of the field.

Moral Goals and Technical Means

Moral goals obtain from moral convictions, not empirical evidence. Of course, we must utilize *technical means*, all the hardware and software and professional expertise available to achieve those moral goals. We know a great deal today about immunizing all children against measles, diphtheria, and other child killers. We know more about the ravages of malnutrition. We know and do more about those problems than ever before. Well baby clinics, food supplement programs, health education efforts, and welfare plans have been established. That's all to the good. However, the goals *themselves* should be natural consequences of what we believe, what we aspire to become, and (conversely) what we disavow. We must always be focused on the goals. There has been confusion in the field, and the confusion has led to unfortunate consequences. For example, experts have been called by the courts to testify concerning whether retarded people have greater opportunities for development in the institution or in the community, or, for that matter, whether it makes any significant difference where they are placed. But the primary question should be whether this society will allow people who have not been judged as dangerous to themselves or others and who have not broken the law to be institutionalized "for their own good" or "for the good of society." That's the prepotent question! Of course, it's true that some people have greater opportunities to develop, or to avoid physical or mental problems, in one type of environment rather than in another. But this is not only true of mentally retarded people. It's true of everyone. What professor will deny that he or she would probably write more books if forced by the dean or department chairperson to spend 20 hours a week in the library or laboratory? Then why don't we require professors to spend more time in the library? To avoid a horrible mess, and to avoid a totalitarian state, people are permitted to do more or less anything that pleases them—just as long as they don't break "too many" laws, or endanger themselves, other people, or society. Such indulgence appears to work well in a democracy. There are people who are relatively happy, relatively free, relatively responsible for how they conduct their lives.

The question remains vis-a-vis retarded persons: Why do we require scientific "proof" that they are entitled to freedom? I assert that scientific evidence is irrelevant to freedom. I assert that all persons, if they are not a danger to themselves or to society, are entitled to freedom. This is a fundamental part of my values, my beliefs. This belief cannot be tested empirically, yet it provides a basis for action. It provides a basis for the formulation of goals, it can be realized in the form of social policy. Camphill Village, an intentional community in rural New York, comes immediately to mind because it embodies the notion of freedom (Blatt, Ozolins, & McNally, 1979). Retarded residents live there by choice—and would probably remain there even if they were miraculously cured. Camphill Village is a model community for a group of about 150 people, about half diagnosed as mentally retarded. Camphill has a lovely modern barn as well as modern homes, work places, and machinery. Consequently, the first-time visitor might be surprised to find that the farm workers, all of whom would be diagnosed as mentally retarded according to conventional criteria, milk cows by hand. Further, a worker is assigned to hold each cow's tail during the milking. What's so modern about all of this? Nothing, but everything. After the cows are milked by hand and the milk is collected in pails, subsequent handling is with the most up-to-date equipment—electronically pumped to an upper level of the barn for pasteurization and refrigeration. Then why the hand milking? Everyone at Camphill Village has a job, a real job, and everything is precisely figured out so that people aren't standing around with their hands in their pockets or playing meaningless games. Thus, they hand milk the cows, because it's much better for people to be needed to milk cows than to have a machine do the milking while they (who could accomplish that work) have nothing to do. This is an example of utilizing technology to implement moral goals, to the best advantage for human beings. A major moral goal is for everyone to work—to be useful to society—and that goal takes precedence over getting the most return on each cow; better we should insist on the most return on each person. I worry about a society that seems to have run amok with its technology. I worry about office building windows that do not open, especially in those communities with few humid days during the summer. I am puzzled when I cannot find an ordinary staircase in many college and office buildings. If, in those buildings, architects had designed staircases that were easy to find and as inviting as staircases of old, the occupants might have been able to do with one less elevator and a lot less energy consumption.

What does all of this have to do with mental retardation? A great deal. Technology is too often perceived not as a means to achieve moral goals, but as a statement in and of itself. If people can be made useless by technology—made useless while cans of peas whirl around innumerable electric openers—then worrying about robots is not as paranoid an activity as some people make it out to be. If the goals are indistinguishable from the technology, then we are being driven not to a better world but merely to a less sweaty world. There is a difference between the goals we stand for and what we merely stand, what we are willing to put up with. There should be a difference between unnecessary and necessary technology, between something useful and a merely interesting gadget, gimmick, or new invention. Possibly, much of the technology that has been reputed to aid us in our work in mental retardation has simply been another way of making the clients or the caretakers less useful to each other or to society. Goals in this field must be primarily judged on moral grounds. Technology must be judged on how well it serves to progress toward moral goals. All other considerations are secondary at best, and sometimes either unrelated or inimical to our goals.

Naderism and the Bureaucratization of Values

With every technical advance or new program on behalf of society, there is the possibility of unintended negative consequences. Witness the great national highway program (and clogged roads), and the great communication networks (and new worries about the effects of television on social discourse). Witness the proliferation of federal, state, and local laws and regulations. Who today does not worry about loss of freedom, about red tape, about the burgeoning civil service? Enter Ralph Nader.

Nader may well be more derogated by American big business than even Karl Marx or Franklin Delano Roosevelt—and Nader is alive, still capable of yet more "mischief." Ralph Nader is neither one dimensional nor uncomplicated. Even to sympathizers his work and influence present characteristics of a mixed blessing. Of course, he provided a great service to Western civilization if for no other reason than by reminding us that, if Charles Darwin was right about the "survival of the fittest," by definition there are times when even the most altruistic survivors must behave selfishly. If "advocacy" is when you work on another person's behalf as if you were working on your own behalf, then "survival" requires you to work (at least from time to time) on your own behalf as if you come first. This is not to say that people cannot rise above their selfish motives and behavior. Our history is replete with great acts of heroism, of sacrifice, and even of martyrdom. But if people were not characteristically selfish, or at least self-interested, then there would not be a need for such words as "sacrifice" and "martyrdom."

What Ralph Nader did was to call attention to the selfish interests of our various industries and government agencies. He reified a well-known lesson, one that forms the basis for most of our laws and practices. For example, we do not ask the trucking industry to set the toll rate on the turnpike, and we do not ask the telephone company to set its own rates. We do not permit the university student to determine when he or she deserves a degree. And we do not permit the university to determine whether or not it deserves accreditation. Nader called attention to certain aspects of our business and government communities that were not sufficiently regulated. Notwithstanding, the "disease" Nader sought to cure—unregulated industry and government—if too vigorously "treated" spreads another disease, one threatening to reach epidemic proportions—bureaucratization.

We observe bureaucratization everywhere—in the paperwork doctors must now attend to, for example, in order for society to control their self-interest. We see bureaucratization in the field of mental retardation and wonder whether the plethora of paper and standards cure or exacerbate the problems they were meant to solve. Once, institutions were unregulated. This lack of regulation was thought to be the source of unconscionable, inhumane conditions. We created accreditation commissions. But what do they do? They seem to be preoccupied with matters such as square footage allotted for each bed or with the fire-resistant qualities of materials used in the dormitories. These are not unimportant concerns, but they are surely secondary to the primary question, about which the commissions and other official bodies remain relatively silent: "Should we have the institution?" Or, "What is going on here that can't go on in the community?" The rationale for institutions and programs used to be connected to what was done and to whom; today it is connected to what the place looks like, how many people are served, and how many people are available to care for them. It seems that we have given up on the idea that we can examine and evaluate the substance of an environment and program. It's as if, because we don't know anything about whiskey but we know a great deal about glass, we should evaluate Johnnie Walker Scotch on the quality, the appearance, and the durability of the bottle.

We should not be misled. The great deal we have achieved with our various commissions and accrediting agencies insofar as the maintenance of standards has little to do with fundamental questions, such as: Is this good for people? Are there better ways? Are we on the right track? That is, we now have the "machinery" to learn more and more about the particulars of the "nuts and bolts" of institutions and their programs, but we persist in learning little about what they do for people and (even more importantly) whether they're necessary. Much of this perceived problem can be laid to movements of the past 20 years to bureaucratize values. Mental retardation suffers not from what we don't know about the institutions but from what we don't know about the world. In this regard, Ralph Nader is of limited help.

> Nader seems to want to overcome…evil by a bureaucratized society, one to be controlled by the people to be sure but, nevertheless, people who would weigh everything, test everything, define everything and be suspicious about anything.
>
> Possibly, at this time what is needed more than… Nader is a good poet who would give us some hints on how to live better with each other…
>
> Maybe we needed Nader when he came along. But I'll take Robert Frost. (Blatt, 1981b, p. 345)

Of course, there are times when the bureaucratization of values might be necessary, times when the bureaucratization of values might insure life. During recent years, courts in the United States and the United Kingdom have ruled that parents in consort with physicians may elect to deprive their children of life-sustaining procedures. Until eventually overturned by California's highest court, the natural parents of a child with Down syndrome were permitted to withhold the necessary surgical repair of his heart. In Baltimore, the natural parents of a newborn with Down syndrome were not challenged by a university medical center when they elected not to permit surgery that could have prevented their child's death 2 weeks later. And in England, a court exonerated a physician who deliberately injected a lethal dose of a drug in a newborn with Down syndrome. The latter two are instances of what might be called the "bureaucratization of death," the former the "bureaucratization of life."

The Department of Justice is prepared to intervene actively in such cases ("Justice," 1982). At least until a newer or stronger bureaucratic edict changes policy, the Department of Justice will vigorously argue in court that parents do not have the right to refuse to permit necessary medical treatment that might prevent the death of a sick child. Furthermore, the Department of Health and Human Services let it be known that federal aid will be denied to any hospital that refuses to provide necessary care for retarded and other handicapped infants. So here we have an instance where a federal bureaucracy—the Department of Health and Human Services—informs the medical community that it is suspected of making bad decisions concerning the protection of human life, and consequently, the bureaucracy will deny funds to hospitals that continue to kill babies. And furthermore, the second arm of government, the judiciary, announces that, when it learns about parents who refuse necessary treatment for their child, it will through the court attempt to save the life of a child whose very parents want to see it killed. In this brief commentary, we have both the reasons why bureaucratizing values causes great harm and why it's often necessary. Here we have instances where at times the disease (bureaucratization) is the cure, and at other times the cure is the disease. Why is it that, in this field, what we do best sometimes causes the most mischief (bureaucratize and litigate)? And why is it that we have the most difficulty in accomplishing that which may help people (e.g., create a normal environment for the disabled or manage a mainstreamed special education program)? Why is it that our institutions do best what other agencies do well (e.g., run laundries), and they do poorly what only they can do (provide living environments for their clients)?

With all of the problems attendant with the bureaucratization of values, I do not want to suggest that people such as Ralph Nader are or were unnecessary. I only want to point out that the bureaucratization of values entails some unintended and undesirable consequences. As I have stressed, though, such bureaucratization is in some instances necessary to insure the preservation of life. Thus the dilemma, a dilemma that certainly does not leave the field of mental retardation untouched…

Reprinted by permission of Steven D. Blatt and the Blatt family.

THE CONTROVERSIES[13]

Some controversies are settled by evidence and rules of discourse, others by statements of faith and values, still others by political considerations. In science, controversy is settled by evidence and laws of discourse. But religion, evidence, and rational discourse usually have little to do with the settlement of arguments. Is the Sabbath on the sixth or the seventh day? And which is the seventh day? In such an argument, what counts as evidence? In order to settle any controversy, it is necessary to first agree on what counts as evidence. And while the "limiting case" can be illuminating, it can also be misleading. For every Helen Keller, there is one who did not have an Anne Sullivan, but nevertheless prospered. But for every Helen Keller, there are many who did have an Anne Sullivan, and perished. It is important to remember, too, that where controversy is concerned, every overstated admiration engenders an overstated malignment; every enthusiasm engenders a countervailing depression. Controversy begets ambiguity as well as heat.

In the field of mental retardation, scientific evidence rarely settles the most important arguments satisfactorily. Rather, those arguments—nature/nurture, cure/permanence—are usually settled by explication of a set of values. We can attempt to settle those controversies by science. We can also attempt to settle them politically, as has been the case, to some degree, in the United States (e.g., Head Start). The political settlement of an argument involves various factions wanting to know about the substance of the argument, so that they can either do something about it or not do something about it. That situation leads to a political controversy.

It is hoped that, out of a discussion such as this, you will be in a better position to place these "controversies" in a more comprehensible context. It is also hoped that, out of such reading, you will be able to view with greater honesty and equanimity the human condition—and accept the idea that you cannot truly look at yourself without disappointment, and that you cannot truly look at others without at least some disillusionment. Possibly, a person's greatest strength is long life; there is time for many starts, many corrections, many opportunities to settle controversies. What follows are commentaries on key issues facing the field of mental retardation.

Nature/Nurture

The nature/nurture argument will not be settled easily. Already, we have a glut of reasonable commentary on the problem. For example, during Walter Lippmann's years as chief editorial writer on the *New York World* and as a regular contributor to *The New Republic,* he wrote about many of the country's serious problems—such as freedom of the press, social injustice, world government, and the nature/nurture argument (Steel, 1980). In a series of six articles for *The New Republic,* Lippmann explored the value and potential mischief of the then relatively new intelligence test, the Stanford-Binet, touted at the time as a guaranteed measure of innate capacity. Lippmann was skeptical, and concluded that the test had been oversold, misinterpreted, and used by some to justify social segregation. His examination of the Stanford-Binet led him to the conclusion that the test simply did not measure innate capacity. He challenged the claims of scientists who were eager to show that they could measure innate capacity, and he also questioned the motives of at least some of them, and—if not the motives—at least the damage they were perpetrating with their pseudoscientific dogma. His articles set up a controversy then, and while the content of such a controversy would probably be different today, it would no doubt be stirred if those same articles were to be published in current issues of *The New Republic* (Steel, 1980).

Gould's (1981) discussion of the nature-nurture argument might have clarified the question somewhat had not the particular argument been so close to the core of the human experience.

There is hardly any other issue that can be counted on more to inflame, enrage, entice, or infect the human mind and spirit than the proposition that differences among human groups and individuals arise from inherited factors, or conversely, from environmental influences. Of course, even the most zealous nativist knows that environment plays a part in shaping character and behavior. On the other hand, even the most rabid environmentalist knows that there are such things as genes and chromosomes, and that what we inherit contributes to our capabilities, physical qualities, and behavior. Realistically, the argument should not be about one or the other (although some debate the issues in just that way). But in reality, the nature/nurture argument has always been much less concerned with whether heredity or environment is the significant factor in determining individual and group differences than it has been concerned with the progress science is making in achieving greater precision concerning the relative weight of such influences.

Gould (1981) suggested two fallacies that interfere with rational discourse on the question: reification and ranking. Everyone appreciates the significance of mentality in our lives. Consequently, we invent the word "intelligence" and assign it to this very complex array of human capabilities. In time, the symbol for mentality, "intelligence," reifies the concept of a contrived, unitary trait for which we have invented a name, and eventually, for which we have invented a way to quantify. This leads to the second fallacy, ranking. If we can take a set of complex, even independent, capabilities and join them under a newly minted label, "intelligence," then we can rank individuals and/or groups by that global attribute. Of course, to achieve an acceptable system of ranking, we must devise some method to assign status—hence, the IQ test.

Added to the impossibility from the outset in achieving a workable designation and measure of what we call "intelligence" are the many other problems associated with the nature/nurture question. Thus, there has been failure standing on the supposedly scientific shoulders of prior failures. Gould, as have others, questioned not only the wisdom of the early measurement pioneers, but in several cases, their academic honesty in the context of today's understanding of what is and isn't proper. Added to the already devastating attacks on the integrity of Cyril Burt is Gould's new information concerning the intellectual honesty of that early 20th century leader in the field of mental retardation, Henry Goddard. Most of the academic scandals in the field of mental retardation during this century, it would seem, have been primarily connected with the examination of the nature/nurture problem. Is it a coincidence?

To this day, the nature/nurture controversy continues unabated, undiminished, and relatively uninformed. To this day, the controversy is dressed in "scientific" clothes, in spite of the fact that these scientific arguments are debated on grounds of faith rather than through the application of scientific methodologies to examine testable hypotheses. Never mind that any number of our greatest scientists have already concluded that the issue cannot be resolved scientifically—not when there are 40,000 genes, not when a gene can barely be seen much less understood, not when the argument is more religious and political than it could ever be scientific. But for the record, I seek here to summarize the issues.

…I have discussed the nature/nurture controversy in terms of the history of the field, the metaphors of mental retardation, incidence and prevalence, classification schemes, and in various other contexts. Here I will focus on what Gould (1981) identified as *The Mismeasure of Man.* Many of our great American heroes believed without doubt that the average White person is superior to the average Black person. Essentially, the Black/White controversy is not greatly different from the more general nature/nurture controversy, and, for that matter, with the narrower question of whether mildly mentally retarded people who exhibit no central nervous system organicity inherit mental retardation or acquire it in some fashion. These kinds of debates have been with us for centuries, differing more about how such variance is measured and why it occurs than whether or not it exists. That is, we have "always" had arguments about ethnic, racial, and religious differences; in a sense, that is what wars are all about, or, to put it more positively, that is what we mean by "nationalism" or "religious conviction." It should also be remembered that the recent "Black Is Beautiful" campaign may have been a strategy that is new to North American Blacks, but that was necessitated by the overbearing and pervasive campaigns that Whites have been conducting ever since landing on these shores. Campaigns informed Indians, Blacks, and immigrants that "Caucasians are beautiful, Whites in general are more capable, Western civilization is better, and Anglo-Saxon and Nordic Whites are best." Fueling these debates, especially on the side of those who consistently found Whites to be superior, were the data collected on virtually every possible anthropometric measure available. The data brought together the monogenists and the polygenists: the one explaining White superiority in terms of linear hierarchies of races that left Blacks low on a phylogenic scale in comparison with Whites; and the other admitting a common ancestry in prehistoric times but concluding that the races had been apart long enough to evolve significant differences in capability and intelligence (Gould). This is by way of saying that those who believed in "one Adam" and "one race" made their peace with those who believed that God had created many distinctly different peoples. What resulted was a "comprehensive evolutionism" that accommodated monogenists and racists and that, during the decades from approximately the Civil War era to World War II, was encouraged by the work of one prominent scientist after another.

For the reader interested in this fascinating history, one which includes the work of Broca, Lombroso, Galton, Binet, Goddard, Terman, and several of our contemporary scientists, you may not find a more informed source than Gould. Suffice it to summarize this section with several opinions about the nature/nurture issue:

1. Our earliest statesmen, philosophers, and scientists were more often than not racists. That is, in whatever ways they achieved, there was a fundamental belief

that Blacks are biologically inferior to Whites, and that other non-Whites are also inferior to Whites.

2. Since early in the American experience, various kinds of anthropometric data have been collected to "prove" not only the intellectual but also the physical, moral, and spiritual superiority of Whites. It's inconclusive whether the "allure" to the scientists was with the problem—the nature/nurture argument—or the numbers themselves. It's enough to note that virtually "everything" was measured, everything compared, every possibility studied.

3. The intelligence test was embraced on these shores and sustained here with far more vigor and attention than it ever received in Europe. While not our invention, it became our love.

4. The hereditarian theory of intelligence, which grew out of the widespread measurement of intelligence, was an American invention, and persists to this day as almost singularly American. It isn't that the idea of inherited intelligence had not crossed the minds of people in the various European and, for that matter, Third World countries, but that such an idea never really sustained the interest or received the almost obsessive popularity that it enjoys to this day in the United States.

5. From Goddard to Burt to various proponents of special drugs and diets, lobotomies, lobectomies, and special educational or therapeutic programs, it seems that the major academic scandals in the broad fields of psychology and special education—and in the narrower field of mental retardation—have revolved around the nature/nurture argument. Unfortunately, scientists working in this area have at times been driven to distrust the data in order to prove a case—sometimes because the scientist was impatient to prove that intelligence is essentially inherited, and other times because the scientist was impatient to prove that intelligence is educable.

6. The controversy continues and probably will continue until we realize that while it is the legitimate task of scientists to examine the nature/nurture argument, the job of the clinician is not to make a determination whether people can or cannot change, but to make it come true that people can change. The nature/nurture argument may well remain of interest to scientists, but it is not useful—and is probably destructive—to those who should direct their efforts to the work of creating and implementing programs that help people to learn.

…Can people change, can they learn, can they improve?

Moreover, irrespective of how much people can learn, what are they entitled to? Irrespective of how much people will achieve or how much they will contribute to society, what are they entitled to simply because they are human beings? The nature/nurture question is truly the beginning and the end for all fundamental discussions of this thing we call "mental retardation." All of this is by way of saying that the controversy will endure—unabated by evidence, and probably without genuine hope for final settlement during our lifetimes, at least.

This section concludes with a discussion of a paradox. The nature/nurture argument can be cast as one that will either lead to support of a "social selection" hypothesis or will lead to support of a "social stress" hypothesis. The "social selection" hypothesis posits that people inherit weak brains through weak genes, and they therefore find it difficult to do well—at first in school and later in the larger society. Those who would be sympathetic to such a hypothesis might term such afflicted individuals as "cultural familial mentally retarded," and they might consider themselves ideological progeny of Henry Goddard or disciples of Arthur Jensen.

On the other hand, there are those who support a "social stress" hypothesis. They believe that there are certain noxious environments that some people were unlucky enough to have been born into; and it's *those* influences that, from early life, blunt an individual's capability for developing normally. The cumulative effects of such a debilitating sociocultural environment may lead to mental retardation. Those sympathetic to such an explanation of how retardation occurs in otherwise physiologically normal people may have as their ideological models such early environmentalists as Itard, Montessori, and Binet. Their modern allies might include Skeels, Kirk, Gould, and Sarason.

The paradox of our contemporary society seems to be that, when all things are considered, environmentalism ("social stress") as a major factor in mental retardation appears to be an appealing explanation for the liberal; and conversely, nativism ("social selection") appears to be the inclination of the conservative. Insofar as questions concerning the mentally ill, however, it seems that the liberals have lined up in support of a "social selection" hypothesis while the conservatives tend to be counted among the "social stress" theorists. In mental health-mental illness, there is perhaps a reluctance among some people (possibly political and social liberals) to "blame the victims" for their own mental illness, or to blame parents for their children's autism. Thus, understanding of mental illness is sought in terms of metabolic disorders or other biological factors.

It may be that it's one thing (it *means* one thing!) to have a defective or weak gene, but quite another thing to have a defective or otherwise awry metabolic system—even if that damaged system obtains from a defective gene. It may be that, in mental retardation, blaming the victim means blaming genes; but in mental illness, blaming the victim means blaming the social-psychological environment. One's position regarding the nature/nurture argument, thus, depends not only on a particular moment in history and the political-social climate of the day, but it also depends on the particular disease or condition under discussion. What is a "conservative" position in one context is a "liberal" position in another. In mental retardation, it appears as if today's "good" guys were yesterday's "bad guys" and vice versa. There is not only paradox here, but the seeds for unremitting controversy. Some see truth in the "nature" evidence; others see it in the "nurture" evidence. So the arguments endure.

Cure/Permanence

Intimately related to the nature/nurture argument is the controversy concerning the curability of mental retardation. Before 1959, mental retardation was *defined* as incurable, irremedial, without hope for even amelioration. Today, the heretofore settled question is left open to discussion since retardation is defined functionally. That is, if a person "behaves retarded" (with low IQ and an adaptive deficit), he or she is retarded; possibilities concerning remediation are neither advanced *nor* discouraged in the definition. Notwithstanding, the very thing that the definition now permits, general practice continues to prohibit. To this day, there is the widespread understanding among many professionals, and among many parents and citizens as well, that mental retardation is essentially incurable, is essentially a chronic condition. To this day, cure is to many people unthinkable insofar as mental retardation is concerned. Is it any wonder that the cure/permanence controversy is so intimately bound to the nature/nurture controversy? The question again arises: Can people change, can they learn, can they improve?

There have been any number of small and large controversies surrounding the cure/permanence issue. The effort toward seeking a cure of Down syndrome, which involves several very distinguished scientists, including Clements Benda and Henry Turkel, has engendered controversy. The arguments concerning surgical procedures with retarded persons once snared such luminaries in the field as George Jervis and other prominent neurologists. The arguments concerning the etiology of infantile autism and possibilities for amelioration, a debate begun by the distinguished pediatrics professor Leo Kanner, is continued to this day by such prominent scholars as Bernard Rimland. And of course there have been many arguments about instructional techniques that are based on the cure/permanence issue—controversies about the desirability of special methods and procedures, special curricula, special *something* that have been designed to prevent, reverse, or ameliorate mental retardation. Although these efforts have proven to be largely unproductive, efforts have not ceased. Skeels and his associates, for example, studied the mental development of adopted or otherwise unwanted children with inferior social histories, influences on their development, and the correlates of intelligence. On the basis of a lifetime of studies, Skeels made a persuasive case in support of "educability." Twenty-five years later Jensen (1973) claimed that any reasonable and proper analysis of the Skeels data would lead to the conclusion that there are strong hereditary factors associated with mild mental retardation.

As the nature/nurture controversy is surrounded by prejudice and misinformation, the intimately connected controversy concerning curability is, if anything, hotter, deeper, and more passionate. In that chasm between rational argument and the goal for understanding lies wasted careers, chicanery, and even academic dishonesty. But amid the rubble dotting that woeful landscape are a few facts, a few good ideas, and many good intentions.

In his Bingham Lecture before the American Psychological Association, Cyril Burt reviewed the history of the mental testing movement and its findings concerning the inheritance of capability (1957). He concluded:

> The child's innate endowment of intelligence sets an upper limit to the best he can possibly attain. No one would expect a mongolian imbecile, with the most skillful coaching in the world, to achieve the scholastic knowledge of an average child. In the same way, no one should expect a child who is innately dull to gain a scholarship to a grammar school, or one whose inborn ability is merely average to win first class honors at Oxford or Cambridge. No doubt, in any individual case the ascertainment of this upper limit can never be a matter of absolute certainty: an I.Q. derived from tests alone falls far short of a trustworthy indication. Hence education authorities, like life insurance companies, have to follow Butler's maxim, and take probability for their guide. They cannot, however, afford to risk a lavish expenditure on cases where there are fairly heavy odds against success. (p. 11)

Burt actually raised interesting questions in this paper, and left several important issues open and deserving of study. But in the last analysis, he was convinced that mental retardation is essentially incurable, essentially permanent. After all is said and done, Burt and throngs of others have decided that we can't make "silk purses out of sows' ears." While history may continue to denigrate Burt and those of similar beliefs, dismissing them as little more than footnotes to the literature (if even that), their skills with pen and voice swayed many, even convinced those in academia. The one sure lesson is that people are ready to believe, to be swayed. Thus, if Burt and his followers represent only a footnote, it is nonetheless a footnote that informs the field.

Pathology/Variance

Do mentally retarded people differ in kind or degree? In psychology, there's something known as "abnormal psychology." There appears to be a need for such a subfield in mental retardation because there is evidence that convinces psychologists that the behaviors of certain people cannot be explained by utilization of general theories of learning and personality. That is, it is believed that people with mental aberrations may best be understood through special psychological theories and hypotheses. Hence, the need for abnormal psychology.

The question before us is: Is there a legitimate psychology of mental retardation? That is, do mentally retarded children learn differently from other children? Are different personality theories required to explain their behavior? Are mentally retarded people not only intellectually slow but intellectually different? It is an important question, and one that has not generated sufficient attention among scholars in the field. Without a great deal of examination of the question, courses in many of our universities and colleges imply that the question has been resolved; that mentally retarded people (like mentally ill people) require a *different* psychology to be understood. Hence, we still find such course titles as "Psychology of Mental Retardation"; and we still find even more prevalent commentary in our literature testifying to or alluding to some sort of "subnormal" psychology.

Around this discussion of "degree" or "kind" are several interesting debates, the Milgram (1969) and Zigler (1969) argument being among the more interesting. These debates focus on whether mental retardation can be explained by developmental theories, motivational theories, cognitive theories, or theories relating to abnormality and pathology. The debate leads to questions such as: Is the root cause of mental retardation motivational? Intellectual? Is there a discrepancy between values and aspirations of children and their families as contrasted with those of the larger society? Or is there a difference—a pathology—contrasting one brain and another? Of course, some mentally retarded people have demonstrably "different" brains; but others seem to be neurologically similar to ordinary people. What else can be said, at least at this time, given what is known?

The literature on personality development, on in- and out-of-school behavior, on postschool adjustment, and other indices of adaptation to society suggests that, even those with significant intellectual weaknesses—those with moderate to severe mental retardation, and also those with associated disorders—are generally people who exhibit normal variations of the "human theme." While it is true that people who might be called severely or profoundly retarded often exhibit unusually maladaptive behavior, and are often disconcerting to others, they still follow patterns of conduct that can be identified and discussed in terms of general learning and behavior theories. Certainly, long-term study of mildly mentally retarded people inevitably leads to the conclusion that they are much more like than different from other people. It might even be claimed that, all things considered, most mentally retarded people differ from others on levels of intellectual attainment and not on the major criteria associated with adaptation to society. Furthermore, even when such differences occur, they seem to be normal variations rather than either abnormal instances of otherwise normal phenomena or attributable to a special subspecies of the human family.

In essence, I am asserting that, for the most part, mentally retarded people do not differ very significantly from other people, except for their mental retardation. Second, I am asserting that, except in rare cases—these associated with people who are also mentally ill or have other very severe disabilities—whatever differences there are among retarded persons and others are differences of degree and not of kind. Finally, I am asserting that there is little use for a special psychology of mental retardation, as there apparently is for mental illness.

Institutionalization/Communitization Normalization/Mainstreaming

In this section several related but distinct concepts are brought together, each of which has been many times defined, clarified, and distorted for mischievous as well as harmless purposes. What is "normal"? Isn't it normal to be "different"? What is "home-like"? Is it like a home, or more like an institution? What's the "normalization approach"? Hiding differences or capitalizing on them? Living with retarded people as a duty (a job), or as a preference (a joy)? Is it "normalizing" to foster: life or death, incarceration or freedom, to be alone or part of the throng, literacy at any price, conventionality at any price? Is it more normal to endure institutionalization or other forms of segregation than to revolt? Is it normal to want to live normally while there is enough life to live normally? Orwell called insincerity the great enemy of clear language. Let's be sincere.

Not only has mental retardation been known since "the beginning," but the very issues facing modern society about what to do with and for people with chronic mental disorders were problems generations ago. McCandless (1979) described a controversy in England more than a hundred years ago concerning the suitability of an institution to treat mentally ill persons, the efficacy of public asylums in contrast to community programs, and the argument between psychiatrists and other medical practitioners on what represents the treatment of choice….

It is difficult to discuss institutions without engaging in controversy. After all, the Willowbrooks and Pennhursts of the world are famous for being infamous. On the other hand, one of the persistent criticisms of the deinstitutionalization movement has been the assertion that the effectiveness of community living has not been well documented. Nevertheless, the ineffectiveness of the institution has been more than adequately documented. I see no reason why vigorous examinations of community placement cannot be achieved in order to settle the question.

Within our inability to develop an adequate database to speak to that question lies a paradox, one that may not only puzzle us but one that may offer illumination. The paradox can also be discussed in terms of another question (possibly, paradoxes are best discussed by indirection): Has there been a conclusive demonstration of the effectiveness of living in one's natural home? Some may think this is a silly question. After all, the overwhelming majority of people in our society live in ordinary homes. What does it mean to document the effectiveness of one's home? Some homes are good; some are not so good. Some homes are good according to so-called objective criteria, but nevertheless, there are people who do not like to live in them. And there are other homes that are not so good as measured against objective criteria, but people nonetheless seem to prefer living there. It is virtually impossible to implement a serious study of the effectiveness of ordinary homes, or ordinary communities, or society.

Of course, many informed people write compelling papers on home life in America (or elsewhere) or American culture. People describe home life in America, or in certain segments of our culture—and even try to do something about it. But where is there adequate documentation to speak to the hypothesis that home life in America is effective or ineffective? It is simply not an intelligible question. It is too large, and it is connected to an almost infinite array of other unanswerable questions. Hence the paradox.

To the degree that mentally retarded people live in ordinary homes and in ordinary neighborhoods, it becomes less and less possible to document the effectiveness of those environments. Of course, one can describe a home, or even a neighborhood, but no one can speak to whether a culture or a normal environment is good or bad. By the very fact that there is such a thing as a normal environment or an ordinary home, the question has been answered. That is what the people want. That is the regularity. Social scientists are infinitely better at describing, analyzing, and discussing variations from the norm than the norm itself. The only way to judge an ordinary or normal environment that is on both objective grounds and also has practical meaning would be to judge it—the home, the community—on institutional criteria. And who wants that? And what good would it do? Put another way, we will know that deinstitutionalization works when mentally retarded people "disappear" in the environment. In the end, that is the true test.

Basically, the institutionalization controversy has been argued in two ways: as a developmental issue, and as a freedom issue. If the advocates for deinstitutionalization have made any serious strategic blunder during the past decade or two, it may have been their insistent, almost perverse, devotion to the clinical (developmental) argument. This devotion generated debates at national and regional meetings, (more or less) scientific studies published in professional journals, and polemics published in newspapers and newsletters affirming or denying that the institution is a better place for people, that the segregated school is a better place for children, that the group home is better or that the mainstreamed class is better.

The "freedom" argument does not address the question of whether segregation or integration is "clinically better" for mentally retarded people. Rather, this argument is based on the conviction that people are entitled to live free in a natural setting, irrespective of what particular environment most enhances their reading capability or vocational aptitude. American slaves were not freed from bondage on the basis that such freedom would enhance their school capability or vocational viability. The slaves were freed on the basis of the belief that people deserve to live free. Historically, the question of freedom has been a perennial subject for discussion in religious and philosophical literature, as well as in poetry and novels. The concept of freedom is at once maddening and elusive for the individual to understand, yet either simple or impossible to achieve. That is, if one denies authority, one is free; if one accepts tyranny, one is imprisoned. It is of course dangerous to deny certain authority, but such denial always confirms one's freedom. Indeed, in the ultimate sense, if one wishes it to be, freedom is the final option. Hence, lives are laid down in its defense, and untold sacrifices are made to insure its continuance. In fact, we might think of freedom as the ultimate gift that can be conferred on the human being. In a way, a person needs to be free to maintain a personal sense of humanness. In a way, the concept of freedom is irrevocably connected to the definition of humanity. In a way, for many people freedom is a more precious gift than life itself.

Let's attempt to lay by the heels the issues surrounding the controversy over institutionalization versus community living and special classes versus mainstreaming. This preliminary discussion should lead the reader to the real debate—on freedom, and the current and future society.

Simply stated, the controversy is between those who believe that *all* children should live in ordinary communities and attend ordinary schools in ordinary classes, and those who contend that children with special needs are best served in specialized programs.

More than a decade ago, Smith and Arkans (1974) presented a persuasive case for segregated special classes for retarded children, especially for those who are moderately and more severely retarded. They summarized the literature both sympathetic and opposed to separate special classes for the handicapped and concluded that the evidence clearly is on the side of those who have resisted widespread mainstreaming of these groups. They acknowledged the various decisions handed down by the courts, the general mood of many professionals and lay people toward integration. They even acknowledged that certain "evidence" had predisposed professionals and legislators alike toward mainstreaming. Notwithstanding, they worried about children with serious problems. They found not only existing regular classes unsuitable for such children, but also various resource programs.

Why? Moderately and severely handicapped children tend to have multiple problems, and consequently they need large uncluttered environments for the specialized equipment and programming they need. Furthermore, moderately and severely handicapped children represent a relatively small proportion of those who require specialized services; and not every school has either the appropriate critical mass of children or the resources to provide suitable specialized programs. Smith and Arkans asserted that regular teachers, with their large classes and limited specialized skills, cannot give proper attention to children with serious, and often multiple, handicaps. However individualized regular classes are, they cannot meet such specialized needs. Nor were they convinced that the lifelong planning that each of these children requires can be accomplished during the school years through participation in ordinary school programs. In summary, Smith and Arkans made the serious assertion that moderately and severely retarded children require specialized personnel, specialized equipment and facilities, often specialized architectural arrangements, very small classes, and unusual auxiliary services that lessen, if they do not entirely obviate, the suitability of regular programs (or even modified mainstreaming programs) for such children.

The questions raised by Smith and Arkans bring to saliency the issue concerning an individual's right to treatment versus his or her right to be different. Such a discussion may get at the core of what it means to responsibly create and implement programs for handicapped persons. Is it more important to provide the very best clinical program possible or more important to insure that the individual will be in a mainstreamed program? "Clinical opportunity" and "integration" are not necessarily antagonistic, but are also not necessarily compatible. That is, if "all" we must worry about is connected with providing the child with the best educational program possible, then Smith and Arkans' criticisms of mainstreaming are immeasurably strengthened. If the primary objective, however, is to provide that child a program in the most "normalized" environment possible, then their criticisms are weakened. Reliance on the "least restrictive environment" covenant is not always helpful in practice. That is, several courts have mandated that handicapped children should be educated in the environment that least restricts their freedom (i.e., that permits them to be most integrated). This environment must at the same time provide those individuals with the most suitable habilitative (i.e., educational) program. Those are fine sentiments, but they lack sufficiently strong or clear advice concerning which priority takes precedence—the need for appropriate clinical services or the need to be free in a normal setting. If the latter takes precedence, then we must necessarily compromise the clinical program. If the former takes precedence—then there must be compromises with an individual's right to be free, to be educated, and to live in a normal environment. This is the issue that must be addressed in any discussion of the treatment of handicapped people.

As noted earlier, there is no empirical documentation that supports the contention that home life is "effective." Nevertheless, an entire body of research is devoted to testing this hypothesis. Many people believe that there is no compelling research to support either approach, integration or segregation, or that the most that can be claimed is that some children fare better in separate special class programs while others do better in ordinary programs. In general, such research, sometimes called "efficacy studies," leads to the conclusion that current segregated programs—essentially special classes and special schools—are of no more observable benefit to mentally retarded persons (or, for that matter, to handicapped children in general) than are other types of class organizations and arrangements (Blatt, 1956, 1971; Robinson & Robinson, 1976).

It is my position that integration is always preferable to segregation. I believe that, in general, people want to live with their families and friends in ordinary communities, and that most children want to go to ordinary schools. I believe that segregated settings are not good for other than temporary periods when a person needs some specific treatment. That is, I believe that it is reasonable to be in a hospital when you are sick, but it is not reasonable to live in the hospital. It is certainly reasonable to be alone when you want to be alone, but enforced solitude and expulsion from society is not reasonable.

As is the case in the debates over nature/nurture and cure/permanence, the debate over institutionalization seems to be unremitting. Those who argue vigorously against deinstitutionalization contend that:

1. The idea of deinstitutionalization is not grounded in an empirical base—that is, there is no evidence that a retarded person's development will be enhanced in a normal community.

2. Some people are so severely retarded that they cannot benefit from any sort of educational programming—they are "custodial."

3. The community is not prepared to integrate profoundly and severely handicapped people.

4. There are both good and bad institutions and good and bad communities, with neither type of setting inherently good or bad.

5. Institutions are more economically efficient than other ways of providing services to people with severe handicaps.

6. The argument for deinstitutionalization is less "real" than political, less grounded in substance than sloganeering.

Proponents of deinstitutionalization counter that:

1. It is probably true that deinstitutionalization is not grounded in an empirical base. There is sufficient face evidence, however, that normal environments are more humane.

2. The idea that some people are so profoundly retarded that they cannot benefit from any educational programming denies the real lesson to be learned from the Wild Boy of Aveyron: that all human beings can learn. It also denies the lesson to be learned from Emile: that all people are noble. It denies the lessons to be learned from the lives of Helen Keller and Anne Sullivan and thousands and thousands of other documented cases of individuals who have changed remarkably when placed in nurturing environments.

3. The idea that the community is not now prepared (or legally required) to accept profoundly retarded persons, and probably never will be, leaves us with moral paralysis. Does this mean that we are to perpetuate injustice? If it does, then what about the people who are incarcerated legally and dealt with according to the legal codes of corrupt governments?

4. The idea that there are good and bad institutions and good and bad community settings is beside the point. Variation in quality is not the issue in dispute. What is in dispute is the question of whether one approach is in principle better than the other.

5. The idea that institutions are more efficient and less expensive than community settings is truly unbelievable. The per capita expenditure for institutionalization in New York State was recently reported as at least $53,200 a year, and there are some state institutions in New York State that spend $100,000 a year per resident. Does anyone believe today that segregation is less expensive than normalization? I would assert that segregation is more expensive than integration both in terms of dollars and in terms of human resources. In this regard, money is less the issue than how we conceptualize the value and the potential of other human beings.

6. The contention that deinstitutionalization is little more than a slogan is puzzling in view of the fact that to this date, estimates made by federal judges, state commissioners, and even people who support continuing the practice of institutionalization indicate that thousands of people are unnecessarily institutionalized.

The institutionalization controversy has been both clarified and complicated by the intrusion of the "normalization concept." Despite its popularity, "normalization" is widely misunderstood and misused. A commonly accepted definition of the term as well as a summary of the basic concepts that constitute its foundation may help to clarify the subject.

> First, normalization means making available to all mentally retarded people patterns of life and conditions of everyday living which are as close as possible to the regular circumstances and ways of life of their society.
>
> Second, normalization means giving society a chance to know and respect mentally retarded persons in everyday life and to diminish the fears and myths that once caused society to segregate them. (Perske, 1977, p. 5)

. . . To the best of Wolfensberger's (1980) understanding, the current usage and original stimulation for the widespread popularity of normalization should be credited to the work of Bank-Mikkelsen, once head of the Danish Mental Retardation Service and a world leader in the field. About the same time that the concept enjoyed its beginning prominence in Denmark, it received strong endorsement and dissemination by Bengt

Nirje and other Swedes. Of course, Wolfensberger himself is mainly responsible for the significant impact of the normalization concept in the United States. There doesn't seem to be much doubt that long before the actual term "normalization" gained popularity, other scholars in the field used it (Wolfensberger). But those earlier examples appear to be rather casual and tangential to the main purposes of those works. Wolfensberger found the earliest mention of the term itself in a 1966 edition of one of Maria Montessori's books. Tracking that clue to the original 1950 Italian edition, Wolfensberger was surprised to find that Montessori actually wrote about the normalization of children. Notwithstanding, even here its mention was quite tangential to the thrust of the main commentary. Wolfensberger also reported the use of the term in a Swiss journal in 1958, its presence in a Canadian journal in 1964, and its appearance in the United States in 1966 in an article by a well-known practitioner in mental retardation, Simon Olshansky.

As Lewis (1973) pointed out, throughout Western history there have been inconsistencies and vacillations insofar as attitudes and behaviors toward people perceived as mentally incompetent. We tend to be vague, uncertain, uncomfortable, threatened, and distraught in the presence of handicapped people. And when such people intrude intimately into our lives, we may even be destroyed by what we find to be intolerable relationships with them. This is not pleasant, but unfortunately it is more accurate than most of us will admit, even to ourselves. At best, there has been a social, economic, political, and psychological ambivalence toward mentally retarded persons. So it was good that Wolfensberger, Nirje, and others here and abroad articulated and fostered the normalization philosophy. It implies attention to helping other people to better appreciate, better comprehend, and better understand the contributions all people (even handicapped people) can make to the quality of their own lives. It implies attention to individual differences—not merely by blurring or ignoring those differences, but by recognizing them and discovering how such differences can enrich our lives, enrich anyone's life. Normalization does not necessarily mean that the individual is to be placed in an ordinary environment without special provisions to meet his or her needs; nor does mainstreaming necessarily mean that every child is to be placed in an ordinary classroom. Normalization does not necessarily mean that a child can get along without special help; nor does mainstreaming necessarily mean that the child can always get along without special teachers, special materials, or special curricula. Mainstreaming has to do with the right each child has to a free and appropriate publicly supported education in an environment that is the least restrictive; but it does not suggest dumping the child in an untenable regular classroom, ignoring special needs, or discounting specialized teaching, equipment, and curricula.

In several profound ways, Vanier has articulated a philosophy that goes even beyond the concept of normalization (Wolfensberger, 1973). Scholar, teacher, activist, advocate, Jean Vanier saw to the establishment of commune-like residences for retarded adults—but not residences where there were "workers" and "clients." Possibly more than anyone else, Vanier was able to overcome what Sarason so eloquently described as "professional preciousness." With gladness, with joy, with the gift and need for sharing, Vanier, the international traveler, made his home with people who share his values of love and friendship—many of those mentally retarded. In an unpublished talk that he gave in Nairobi, Kenya, in 1974, Vanier remarked:

I have had the grace and joy to live with mentally handicapped adults over the last 10 years. With friends, we have been able to create some 45 small homes for men and women who were either roaming the streets, locked up in asylums, or just living idly—though frequently in a state of aggression or depression—with families who did not know how to cope with them. These homes of l'Arche are in France, Canada, the United States, England, Scotland, Belgium, and Denmark, as well as in Calcutta and Bangalore in India; our first home in West Africa is just beginning in the Ivory Coast. Each of these homes welcomes and finds work for eight to ten handicapped men and women and for their helpers or assistants. They try to be communities of reconciliation where everyone can grow in activity, creativity, love and hope. Some of the handicapped people leave us and find total autonomy; others who are more severely handicapped will stay with us always.

It is this experience of daily living, working and sharing with my handicapped brothers and sisters that has made me so sensitive to the question of their contribution to the development of our world. A man or woman can only find peace of heart and grow in motivation and creativity if he or she finds a meaning to life.

What normalization has done for retarded persons, Jean Vanier has done for other people, seeking ways to share their lives meaningfully with those who might need them. What mainstreaming and normalization have done for special education, Jean Vanier has accomplished for humanity.

The normalization concept, possibly more than any other concept connected with deinstitutionalization, provides the fuel for the philosophical argument against institutionalization. In addition, the trends toward deinstitutionalization and mainstreaming are connected intimately with the concept of "least restrictive environment." They were fostered after the institutional scandals of the 60s and the Civil Rights movement of the 70s. They are connected with the consumer movement, citizen advocacy, and the generally heightened political activism of the public. Deinstitutionalization, normalization, mainstreaming, zero reject policy, Public Law 94-142, or any other permutation of what has almost become an Integration Revolution in the United States had been very much influenced by research concerning where people learn and grow best, what people want, and what people need. These particular arguments cannot satisfactorily be resolved by science, as they cannot be much better understood by what science uncovers. Stated another way, the integration controversy is not one of those dilemmas that presents us with a puzzle to solve as much as it is one that presents us with an opportunity to expose our values. The integration controversy has to do with how we want the shape of the future society to be rather than with what the evidence is that will dictate the future society. The integration controversy is one of those arguments that is almost completely in our hands. It has little if anything to do with what is "best" for people and virtually everything to do with what people want to make of their lives.

Notwithstanding the longevity of residents in institutions for mentally retarded people (and in the United States, mortality rates are commendably low), in a metaphorical sense there is more "killing" than "living." Here, of course, I refer to psychological killing and psychological living. At one time, people feared to go to hospitals because there was essentially one reason for going (or, at least, one consequence of going)—to die away from known people, to spare the living from the sight of death. In a way—at least metaphorically speaking—this remains the major role of the institution for retarded individuals. We spare from the living the sight of psychological death.

When there is nowhere to go but the ground which inevitably comes to each of us, one waits for death. That is what is wrong with the convalescent home. That is what was wrong with the old hospital for the "incurables." And there actually were hospitals with such names and purposes. There are hospitals today with similar names, but the names are embarrassments now, and are always explained as historical artifacts that do not reflect the character of the institutions they stand for. But even this embarrassment does not extend to the institution for mentally retarded people, which even today is called a "hospital for the incurable," a place to die, not a place to be cured (certainly), a place to be admitted, but rarely released, just as the institution is today's version of the Hospital for Incurables, so the segregated class is a permutation of that same idea. At one time, the American institution was universally accepted, if not always admired. At best, today it is universally acknowledged as an inadequate temporary compromise with minimal standards. Likewise, the segregated special class and school used to be called the placements of choice, until newer standards and values adjusted the conception. *Aun aprendemos;* we are learning.

In the field of mental retardation, possibly more than in others, time should be spent grappling with our controversies. In that chasm between facts and rhetoric, we may find wisdom. But in our field, there are many issues where facts are not sufficient to discuss the truth. In our field, facts often become truth only when they are tested by articulated values. In closing this chapter, I should openly acknowledge—even if it is obvious—that my biases are explicitly shown. It is difficult if not impossible to discuss the fundamental controversies of the field without showing bias, and it is critical to air these major unresolved—yet insufficiently addressed—controversies.

Reprinted by permission of Steven D. Blatt and the Blatt family.

Part 4
In and Out of the Professions

Fred Kaplan

Editors' Introduction to Part 4

Burton Blatt performed many professional roles in his career: public school teacher, university professor and department chair, center director, state mental retardation director, university dean, professional association president. Whatever role he performed, he never refrained from commenting on the professions in which he was involved. Nor was he reluctant to speak his mind openly and honestly, even at the risk of being controversial among his peers and colleagues.

Part 4 of this book contains some of Burt's writings on the professions. The first two selections, "This Crazy Business" and "The Industries," provide his reflections on mental retardation professions and the field generally. The final excerpt, "If People Could Heed Good Advice," was based on a lecture given in 1984 through the J. Richard Street Lecture Series in the School of Education at Syracuse University. Although the lecture was addressed to university colleagues, this lecture contains some good advice that all people should hear, if not heed.

THIS CRAZY BUSINESS[14]

The contents of this chapter derive from activities during my years as an administrator in government and academe. Essentially, the plan is to present a personal analysis of this crazy business we call "mental retardation." It may strike some readers that this chapter's organization is the reflection more of idiosyncratic conceptualizations than of logical processes. I must admit that I believe that, in this crazy business, one fights general craziness with any resources at one's command, even those which are paradoxical or illogical. In this regard, my long suit has always been independence. Some people may define such resistance as hostility, a transference mechanism, or whatever; I choose to interpret their definitions as other examples of this crazy business. In a world of continuous war on peace, where people incarcerate, and even kill each other, because of labels ascribed to or withdrawn from human beings, should anyone be surprised to read here that I call this business crazy, that there may be some who will think me crazy for it, and that I would find such reactions to be but additional illustrations of the craziness in our field?

Dreams and Means

One should start at the beginning, and the beginning for me must include the language of theory, laws, beliefs, and prejudice—statements of principles—goals and their pragmatic translations. So, first the principles and goals and, secondly, with a degree of diffidence, how I have interpreted them.

Ideas

It seems entirely reasonable to suggest that goals represent important ideas to be achieved during some future period. Stated another way, I envision the term "goal" as including to some degree, and embodying but not encapsulating, such other terms as "objectives," "hypotheses," "dreams," and—most of all—"ideas." At least while I write this chapter, I have persuaded myself that there are compelling ideas that seek expression, that there are people in this field who agree and disagree with these ideas, that one way of gaining a perspective on the "mental retardation" business is to evaluate those ideas.

The ideas are everywhere—in the literature, at the conventions, in the academy, in the field. Typically, we express them as researchable hypotheses or as pragmatic goals. Typically, we find them substantively discussed: (1) as the educability hypothesis, or the nature nurture controversy, or the human potential movement; (2) in agreement that human beings are entitled to fundamental services and opportunities, or that there should be options available to all people; (3) in the belief that the state has certain responsibilities to the people, and the people have certain rights; (4) or as more specific goals, such as the recently publicized White House hope to reduce the incidence of mental retardation by one half by the year 2000; (5) or as very general goals, such as to guarantee each person the right to be born healthy, the right to habilitation, the right to the least restrictive placement, the right to an appropriate education, or the right to equal protection and due process under the law.

There are goals, objectives, dreams, and hypotheses; but, at the beginning, there must be ideas. Unfortunately, one reason why many ideas are timeless and persistent, yet feeble, is that they haven't fully existed in reality; we don't feel compelled to implement them. And one reason why we aren't so compelled is that ideas, like people, are themselves mixtures of weakness and strength—which itself may be an important idea. Possibly, such mixtures are inevitable, the products of dissonance between intent and practice, noble hope and dismal realization, and shared bitterness. The lesson is plain. Be humble or one has very little to rely upon.

The following are some ideas that I feel are now in the air, not always because they are loud or striking but, rather, because they are fundamental and each possesses the sound of truth:

The idea that each human being has unique value. Not only is each person educable, not only is capability a function of practice and training, motivation, and expectations, not only must all developmental programs be individualized, but so must one's life objectives. This is by way of saying that, although we believe that people can change, an individual's value as a human being isn't bound to his educability but to the intrinsic and inalienable right to be respected—because he is a human being, if for no other reason.

The idea that children represent our great hope to improve society. An individual is born and he dies, and during the interim, he struggles to realize his gifts, while the group—the government, the bureaucracy, what we call society—seeks to trap him, tame him, certainly standardize him. But, sometimes for good and sometimes for bad, there have always been people who would not be molded. They cause us problems; yet they are our major investment for the future. The dilemma has always been to know who should be molded and controlled and who should be as free as the wind, who is dangerous and who is our prophet. And so we encourage freedom and individuality, while we weed out those who appear to be dangerous and maladaptive, while we pray that serious blunders have not been perpetrated in the name of society. And children must always exemplify humanity's universal continuing enthusiasm for a better future; therefore, if we fail with them we fail with everything.

The idea of the creative person. Each human being has a will to live, but also a dream to express himself, to realize his individuality in unique ways. Someone once said that living well is the best revenge. And, I truly believe, if we can agree that "living well" means living in one's unique manner, that living well is the only way. It's not enough to live, to exist, to be; all people seek to unfold, work to create something, and struggle for a principle or some different future.

The idea of freedom. A jaundiced assessment of our culture is that we revere life but disdain freedom. In our zeal to protect the weak, the aged, the so-called handicapped, and the ugly, we segregate and separate and stigmatize and make pariahs out of legions of people. We build industries to incarcerate—out of sight and out of mind—the blind and the retarded and so not only do we accomplish little to help them "see" and understand us but we preclude any possibility that we—the sighted, the brilliant, even the humanitarian—will "see" and understand them. Where is the liberty that our fathers wrote of in our declarations and constitutions? Where is the liberty that children every school morning across America claim their country guarantees for all of its citizens? Where can we find total implementation of the principle that a human being is entitled to freedom under the law?

All Ideas Have Histories

Each of these ideas has a history, long and bloodied. Wars were fought and lives were lost because of them; the idea that all people are entitled to freedom under a just law is one that has turned red the soil of most lands. So, today, these ideas struggle against other powerful ideologies, moving ahead, then falling back, in favor during one generation and out of favor in another. Today, at this very moment, it is no different, except for the difference in time and perspective. However, ideas dealing with freedom, individuality, human values, and human resources continue to intrude into public consciousness, crying for legitimacy and support.

I have learned that one way to at least partly understand what our values are is to read the papers and listen to the public communicators. As the saying goes, look it up in the newspaper; everything begins with the birth announcement and ends with the obituary. Unfortunately, people may draw wrong conclusions from discrete facts; hence, this attempt to relate "word" facts with "deed" facts. It's necessary; for as all ideas have histories, so do all people. But some leaders tend to think they don't, that each day is a clean slate in a new world.

The following items have appeared in our New York State newspapers in recent months:

> A bill passed last month by the state legislature and sent to the governor for signature changes the names of all department facilities for the mentally retarded from "State School" to "Developmental Center." (*Mental Hygiene News,* 1974, p. 1)

No longer will we have to contend with the Syracuse State School, the Willowbrook State School, the Letchworth State School, the Wassaic State School, or the Newark State School. Rather, there is a new model; new progressives and humanitarians appear to be in control. We now have the Willowbrook Developmental Center and the Letchworth Developmental Center. We change the names and, as if by magic alone, things are expected to get better.

> The playground of the Syracuse Developmental Center is going to be remodeled stressing safety and more creature comforts. Protruding bricks removed from all play areas and smooth epoxy applied to the sides of the slide to prevent abrasions are just two of the improvements to be made according to Al Clinton, assistant business officer of the Center. Improvements are being made to provide more safety to the retarded children that the Center serves. (*Syracuse Herald American,* 1974)

Some who read this announcement in our local paper remember that the Syracuse Developmental Center (formerly Syracuse State School) was once the oldest unremodeled and unchanged state school for the mentally retarded in North America and, just a year or two ago, it was torn down and rebuilt at an expenditure of approximately $25 million. The aforementioned playground, constructed at a cost of several hundred thousand dollars, received more than one national award for its innovativeness. Unfortunately, children couldn't play in this playground without submitting themselves to unusual physical dangers. Essentially, this award-winning playground built by the New York State Department of Mental Hygiene was, and probably still is, "unplayable."

> A State Comptroller's investigation of Matteawan State Hospital in Beacon, N.Y. has uncovered a pattern of fraudulent transactions and irregularities, including the bilking of inmates through doctored commissary records. ("*A Matteawan Audit,*" 1974)

Mental health and mental retardation are big business. In each state, not only is the state itself the "biggest" purchaser of new construction, but the state is in the position to offer millions of dollars in food, linen, garbage, you name it, contracts. Further, state employees handle transactions involving millions upon millions of dollars, oftentimes "on behalf" of incompetent, or presumably incompetent, inmates. So the *New York Times* reports that "A Matteawan audit shows inmates were defrauded." What else is new?

> It was a scientific experiment. For 30 years Federal health offices allowed 400 poor Black men known to have syphilis to go untreated despite the discovery that penicillin could cure their devastating disease….
>
> In 1967, coercion was charged in conjunction with a study in which live hepatitis virus was injected into mentally retarded children at Willowbrook State Hospital on Staten Island. ("All in the Name of Science," 1972)

Probably also reflecting its revulsion from the above kinds of human treatment, all of it despicable, probably some of it criminal, the *New York Times* headlined the above article by Jane Brody, "All in the Name of Science." Yet let's now read a portion of a recent editorial in that same newspaper, reputed to be, and deservedly, the paper of record. Let's read the view of a newspaper that is not too modest to claim that it publishes "All the News That's Fit to Print."

> A wasteful dispute has long been seething between civil libertarians and elements of the psychiatric profession. The issue, in effect, is whether the mentally ill should ever be hospitalized against their will or must at all times be left to their own resources as a recognition of their rights as free citizens. ("Civil Liberties for What?" 1974)

Why did the *New York Times* print this lead editorial, titled "Civil Liberties for What?" With the world at war, Watergates, impeachments, runaway inflation, pollution, crime, Henry Aaron and the new baseball season, with a whole world of problems and happy and sad events to choose from, why did the *New York Times* feel compelled to report to the world that mental patients really need communities away from typical society, preferably located in the country? Apparently, even the *New York Times* can be misled, possibly by a few influential colleagues or, just as possibly, by a great many Mr. and Mrs. Citizens who plunk down their 20 cents on weekdays and dollar bills on Sundays for the privilege of not only reading the paper of record but giving it advice.

Apparently, the people of New York City have "had it." So too, apparently, has the New York State Department of Mental Hygiene. For, in an April 28, 1974, front page article, also in the *New York Times,* it was reported that the "Department of Mental Hygiene, in a private memorandum and directive, has made a major change in its policy by telling its hospitals that 'we should not take the initiative in discharging the patient to the community.'" Why, after the scandals of Willowbrook and Letchworth, the reports of joint commissions, with a new morality and in a supposed era of concern, does the *New York Times* ask us to slow down, if not apply the brakes? Why does it appear that the State Department of Mental Hygiene is doing one of its familiar herky-jerky about-face dances, tiptoeing in a 180 degree turn, skimming over the issues and principles that honest people would not ignore? Well, the Department of Mental Hygiene not only has "had it," but was "had" by the "anarchists," the too-liberal psychiatrists, the reformists.

When they were persuaded to evacuate some of their more embarrassing units, they were not told that many people would be unimpressed with the idea that mental patients should live in ordinary neighborhoods, especially unimpressed if the designated neighborhoods were theirs. The Department of Mental Hygiene apparently never did develop a contingency plan that would permit them to deal with community resistance. Further, the Department of Mental Hygiene doesn't quite understand that, when mental patients or state school patients are released, it would be best to diversify their placements, not consolidate them in one or a few locations. And when the residents of Long Beach, New York, complained to the State Department of Mental Hygiene that, in fact, the department was creating new quasi-institutions in the community with the purchase of converted motels or hotels for subsequent assignments of large numbers of mental patients to these facilities, the State Department of Mental Hygiene responded with lectures to the citizens on their moral responsibilities and the need for increased community acceptance and goodwill.

The irony of it all is that the community laypeople had a much more insightful analysis of the situation, the problems, and possible solutions, than the state department professionals. The community group said, "OK, send your mental patients into our neighborhoods. However, if you want them to live in a normalized fashion, in ordinary neighborhoods, don't congregate them together. Permit us to continue to have normal communities—not places where there are large numbers of peculiar or different people, herded together in abandoned, dilapidated, or second-rate hotels."

The State Department of Mental Hygiene did not heed the community's advice, then pleas, then threats. They merely lectured at the community: to be good citizens, to accept differences, to have forbearance, to understand, to possess all of those virtues that the professionals in the state department seemed to lack themselves. So we had the backlash, and a new and strange coalition of conservative average citizens—people such as our own mothers and fathers, our friends—and the *New York Times.* One wonders—and those who answer the question negatively are probably correct—will they ever cease? And so, we have a new state policy to slow mental patients' releases. Don't suggest discharge to them lest they request release. Cool it, boys; the natives back in the boonies are getting restless. Even the New York City sophisticates have "had it"….

Rebuff after rebuff; yet the dauntless state department continues to seek solutions to the problems of this crazy business. Like Don Quixote jousting with windmills, our mental health leaders, ever sensitive to both the community and current professional metaphors and slogans, would evacuate institutions by creating new ones in the community, would evacuate them altogether. So they claim, but they don't have an analysis of what must follow. They are dedicated to "integration" and "humanization," as they integrate inmates by segregating them in nursing homes, and humanize the large institution by dehumanizing the community. Unfair? Probably! Is there another way of analyzing this news? Certainly. Yet does the department deserve the censure? No, if nobody deserves censure for what we have perpetrated; yes, if anybody deserves censure….

So, again, what else is new? Problems occur, statements are made, tempers rise, newspapers report, commissions are appointed, funds are allocated, and the more things change the more they remain the same, except, things remain the same differently from the ways they remained the same before. And, so it seems, that's all the people want. Things can remain the same so long as the color and rhythm of the sameness change hues and tempos from time to time. The major task is not to change but to satisfy everyone: first, the conservatives, but, also, the radicals, the conservatives, because they are in control and pay the bills and the radicals, because—if they are not under control—they will try to upset the delicate balance between no-change that appears as change and no-change that's discovered for what it is. Satisfy everyone, those who pay the bills because they pay the bills, and those who are potentially, or really, irritating to the true power groups.

The ultimate aim is to not only "freeze" the present but establish some type of "warrant," a hold on the future. It appears that one of the goals of a large segment of our society is to guarantee to their progeny what was guaranteed, and later delivered, to them—places of relative prominence and affluence in their society. And who could question that ideal? Who doesn't want to prepare for his coming generations? Who doesn't want a world for his loved ones that is at least as safe, and cozy, and comfortable as it was for him? The answer is obvious: those who never had anything, those who want something different for their children, if not for themselves. So there is a conflict between variance and invariance, between the haves and the have-nots, between those who are more and those who are less selfish, between those who have more to protect and those who have more to gain, between the power block and the powerless, between the *New York Times* for the underdog and the *New York Times* for the overlord.

All ideas have histories, and the proper study of the histories may illuminate for us not only what occurs in the "name" of certain ideas but what the ideas actually mean. That's the first lesson; a goal or an idea is nothing without its history, and then it's only something in a special context and perspective. Therefore, let's continue examination of a few of the more provocative ideas that we seem to be romancing at this time. And if these love affairs weren't made in heaven, there may be a more appropriate place to bear witness to such unions—and if not to the marriages themselves, to what they have become.

Mainstreaming, the Community, and the Teachers' Union

As enunciated again and again, during informal discussions and in official or scholarly documents, our nation's educational leaders have now decided that handicapped children are best served in integrated settings. "Mainstreaming" will be, if it isn't now, the law, if not the practice, in this land. The Regents of the University of the State of New York urge a greater commitment by society to the education of handicapped children, with the primary responsibility for programs placed with local school districts and as integral facets of public education (State Education Department, 1973). The litigation in our field exemplifies the centrality of the "integration-mainstreaming" issue (Collings & Singletary, 1973; *Syracuse Law Review,* 1972).

An analysis of the official reports of the various public committees and commissions responsible for formulating national policy on behalf of the handicapped indicates the marked escalation of concern about the integration issue. From the first annual report of the National Advisory Committee on Handicapped Children to then United States Commissioner of Education Harold Howe II in 1968 *(National Advisory Committee on Handicapped Children,* 1968) to its subsequent reports to later Commissioners James E. Allen, Jr. *(National Advisory Committee on Handicapped Children,* 1969) and Sidney P. Marland, Jr. *(National Advisory Committee on Handicapped Children,* 1970), mainstreaming does not appear to be an important issue, at least an issue that deserves identification in annual reports. Contrast its virtual total absence during the late 60s and early 70s with the most recent report of the Committee *(National Advisory Committee on Handicapped Children,* 1973). Now, priority recommendations reaffirm the Constitutional right of all handicapped children to a tax-supported appropriate education, regardless of their physical or mental capabilities. Further, the Committee now urges that regular education environments should be made available and, when there are differences between, for example, parents and school authorities, due process procedures should be operational to insure an equal educational opportunity for each child.

A comparable analysis of *MR '67* (President's Committee on Mental Retardation, 1967), the first major policy statement of the President's Committee on Mental Retardation, and all of the subsequent reports, including its most recent one in 1974, *Silent Minority,* illustrates a major shift in policy discussions from an earlier deficit-oriented and categorical segregation model, based on the assumption that handicapped people need special and separate services to be delivered by professionals, to an avowal of principles of: advocacy, normalization, least restrictive alternatives, due process, and rights rather than privileges. Witness that, in 1967, the President's Committee appeared to be very proud of the fact that there were nearly 700,000 children in special classes for the educable and trainable mentally retarded. Note that, in 1967, there was little distinction made between special class and special education; special education was special class. Note, again, how "needs" were discussed in 1967, in terms of more services, not "open" or integrated services. And, although in 1974 the realities for people with special needs may not be very much different, the rhetoric surely is—with the language today expressing concern for an individual's rights, his freedom, his entitlements, his need to be a part of a world that includes rather than excludes him.

I don't know of a professional organization, or a municipal, state, or federal system or agency, that is plainly antagonistic to the mainstreaming principle. Certainly, there are individuals within those organizations and programs who take a dim view of the mainstreaming movement. However, mainstreamers seem to have the segregators on the run, at least for now. Or do they really?

Item 1: A debate is currently smoldering in Syracuse, and it will probably rage again as it did a year or two ago. It's a complicated matter, as all of these things are; suffice to say, I think there is one group that wants a special school for the trainable retarded and another group that believes that a special school is neither desirable educationally nor responsible fiscally.

Although they have difficulty in believing they've won, the special schoolers have won; the Syracuse City Council, the Board of Education, and the school administration have all agreed that a special segregated school for trainable children is necessary, desirable, and defensible. Those of us who have raised questions concerning the need for a separate school, during a period of significant pupil enrollment decreases (e.g., a 600 drop for 1974-75 alone) and in a supposedly new egalitarian era, have been accused of insults against children. It seems ironic, at least to me, that in an age when unusual efforts are being exerted by local communities to integrate, for example, Black children, more unusual efforts are being exerted to segregate retarded children. While the courts in Boston and Detroit insist that minority youngsters be integrated—irrespective of long bus rides and significant program modifications and costly expenditures—the Syracuse City Fathers continue their plans to segregate handicapped children, whatever the costs.

Item 2: Syracuse is in Onondaga County and, reflecting the same "disease" of that city, the County Board of Cooperative Education (BOCES) has been seeking citizen approval for an additional new segregated school for the handicapped and for those youngsters enrolled in what was once called vocational education but now is referred to as career education. Probably, more out of anger in again having their "pockets picked" than for any reasons concerning principles or morality, the voters recently turned BOCES down—for the first time in New York State history denying a BOCES program the opportunity to expand its segregated mission.

Why does BOCES want a new school? Again, the polemics run rampant during these kinds of discussions and, trying to be fair but probably not succeeding very well, I should point out to anyone who hasn't noticed that I am singularly unimpressed with any efforts to expand or strengthen segregated settings for people. Having said that, I can now claim that the special education officials in the county want a new school because, since the beginning of organized society, bureaucrats want larger budgets, more staff, bigger and newer facilities, and control. Certainly, the current segregated school for the trainable mentally retarded in Onondaga County is inadequate. It is old, crowded, inaccessible to many families, and inappropriate. On the other hand, the only virtues I can see in constructing a new school is its newness and, possibly, its greater square footage per child. Yet, irrespective of its newness, size, or even beauty, a segregated school is still a segregated school; it will be centrally located and, therefore, inaccessible to many families; it will not permit the integration of the handicapped with the nonhandicapped and, as importantly, vice versa. However, exactly as with the Syracuse group, time is on the side of the county segregationists. Someday they will have their new school, if not after the new referendum, then the referendum after that, or the next one, or the next one.

Item 3: Ideological banners fly from the public relations staffs of the New York State Department of Mental Hygiene, proclaiming: deinstitutionalization, community programming, advocacy, priority reassessments, normalization. Yet, in the city of Syracuse alone, during the past 3 years, more than $50 million (plus millions more in interest) has been expended by the State Department of Mental Hygiene for the creation of new segregated institutions.

The Syracuse State School, created in 1854, the oldest state school for the mentally retarded in North America in continuous operation on its original site, has now been torn down and rebuilt, almost brick by brick, on that site. Where, formerly, it had a resident population of 250, the new state school is built to serve 750 residents. Permit me to remind you that not only is the facility larger but it is no longer a state school; we now have in our community a brand new concept as well as facility, the Syracuse Developmental Center, that has replaced the old state school. Similarly, what was once the small, essentially outpatient, Syracuse Psychiatric Hospital is now the brand new $25 million Hutchings Psychiatric Center, capable of "bedding down" 750 inmates.

Item 4: "Everybody" in Syracuse had agreed that we should return state school residents to the community as quickly as possible. Therefore, the school's director acquired a small residential facility to develop as a group home. Neighbors-to-be learned of this plan and, very quickly, drew up a petition which they presented to Mayor Lee Alexander; said petition denying any hostility to the concept of community integration but, on the other hand, providing a number of compelling reasons why this community residence would be inappropriately placed in that particular neighborhood. Mayor

Alexander agreed with the petitioners. End of group home plan. And, when I was interviewed on television soon after the mayor's decision, I received a number of rather hostile calls and letters, the following among them:

Dear Dr. Blatt:

You should live next door to mentally retarded like I do. On the weekend they go all over surrounding streets, scavenging big pieces of metal trash and wooden trash (they have superior physical strength to make up for lack of mentality), and so on Sunday the peace of the Sabbath is broken by their hammering on it (trash is picked up Monday a.m. in our neighborhood).

One looks about 30 and plays like a little kid. The other looks about 7 or 8. He thinks he is a method of transportation all the time. And goes down the street making like a motorcycle, an airplane, a racing car, etc. Sometimes he just stands and yells as loud as he can yell. They both do this.

They have not one but two dogs that bark 24 hours a day.

I say these people have no business living in a normal community—whoever sold them the house should get a medal!

I say these people should be provided with a community of their own; live with their own kind.

I understand there is one at Liberty, New York. I sure would like to be able to send these people there.

(Signed)

Has had it.

Item 5: Now, the most puzzling for last, the quintessential hypocrisy for the finale. My friends in the Syracuse City Schools, many of whom have been students in my classes, others of whom have served with me on committees, a few of whom are—truly—my friends, collectively agree that handicapped children deserve to be integrated in regular programs. Yet circumstances and promises made by their predecessors force them to support the construction of the aforementioned new segregated school for the trainable in Syracuse. Yet precedents, teacher prejudices, and practicality require them to continue their elaborate segregated special-education program. However, if they had their way in the best of all possible worlds, they would integrate more children with special needs, especially the mildly handicapped. Similarly, members of the Board of Education agree fully with the concepts of mainstreaming and normalization.

And, as if to add insult to injury, in spite of public pronouncements in support of the principle of integration, the Syracuse Board of Education, with the concurrence of school officials, has entered into a negotiated agreement with my friends in the teachers' union which discourages school authorities from requiring regular class teachers to accept handicapped or disruptive youngsters in their programs.

It is the ultimate non sequitur to claim to foster integration in a system where those same claimants support segregation. Not only is this crazy business, but it is also funny business.

The Year of the Child and Other Indecencies

Surely, there are reasons, related chains, that make indecencies almost inevitable. The reader has a right to ask why these indecencies occurred. I have some notions to "explain" them and you probably will develop yours. But I don't have truths, and you might not find those either. Someday, maybe, but for now, I only claim to collect and publicize indecencies, not adequately to understand them.

Item 1: Sometime during the spring of 1970, an administrator in the Massachusetts Department of Mental Health was in San Francisco. Upon his return, he remarked to colleagues that the California Chinese seem to always have a Year of something or another, and he suggested that this would be a good time for Massachusetts to have the "Year of the Child" (Task Force on Children Out of School, 1972). The idea caught fire. The commissioner of mental health announced that 1971–72 would be the "Year of the Child" in the commonwealth. Finally, attention would be given to the needs of children, priorities would be reordered, and an increased proportion of the department's resources and programs would be allocated for children.

Unfortunately, this commitment to children was made after the Department of Mental Health had submitted its budget requests to the legislature. No resource shifts would be possible. Additional state assistance was equally impossible. Additional federal funds to meet the commitment didn't materialize. The "Year of the Child" was never more than a gigantic hoax, a public relations ploy created out of innocence, "implemented" by the cynical, and finally exposed publicly amid embarrassment and frustrated disclaimers from the insiders and righteous anger from the muckrakers. The grand objective, the beautiful logo on thousands of wall posters, the fervent promises made, were all garbage, like confetti after the parade, like a kewpie doll the morning after in the noon day sun. All this from the chance notice of a wall poster in a Chinese restaurant. How easy it is to do something, and how difficult to accomplish anything.

Item 2: I can hardly wait to complete this next section on advocacy. In my study, I am surrounded with piles of books, monographs, chapters and papers—all dealing with the definition, theory, implementation, and practice of various forms of human help we now term "advocacy." Who really knows but that, when I finish this section, I will find a paper I wanted to use earlier but is now hopelessly irretrievable in a morass of advocacy papers. But, to paraphrase what a colleague once said in an entirely other context, "Do we have a knowledge explosion on advocacy or merely a paper explosion?" One wonders, and here's why.

Wolfensberger described the various advocacy roles for children, including those that are primarily instrumental, some instrumental and expressive, and even one that is primarily expressive, the advocate-friend (Wolfensberger, 1972). As he and others noted, there are advocates who assume roles as guardians, friends, adoptive or foster parents, legal advisors, and "helpers." However, the one characteristic advocates must have in common is a partisanship, a primary interest to serve the client. Literally, the advocate is one who pleads the cause of another person, not conflicted by self-interests or loyalty to an organization or to one's profession. This partisanship, as a matter of fact, is one of the significant factors in the case Wolfensberger makes for the utilization of citizen-nonprofessional advocates on behalf of people who are mentally retarded.

The idea of advocacy has so captured the thinking in our field that, as happens to all good ideas, there are now groups attempting to appropriate—capture for themselves—the idea. Why must the advocate be professionally disinterested and nonpartisan, preferably a layperson? Why indeed? Wouldn't it be best for an advocate to be a spokesman for the deliverers of services so the program as well as the advocate can be held accountable for the work of the system? Would it? Some people think so.

As a matter of fact, the Regents of the University of the State of New York not only believe this but have developed a sure-fire method to implement an advocacy system that, in my opinion, will only lead to the destruction of the concept of advocacy in the public schools of New York State. The Regents have designed an ingenious method to co-opt an idea intended to serve clients but which now would serve the providers (State Education Department, 1973). They recommend the creation of a new advocacy system for children with handicapping conditions. They claim that a good advocacy system requires strengthened cooperation among agencies in the public and nonpublic sectors. Therefore, to be effective, any system of advocacy and service delivery must provide for cooperative arrangements agreeable to the commissioner of education and to those people responsible for the supervision of institutional programs at the state level. Consequently, the commissioner of education should be given the responsibility for the overall supervision of programs for handicapped children. Further, the state-wide system of advocacy should be vested by statute with the commissioner of education, and "…local school districts, BOCES, and other state agencies (should) have a proper role to play and that, wherever possible, parents represent the starting point."

Imagine a state-wide advocacy system, where the advocate is employed by the state yet uses his expertise or services only to serve his client, with the chief advocate being the commissioner of education, and with other state and local agencies and individuals having proper roles in that system—including last, but including wherever possible, parents. Just imagine!

Item 3: During the past several months, the R. J. Reynolds Tobacco Company, manufacturer of Camels, has been conducting a vigorous advertising campaign to attract the "honest and independent" smoker. Each of the advertisements in this series began with the question, "Can you spot the Camel Filters smoker?" The scene is in an airplane, at a party, or on the beach. Various people are pictured, saying something or doing something or appearing in some distinctive manner. The reader is to deduce who smokes Camels and, presumably, why. Surely, you have seen these ads. I have but, as with most advertisements, my observations were mindless; for so much of today's reading, advertisements or otherwise, mindlessness is a fairly safe and respectable condition to be in. If not for Liz Smith, an attorney who is a member of our Center on Human Policy staff, I never would have noticed that a particular Camel ad was vicious, bigoted, and unfair—but as typical of our culture as apple pie and baseball games. Among five other people on the beach, ranging in "beautifulness" from zero to everything, is Tyrone Shulace, "beach pest." We are told in the ad that the "58" on his shirt stands for his IQ. Further, Tyrone thinks that "off shore drilling is something marines do." He smokes "Huffn Puff" super filtered cigarettes. Obviously, that makes him retarded, unappealing, and deserving of whatever ridicule is heaped upon him.

Liz Smith wrote to the president of the R. J. Reynolds Tobacco Company…. Within a week, she received a reply from…vice president and director of marketing for the company. He was apologetic. He said that:

> We do our best to create advertising that will appeal to large numbers of people. We have found one of the best methods to be humor. The "Can You Spot" ads are intended to be much like a cartoonist's caricatures with the larger-than-life portrayal of the subjects not meant for literal interpretation.… We have a great deal of empathy for the kind of public spirited work you are doing

(our company supports local organizations involved with mental health).

And, I think [he] is right. This ad will appeal to large numbers of people. It will be thought very humorous. And besides, R. J. Reynolds does have a lot of empathy for the kind of public spirited work we are doing. And, I am sure, the company supports local organizations involved with mental health. They're as clean as a hound's tooth.

Item 4: Behavior modification, operant conditioning, behavior shaping, there are those and other names for a relatively new technique that has fast replaced psychotherapy as America's mental aspirin. The following bizarre story (*Miami Herald,* 1972) is not intended to repudiate the importance or effectiveness of behavior modification techniques. There is no intention, at least on my part, to dissuade the reader concerning the great promise this method holds if used judiciously and appropriately. Rather, the Miami Sunland Training Center scandal is another indication of good ideas gone awry, good intentions misanthropically realized, potentially good people turned sour.

Sunland Training Center, in Dade County is a state institution in Florida, domiciling 900 people, each labeled mentally retarded. Like most state institutions, some of the residents are very retarded, some mildly retarded, some "retarded" only because they had once been labeled retarded. As in most large institutions, the age range represents a very wide spectrum indeed, young children to adults; and the range of behaviors represented at this institution is uncommonly broad and multidimensional. In essence, Sunland has a very heterogeneous group of residents, some of whom are at least adequately identified by the label "mentally retarded." Enter into this scene a new superintendent, one with a good reputation for "getting things done," for doing the right things, for being truly concerned about the mentally retarded. Enter also a psychologist who is given a free hand, who believes he has answers to the developmental problems these residents present, who is strongly devoted to behavior modification techniques as the foundation, the beginning direction, for behavioral improvements.

The consequences: homosexuals compelled to wear women's underwear; "thieves" who steal Cracker Jacks required to eat bars of soap and wear special signs noting each as a "thief"; those found masturbating, forced to masturbate in public; one inmate, who defecated in his pants while in seclusion, required to hold his soiled underwear under his nose before washing the pants out in the toilet; another "thief," caught stealing Sugar Pops, placed in restraints except to go to the "potty"; another boy who didn't want to go to bed locked up in a seclusion room; and on, and on, and on—children cleaning up their own vomit, rinsing their mouths with soap, denied meals, denied "privileges," tortured. Surely, this is not what Skinner planned for a new Walden. Surely, this is not what Barrett, Lindsley, or Sidman envisioned. But, in this business, good ideas are often spoiled and altruistic motivations are corrupted.

Item 5: A letter to the author.

> In reviewing your book, *Souls in Extremis,* I am informed that the pictures in "Central" State School are in reality…State School. I would suggest that the material is quite out of date…the conditions you mention have definitely changed.
>
> One of my main criticisms would be the picture of the Community Store. I cannot identify the page as it does not have a page number, but the entire paragraph there is incorrect. The interest for residents is strictly regulated by law. There is a small amount left over because of bookkeeping

difficulties. This amount is never used for the Community Store, never used for a retirement banquet, employees' gift fund, etc. The purposes for which this money is used must be itemized and presented to the Department of Mental Hygiene for approval. I take strong objection to this. (personal correspondence, January 3, 1974)

But here is an entirely different letter, from the above superintendent's immediate supervisor:

By chance, I must confess, I was going through the Department library and found your book, *Souls in Extremis*. I have not been able to start reading it yet but was caught by the picture in the chapter, "A Photographic Essay, 1971," by Mark Blazey. What struck me was your straightforward description of Community Stores and the use of money for the benefit of employees. This came to my attention last Christmas when I found that these funds were used to pay for employee Christmas parties. I am enclosing a memorandum which was sent out concerning this problem and I think procedures are such that this misuse of money should be a thing of the past.

**State of…
Department of Mental Hygiene**

February 15, 1974

**Division of Mental Retardation
and Children's Services**

Memorandum No. 74-5

TO: State School Director, Deputy Directors for Administration Central Office Distribution Schedule 2

SUBJECT: Review of Community Stores, Donations and Patient Accounts by an Institution Ad-Hoc Committee

No proposed budget for community stores, donations, or patient interest accounts for fiscal 1974–75 will be accepted unless reviewed by a Committee whose size shall not be more than seven (7) members and whose membership shall consist of one-third parents, one-third residents, one-third employees, and one member of the Board of Visitors.

The Division policy will be that all funds from these sources shall be used primarily for residents' benefit. Recommendations will be made to the Director who will make final decisions.

Each institution will notify Dr….'s office in writing upon the selection of their review committee.

This memorandum will be in effect until superseded by future directives.

The supervisor adds:

I am also enclosing our memorandum on burials and maintenance of cemeteries (also discussed in book, with our treatment similarly criticized by aforementioned superintendent) which hopefully will start solving this problem.

August 12, 1974

**Division of Mental Retardation
and Children's Services**

Memorandum No. 74-30

TO: Directors, Deputy Directors, Clinical and Deputy Directors for Administration of all Division of Mental Retardation and Children's Services Facilities Regional Directors Central Office Distribution #2

SUBJECT: Burials and Maintenance of Cemeteries

It has come to the Division of Mental Retardation and Children's Services' attention that many graves in our institutional cemeteries are unmarked or marked only by a number. To correct this situation, the Division of Mental Retardation and Children's Services enunciates the following policy:

1. All graves in Mental Retardation and Children's Services' facility cemeteries will be distinguished by a marker with the person's name, date of birth and death, and appropriate religious symbol. No numbers will be used.
2. All burials will have a religious ceremony, unless such a ceremony is waived in writing by parents or guardians.
3. All state cemeteries will be maintained, and whenever possible, no new plots will be opened and community cemeteries should be used.
4. All graves, whether in state or community cemeteries, will be distinguished by a named marker.

The correspondent continues:

> The other things that are photographically highlighted are obviously more difficult given the inertia of the system. However, we have a number of projects which I hope will make some dent in the problem. (personal correspondence, August, 16, 1974)

The institutional superintendent claims that I am unfair, that the problems we portrayed have either been corrected previously or were never present. Her supervisor informs me that he has observed the same institutional abuses we described. He also tells me that, given the inertia of the system, other aspects of this photographic essay will not be corrected easily. Yet I am threatened in a subsequent letter by the superintendent who warns me that, because she is an advocate for the residents, she intends to "pursue this (our) transgression further." We have been waiting and, although I have heard several rumors that I will be sued, our last communication from this superintendent was January 23, 1974. Who is deceitful? Who are the advocates? And if, as claimed, the superintendent is an advocate, what does advocacy mean?

Innovation Is the Name of the Game

Innovation is the name of the game, but it's not the stuff in the game. We may convince ourselves that we are truly in an innovative era in mental retardation. There is a plethora of monographs, books, and full journals devoted to innovative approaches to evaluating, placing, treating, dealing with, serving, and counting the mentally retarded; there are even claims that innovative approaches to paying for it all are now available. We read about innovation in special education (Aaronson, 1972) and innovation in other mental retardation settings (Stedman, 1971) and we are tempted to believe. However, notwithstanding instructional materials centers, engineered classrooms, "hot" new dyslexia treatments, the effects of early educational intervention programs, new directions, and exciting frontiers emerging, notwithstanding the wish to believe, the jaundices and disappointments of the past remain, and therefore one tends to doubt. It isn't that we don't want to believe; we do or, I should say more correctly, I do. It's not that the evidence isn't piling up; we now have a *Mental Retardation Source Book* (Department of Health, Education, and Welfare, 1973) and, believe it or not, I am currently serving on a committee that is optimistic enough to think it can develop a Mental Retardation Fact Book. Who would have thought that?

Nevertheless, I don't think that there is very much innovation in our field: first, because innovation requires new ideas (that's always a rare commodity) and, secondly, because we seem to be deliberately planning to achieve the antithesis of innovation and diversity.

Essentially, ours is a monolithic system, a single block of ideological stone; ours is a massive and solid, uniform, no-option, no-alternative, slot machine type of strategy that would seek the single best method, the single best procedure, the single best something or anything (Blatt, 1973a). The Monolith is not the special class, or even the segregated institution, or any other special setting or procedure or model. Rather, the Monolith is the one way, the unavailability of alternatives for clients, families, therapists, and others concerned with the education and treatment of people with special needs. The Monolith supports "innovative" programs that evolve into either carbon copies of what is currently available or distortions of something that was once good, bad, or indifferent but will, surely, become tomorrow's new fad or the "magic" of the next modern-day alchemist. One thing that I've learned from all of this is the value we must assign to truly creative thinking and planning; it's an infrequent occurrence, often unrecognized, usually feared, and commonly disdained.

Definitions, Labels, Incidence, and Prevalence

Wedged by Executive and Squeezed by Academic Views

Years ago, when I first began seriously to study institutional life, I learned that, in New York State, residents of state schools were labeled "material" and their attendants and supervisors were labeled "items." More recently, while attending a meeting on the so-called geriatric problem in mental retardation, I learned that human beings are called "inventory" by some state department employees who have been designated responsible for their care and humane treatment. During the years, I have learned that labels are important, because they picture the feelings we have for people and things, and because they serve to peel away the concealment of our prejudices.

Labels may not be of consequence in a clinical setting; in fact, their usage with individuals should be restricted, if not discouraged. However, there are people who need service and the administrative assignment of resources to programs and groups requires the utilization of identifiers, labels. We can't even discuss policy priorities, much less programs, without naming people and things. For better or for worse, we have and will continue to have, and suffer with, labels. Hence, we will need to contend with an "epidemiology" of mental retardation—notwithstanding the knowledge that mental retardation is neither a disease nor a condition with "lawful" characteristics.

The labels we use are critical in understanding that epidemiology, because incidence and prevalence estimates have little meaning when separated from a definitional context. Therefore, notwithstanding the President's Committee on Mental Retardation, which has reported that there are 6 million mentally retarded individuals in the United States (a convenient application of the 3% estimate) and other approximations, I believe it remains essential for us to review what else may be known about these complex matters. I begin here with where I began the chapter itself, discussing metaphors, language, and the relationship between our words and our values. We should begin by noting again that incidence and prevalence data are not grounded only in objectively derived disease entities.

The American Association on Mental Deficiency has recently revised its definition of mental retardation. Before 1959, there was more or less general agreement that the incidence of mental retardation is approximately 3%. That is, mental retardation was assumed to be normally distributed in the population and it was further agreed that the psychometric "cutoff" would be 75 IQ or one and one half standard deviations away from the mean. In 1959, the Association's Terminology and Classification Committee, chaired by Rick Heber, redefined mental retardation and, included in the revised definition, there was the statement that subaverage intellectual performance refers to a psychometric score which is greater than one standard deviation below the population mean on tests of general intelligence (Heber, 1959). With that change in definition, 16% of a typical population would be, psychometrically at least, eligible to be designated as "mentally retarded."

In 1973, a subsequent committee of the Association, now chaired by Herbert Grossman, again revised the definition to include as mentally retarded only those who are "significantly" subaverage in intellectual functioning, where "significantly" means performance which is two or more standard deviations from the mean or average of the tests (Grossman, 1973). With the figurative, and possibly literal, stroke of Herbert Grossman's pen, a committee sitting around a conference table reduced enormously the potential incidence of mental retardation, never having to see or dose or deal with a client, only having to say that, hereinafter, mental retardation is such and such rather than this or that. We cannot redefine measles, or cancer, or pregnancy with such external procedures. It's obvious; mental retardation and emotional disturbance, and even such seemingly objective conditions as blindness and deafness, are less objective disease entities than they are administrative terms; they are metaphors more than anything else.

It is important to understand that merely having a low IQ neither legally nor functionally jeopardizes how society views a person or deals with him. Sixteen percent of the population have IQs below 85; 3% of the population have IQs below 75; but probably no more than 1% of the population are ever in their lifetimes administratively adjudicated as "mentally retarded." This is by way of saying that the incidence, prevalence, and characteristics of mental retardation depend upon such influences as definition and criteria, program supports, cultural value, social class, and other factors that have more to do with political and administrative rather than biological or psychological matters. This situation exists across all so-called disability areas, and, consequently, estimates of various categorical handicaps vary from study to study, from culture to culture, and from time to time. Disability means no more or less than being placed in a special class, a special program, or a special category or setting, as a consequence of that disability. The most relevant definition of a disability must refer to the fact that it is essentially administratively determined.

Incidence and prevalence estimates, predictions of program needs, and cost-benefit analyses are extraordinarily hazardous when dealing with these diverse administratively defined populations. For example, in one state, attempts are made to integrate so-called educable mentally retarded children in regular grades; in another area (e.g., Prince Edward Island, Canada) such youngsters are in regular grades and are not even thought of as "mentally retarded." In yet another state, every effort is made to place as many children as possible with IQs less than 75 in special classes for the mentally retarded. Then, we might ask, what is the prevalence of mental retardation in the public schools when, on the one hand, there are school systems that deliberately attempt to identify such children as retarded and others, equally interested in their well being, that deliberately attempt to integrate such children fully into the mainstream of educational life?

…The ostensible purpose for defining groups, labeling individuals, and developing incidence and prevalence estimates is to serve better those individuals defined and labeled. If labeling does not lead to services, and it often doesn't, it reduces what might have been a helpful procedure to a pejorative and detrimental act.

…In a perverse and ironic manner, we may be fortunate that needs seem always to be bottomless, endless, and never met. That is, we haven't suffered from an overabundance of services for so-called handicapped people. On the other hand, especially with limited resources—which we will probably always have to confront—it may be useful strategically to place those resources where they can do the greatest good for the greatest number.

While many experts in the field of mental retardation have argued that, for example, 16% or 3% or 5% or 2% (AAMD) of the population are mentally retarded, or "psychometrically mentally retarded," our own study indicates that a 1% estimate is more valuable for program planning and development. Similarly, estimates as high as 20, 30, or 40% in the relatively new category "Specific Learning Disabilities" are provocative, certainly, but do not appear to be helpful in program planning. Further, prevalence estimates of various types of handicapped children (not including the new general category, "Learning Disabilities") conclude that approximately 10% of all school age children are "handicapped." Unfortunately, there are problems with this estimate for the same reasons that epidemiological data on mental retardation have never provided satisfactory guidance for program planning.

The studies that have been completed indicate that there are important differences between what we might call "administrative disability" and "objective disability." As mentioned, a clear example of this dichotomy is the discrepancy between psychometric mental retardation (at least 2% of the total population) and administratively designated (or known) mental retardation (approximately 1% of the total population). Therefore, taking these factors and their resultant problems into consideration, I believe it is reasonable to consider using population estimates that are based on available studies of known cases in the various disability categories.

From our own demographic studies of mental retardation, our evaluation of the epidemiologic literature in the field, and from a careful analysis of the data obtained from both our Head Start questionnaire survey and our observational studies of selected Head Start programs, we estimate that 1% of the total population (incidence) need special services because of their mental retardation, another 1% require it because of behavioral disturbances, and another 1% because of moderate and severe sensory and/or physical disorders.…We would not include the so-called speech-impaired in such designations; nor would we include the so-called learning disabled.

We believe it is not in the best interests of either the children or the programs to label children with mild disabilities, who could otherwise be adequately dealt with in ordinary classes, as "handicapped," "retarded," "speech-impaired," etc. We believe it is in the interest of both the children who have been so labeled until now and those others who are now denied a normal interaction with them, to reserve the categories of handicap only for those who have such severe and moderate needs that they will not be able to be served adequately in ordinary classes under ordinary conditions. For that group with such special needs, we estimate that there is no more than a 3% incidence across populations and age categories, and possibly, a 4% and no more than 5% prevalence during the preschool and school years. Therefore, mild speech impairment, as mild retardation or disturbance, could not be considered a handicap requiring special attention in the traditional sense. Those children with mild disabilities should be served within the context of regular school settings. Those with severe or moderate speech impairments will be found to have general language disabilities and, more probably than not, learning, behavioral, sensory, or physical disorders.

Obviously, the above recommendations will not solve all of the difficulties inherent in estimating the incidence and prevalence of conditions that are grounded more in political-metaphorical issues than in scientific ones. However, at least in some modest manner, we may be able to reduce the harmful effects of unnecessary labeling and the resultant stigma to many children and their families. We may also move from a disease-oriented planning model to a developmental model, one that seriously considers the benefits of integration and decategorization of both children and programs, one that is committed to the concept that people are educable, that development is a function of not only endowment but training and opportunity and encouragement….

Concepts of Mental Retardation

Mental retardation is not something that can be simply and scientifically defined, discussed, dissected, applied, or studied. Mental retardation is related to our very understanding of humanity, of human potential, of educability, of equality, of rights and privileges, of everything we are and everything that relates to us. Asking someone to comprehend a concept of mental retardation is akin to asking him to comprehend a concept of spirituality or decadence, beauty or ugliness, strength or weakness, good people or bad people. Mental retardation can't be encapsulated and pictured by IQ parameters, or even etiological descriptions, or behavioral assessments. It must always be anchored to other people, a community, values, expectations, and hopes. Therefore, the epidemiology of mental retardation can only be discussed in a psychological-social-political-economic context. Further, the economic factor, or any other factor or problem, can be appreciated only in this same context. Unfortunately, we have neither a manual on terminology and classification nor a curriculum that will permit us to shortcut this conceptual process.

Also unfortunately, one's concept of mental retardation may impair seriously otherwise good judgment. Prejudices concerning those whom society calls "mentally retarded" may cause even the most distinguished and wise among us to do thoughtless things and issue silly pronouncements.

Reform or Revolution

I've asked the question many times, yet there is no answer for me. Possibly, there is no answer because I'm not pleased with the answers I see. I cannot tolerate the invidious comparison between the promises made and the institutions created. And what were the promises that our field was to keep? What did the institution, the special education program, the community mental health-mental retardation movement contribute? We have been faithful, some have worked unselfishly, some have raised large sums of money, many have supported humanistic precepts and philosophies on behalf of people with special needs. What good was to come of all of this? The hope then, and remaining today, was that people would gain strength, would deepen their optimism and faith in the human ethos, would develop more genuine concern for our brethren, would eventually have the wisdom to believe that all human beings are equally valuable, and that our work is not to judge who can or can't change but to fulfill the promise that all people can change, that each person can learn. The promises made were to coalesce around the demonstration, especially to those of us most intimately involved, that society is each person, not multiplied but singular, each person unique and valuable.

Yet what have we created? We find that, in institutions and in many special schools, both the caretakers and the clients victimize and are victims. In the institution, and in many special school programs, there are not sufficient options for children, for families and, equally important, for staffs. In plain fact, the research available confirms the shambles that too many special programs and facilities are.

Yet, in spite of powerful critical reports on institutional life (Blatt, 1973a), and the scientifically questionable but numerous reports on special class life (Blatt & Garfinkel, 1973), we continue to build more and more institutions and pass more and more mandatory rather than permissive special education laws—regardless of the well-known fact that we have yet to demonstrate either the efficacy or moral rectitude in continuing, much less encouraging, those segregated programs. To turn to an earlier theme, such proliferation on the basis of trivial evidence is but another illustration of the monolithic influence.

We have made too many concessions, we have so bent the data to suit our ignorances and confusions, we are so anxious to please the people, that we lie to spare them the anxiety we feel because of what we have created. I'm expecting that, at any time now, somebody will propose a new concept, a remodeling of the old French triage system for sorting out and treating battlefield casualties. However, the neo-triage model will deal not with the militarily wounded but with those whom bad luck, accident, and society inflict their insults upon. I'm expecting to read someday an "erudite" paper advising us to set aside the hopeless, for their very designations demand we should not waste time with them; and, we might best benignly neglect those who will probably do as well without us, those who puzzle us, or those whose problems—although real—do not fully incapacitate them; and, consequently, we should reserve our resources and energies for those who most need our help. Possibly in war, triage is a valid concept; where some will live and some will die, and resources are particularly scarce, the whole thing—ghoulish as it may be—makes at least a little sense. However, when the new triage is trotted out, will there be anyone to say, "But we are not at war"? And will there be anyone else to say, "No, we are not at war. Yet we should have been. It was always a war, but most of us thought of it as merely a debate"?

Reprinted by permission of Steven D. Blatt and the Blatt family.

THE INDUSTRIES[15]

In our personal lives, we are confronted with electric can openers or egg beaters that make people useless, exercycles and rowing machines that make us foolish, and elevators that make us flabby. We build buildings without windows, play games on our television sets, own cars to take us to the railroad, and build highways to encourage us to consume more gas and buy more cars for our journey to the Good Life. America seems to believe that it's better to spend money than to conserve it, better to find a complex solution to a problem, better to have "bells and whistles" on the game or the machine than to make it clean and functional. For generations, America's industries have profited greatly from our seemingly insatiable desire to spend, accumulate, consume, and discard. Even in sit-down restaurants, you will find in many places that the "china" is paper and the "silver" is plastic.

Likewise, consumerism infects the profession. At the annual convention of this society and that association, I get the feeling that I have been surrounded by the descendants of P. T. Barnum. Buy the "walking beam" and you may cure learning disabilities, buy the trampoline and you may cure reading failure, buy the new curriculum in music and you remediate arithmetic failure. Buy the reading series and you obviate the publisher's business failure. Like a pedant reviewing a concert with the complaint, "The Mozart symphony was fine, but the violinists' chairs were too far apart," we work on the chairs of life and ignore the music. To say that technology is misplaced is not an overstatement.

Yet there *are* professionals, technicians, and administrators who solve rather than create problems. Biklen and his colleagues at the Center on Human Policy at Syracuse University have written several guides concerned with the problem of mental retardation. For example, Biklen's (1977) *The Elementary School Administrator's Practical Guide to Mainstreaming* reached thousands of school principals and other administrators, hopefully to ease the way for the effective integration of handicapped children into ordinary school programs. There are other authors, too, who take seriously the idea that the biggest problem we have in the field of special education *isn't* money. For example, Don Caston, lecturer in charge of the Handicapped Education and Aid Research Unit of the City of London Polytechnic, has published a number of books and brochures that provide guidance to teachers and others in developing simple aids for handicapped persons. Their motto: It Isn't Clever to Spend Money. And they demonstrate that simple (and profound) declaration in numerous ways, especially by providing first-rate programs for disabled people. Thus, I don't want to leave you with a sense that all is lost or that nothing is done adequately. Quite the opposite; many things are accomplished in a splendid manner. Notwithstanding, I prefer to dwell on the great deal that needs to be corrected rather than on the impressive work that has been done in this field. Other books, other formats and forums, deal with those more pleasant (sometimes extraordinary) situations.

Why do the monopolies and monoliths thrive in our culture? For one thing, there are great fortunes to be made. For another, we don't take seriously enough Don Caston's dictum regarding the expenditure of money. Similarly, we don't take seriously the fact that it is not necessary, desirable, or effective to look for complex solutions to problems that may be amenable to more simple explanations. We should remember that common things occur commonly; or, as the old adage teaches us, when one hears hoof beats he should look for horses not zebras. This can be illustrated by the response I heard in 1982 from the University of Chicago psychologist, Bruno Bettelheim, to a young teacher who wanted advice about a child who banged his head when things weren't going his way. Bettelheim's off-the-cuff advice:

> Obviously, he needs to bang his head. The environment doesn't please him. Rather than try to convince him not to bang his head, or rather than to try to prevent him from banging his head, why don't you bring a pillow from home and place it between his head and the wall the next time he starts banging his head.

So many of the problems we encounter with retarded children require common sense, observational skills, and a teacher who deliberately and regularly thinks hard about the children in class or the clients at the clinic. It's much easier to *do something* about a problem, and it's much easier to *spend money* on the problem than it is to think hard and well about the problem.

…Although the field of mental retardation is hardly ever described as a monolithic industry, when you stop to ponder it, the idea cannot easily be dismissed. And while even monolithic industries may contribute to civilization, is there ever one that cannot stand criticism? A little criticism is better than no criticism, and leaders in our field may profit from a little criticism. The Nobel laureate Isaac Bashevis Singer tells the story about his grandfather who was asked the question, "Why is there a devil?" After all, if God is so omnipotent, so all-powerful, why did he permit the creation of the devil? He responded, "God not only created the devil, he needs the devil. God too needs critics." If God needs critics, don't we in the field of mental retardation surely need critics?

It may be that we in this field should consider the possibility that we have suffered with our own Vietnam. We have suffered with authorities who cut corners, academics who piously ignored the obvious, jurists who looked the other way, administrators who made excuses, and the people who pretended not to know that things simply were going sour. We in the field of mental retardation spend too much time measuring how well children drop marbles in holes, ignoring all the time the holes they live in, and the holes we professionals got ourselves into. We have spent our resources fighting for the clinical needs of retarded persons, when the quintessential issue has always been connected to civil rights. Our "enemies" exacerbate problems, and we minimize them—or vice versa; but we're never in agreement on either what the problem is or how serious it is. And unfortunately, most of us lie about what we see, what we think it means, and how we feel the problems might be solved. There are dilemmas, there are paradoxes, there are experts who argue with experts—to such an extent that the nonexperts wind up being the experts. The courts intrude, often focusing not on compelling problems, but on those narrow issues which they are empowered to judge, issues that may not necessarily be most important, may not be important at all.

These are a few of the reasons why this is not a charitable chapter…. This chapter deals with the "business" side of the field, with that and other sides that are neither discussed in textbooks nor analyzed at professional meetings with sides that some would rather leave unremembered—with sides that we must seek to understand better if we are going to understand our problems better, and ourselves better.

Treatment, Research, and Training Professionals

Mental retardation has always been an industry, and its professionals (like other professionals) have not been shy about living off it and (insofar as the leaders are concerned) controlling it. Consequently, it should come as no surprise that political and self-serving considerations have always been important to policy developments in the field. By analogy, an interesting example is the commentary offered by Cartwright, a prominent Southern physician who lived during the American slavery conflict, to "explain" the slave's character. Cartwright was puzzled why slaves tried to run away, but he finally figured out the cause: It was a mental illness characterized by the desire to flee, what the good doctor called "drapetomania" (Gould, 1981, p. 71). The Black could no more control his insane need to flee than he could his love of a kind master. The cure: Slave owners should avoid either extreme cruelty or permissiveness; that is, their slaves should be treated like children if the disease were to be controlled. There were other "scientific" explanations of slave behavior, and "scientifically authenticated" treatments, just as today there are "scientific" explanations of the behavior of mentally retarded persons and "authenticated" treatments for their deficiencies.

Elsewhere, I developed the argument that education is a monolith, "no more capable of dealing with revisionism than any other monolith" (Blatt, 1977, p. 17). Education is a monolith as medicine is a monolith and other professions are monoliths. Hence, it should come as no surprise that a field such as mental retardation, powered by professionals, is monolithic. Let us look at those characteristics of the professionals who serve us, often with distinction, and it will be difficult to escape the conclusion that the ways our professionals are trained, the ways they are rewarded, the ways they protect themselves, the ways they perceive themselves, and the ways they are perceived by society among many ordinary citizens, as well as within the professions, the beliefs that:

1. There is a right way and a wrong way; there is established practice and quackery.

2. There are rules, regulations, customs, and values, from which there should be no significant deviation.

3. The public judges professionals by how closely the teacher, for example, behaves like others in his or her profession.

4. In unity there is strength; with a common agenda there is purposefulness; with common methods and procedures there is verification.

Not everything is bad about monopolies and monoliths, but it must be pointed out that in private industry there are laws prohibiting contrived orthodoxy. The opposite obtains in the professions. The greed of Rockefeller, Carnegie, and other oil and steel barons caused the creation of the Securities and Exchange Commission and the various antimonopoly measures in the United States. The professions, on the other hand, not only continue to strengthen and refine their monopolies, but society praises them for their efforts. In the professions, monopolies are believed to be the antidotes to quackery and its permutations, despite some indications that they may also contribute to the disease. Teachers are required to complete certain courses before they can be endorsed to teach. Teacher groups are increasingly proclaiming that certification doesn't go far enough. Teachers now want to be licensed—in the same fashion that doctors, nurses, and psychologists are licensed. What may have begun as measures taken by the state to protect the public—licensure—are now viewed by teacher organizations as measures necessary not only to protect the public but to give enhanced status to the teachers. While teachers are waging battles to achieve licensure, doctors are waging battles to control the sizes of medical school classes. Each group is nurtured by its own distinctive unions—those of the teachers more resembling the union, that of the physicians more resembling the exclusive club. Should we trust the man who works with too obvious zeal to feather his own nest? Or is it better to trust those who don't trust him?

The above comments may seem unfair and one-sided. No doubt, there is another side to the arguments concerning teachers' and doctors' unions, licensure for professionals, orthodox treatment practices, and conservatism in the professions. But of course, such professional perspectives are represented in most textbooks in those fields. I am assuming that you will examine that other side. The point here is not to present a balanced picture, laying out the good that professionals accomplish with each instance that I note a problem. Rather, I am making the point that treatment, research, and training professionals in the field are, for the most part, represented by large organizations that have powerful voices in federal and state legislatures. Indeed, those organizations employ substantial numbers of people to lobby on behalf of their members. And representatives of those teachers, doctors, nurses, social workers, psychologists, and administrators are not able to make their cases merely on the self-evident good works that their clients accomplish. There is an array of lobbyists, public relations specialists, and legislators who spend much of their professional lives convincing America that those professionals are necessary to foster the public good. And while of course that's all true, embedded in those claims is a degree of hyperbole cloaking self-interest. The professionals can take good care of themselves. The reader need not be unduly fearful for their future welfare. Better to pity the critic.

Most of society operates on the principle of "interchangeable parts." Certainly, industrial hardware is built and maintained on that principle. And oftentimes, human beings are viewed as interchangeable, especially those who are employed in "unskilled" and "semi-skilled" jobs. To a degree, even those in skilled and technical fields are trained and employed as if anyone with certain skills can take the place of anyone else with similar skills. The concept of "interchangeable parts" so permeates our society that it is rarely noticed, much less challenged. Some examples:

1. Rigid salary schedules for virtually all blue collar and technical workers. Furthermore, for most school teachers, social workers, nurses, and state and federal administrators, salaries are determined by the position one is slotted into and the years he or she has served in that position.

2. The ever more widespread utilization of objective competitive examinations for skilled and professional positions.

3. The popularity of competency-based instruction programs.

4. Unionization.

5. Stipulated procedures for arbitrating grievances.

6. Standard benefits programs.

7. Rigid retirement practices.

Of course, many of these practices—such as well-publicized stipulated grievance procedures, salary schedules based on seniority, and worker protection programs—were created because of employer abuses. It isn't an accident that unions have become remarkably powerful in the United States. Nor is it accidental that local, state, and federal salary schedules are for the most part determined by seniority. And of course, the civil service system is built on competitive examinations. These programs have accomplished good, and many would argue persuasively about the necessity for their creation and continuance. But at the same time, these practices reflect a society that employs individuals as if one person were interchangeable with another. In a fashion, the field of mental retardation not only employs its personnel as if one doctor (or teacher, or administrator) is interchangeable with another, but it also creates programs as if one developmental center in a state is not different from another, as if one regional center is not different from another, and as if one group home is not different from another.

The practice if not the theory of "interchangeable parts" is widely accepted in the field of mental retardation. This practice may be considered to be one of the primary problems in the field. Getting back to the fundamental principles, if all people are valuable, and if all people are different, wouldn't it appear that the main goal is to utilize humanity's many talents differentially?

Builders and Architects

When a vice president of the United States was forced to resign on threat of criminal prosecution for accepting bribes, it may or may not have been noticed by the average citizen that *every* participant involved with him in an alleged illegal "payoffs for favors" schemes was either a builder, an architect, or a land developer. It may not be noticed by most observers of bureaucracy that, year in and year out, the state is the largest customer of architects, builders, and land developers. The state appropriates money not only to provide services but to build facilities to house those services—with enthusiasm if not always in the public interest. It isn't necessarily true that state functionaries are crooked, but land acquisition and construction represent the biggest of big businesses. And where there is big business there is sometimes a compromise with, or even a disregard for, legality. Always, there is temptation.

In mental retardation, institutions (and now community facilities) have kept many an architect, builder, or land owner solvent. In several states, facility development is a billion-dollar industry. Of course, not all builders and architects are venal and avaricious. There are many who work very diligently to create healthful and beneficial environments. …

A community based on the proposition that people with special needs can help themselves, as well as being helped by others, to be more self-reliant—that is an idea worth examining and working hard to achieve. The ideas of Gilroy and Sokoloff provide a ray of hope and an inspiring example of what *can* be done by the builder and the architect.

Merchants and Manufacturers, Organized Labor, and Bankers

What does the proletariat have to do with the bankers? Or with the merchant princes? Of course, most people have observed that the leaders of organized labor are as powerful and well known (if not quite as affluent) as chief executive officers representing the Fortune 500 companies. So in a sense, there is a relationship between labor and business. The relationship between the banker or the captain of industry and the mental retardation professional may not be as obvious. The leaders of a state employees' union are not, after all, as well known as the presidents of major industrial unions. But one fact connects all the "players"—all benefit from the mental retardation industry. The bankers raise the money to build or refurbish the institutions. The merchants and manufacturers fuel those institutions. And labor services them. These are not "cottage industries," but important and powerful in every sense. Consequently, there is great interest in the business and labor community whether there will be a deinstitutionalization effort or not in America. Why? It does not require mathematical wizardry to deduce that 6% (e.g., an architect's fee) of $20 million or $30 million (cost of constructing an institution) is a great deal of money. A construction program of this magnitude requires major contractors, suppliers, land developers, unions, and, especially, banks, which earn millions on the capital they raise to finance the enterprise. The question is: How can we terminate institutional building programs when, in many states, they are the sources for political support and patronage? In an analysis I did for a paper co-authored in 1977, the economics of mental retardation were likened to the game of Monopoly (Blatt, Bogdan, Biklen, & Taylor).

…Mental retardation is a bigger industry than ever, and the country has experienced an unprecedented inflation. For example, the New York State Office of Mental Retardation and Developmental Disabilities budget was approximately $1 billion in the early 80s, and it is getting bigger. In 1965, the care of a mentally retarded resident in New York State approximated $4,000 a year. In the early 80s it was $60,000, with at least one or two institutions spending $100,000. In a sense, costs are not only inexplicable but also incalculable. Precise figures hardly matter.

Parents especially are up against it. It isn't that all merchants who serve handicapped persons are out to gouge them, but they surely are out to survive, to make a living, and, if they can, to make substantial profit. As Calvin Coolidge once said, "Business is the business of America." Well, those who manufacture wheelchairs in this country not only have very good businesses, but businesses without a great deal of competition. Read what Hutchinson (1982) had to say in a recent issue of *The Exceptional Parent:*

> I have been in the process of buying my fourteen year-old cerebral palsied son a wheelchair since last March, which is eight months ago. This chair is a custom chair. I will not name the company. It is also motorized. He and I are frustrated at this point…. The cost of the chair is $3,450, which includes a $75 fee for measuring him. You can get a two-seated motorized golf cart for $1,900, a small farm tractor for $3,000 and a darned nice used car for $3,400…. We have for some time been concerned about the high cost of wheelchairs and the possibilities for competitive abuse in a market characterized by substantial sales to public institutions, significant under-writing by third parties and consumers who are at competitive disadvantages due to their absolute need for the product. In other words we are indeed a captive audience.

In my case my insurance will pay most of the cost. That is not my problem. In March I was told I would have it in two months. By mid-July my son was asking every day. By August he was hoping he would have it for his birthday, August 7th, then in time to start school. It is now past Thanksgiving and he still does not have it. Maybe they will be kind and let him have it by Christmas…. I was told by an agent from the FTC that those that sell wheelchairs make 30 to 40% commissions on these chairs. That's a lot of money on a $3,000 chair.

Pork Barrels and Politicians

It was during a year of leave from academe, as Massachusetts director of mental retardation, when I may have lost my innocence about government and "men of affairs." For sure, what I experienced during that leave reified my disillusionment with a state's ability to offer direct services to people. It was during this leave when sufficient data were collected to lead me to conclude that there is no hope for institutions, that there is no hope to truly reform them, that there is no hope that sustained good works can be accomplished in state schools for mentally retarded persons. It was also during this leave when I experienced firsthand the ways in which politicians and their hangers-on operate. First, the hangers-on.

I hadn't been in the job very long when I had an insistent visitor, an angry man who wanted to know why I was harassing him. Not recognizing his name, face, or anything about him, I expressed puzzlement and the observation that he probably was mistaking me for some other bureaucrat in the building (and who could blame him for that?).

"No, you're the guy. I have been selling tile to the Commonwealth of Massachusetts for many years. I have not only built a wonderful business, but I have paid my dues to the party and to many philanthropies. I am a respected member of this community, and you are ruining my business. You are ruining my life."

Possibly, the recounting here is a bit melodramatic and not "exactly" how it occurred in my office in the State Department of Mental Hygiene in 1968. But, essentially, this rendition conveys what occurred. By my efforts to stop the building of large institutions, by my reactions to the various plans that were presented to a committee concerned with new facilities in the commonwealth, this man's business was being affected. And he wasn't going to put up with it! I was informed that he was the closest personal friend of Governor so-and-so, State Senators X, Y, and Z, and distinguished and powerful politicians 1, 2, 3, and 4. Whether our industrialist actually knew all of those important personages, much less whether *they* counted him as close personal friends, isn't germane to the point here. While the *works* of government are fueled by the taxpayers, those who govern are personally sustained by private resources from industry, commerce, and even philanthropies and other nonprofit organizations such as universities. The people pay for constructing the state's facilities, but the vested interests—usually legal vested interests—support those who execute those works. There are two types of pork barrel: the one into which the Congress, the state legislature, or county assembly dips *for* their various constituents; and the one from the lobbyist, which is distributed to the executives and legislators of our federal, state, and local governments. Mental retardation, like every other important enterprise, engenders a lot of business. It *isn't* supposed to be a business, and it usually isn't a business. But it always engenders a lot of business. And where there's business, there are winners and losers, favors given and favors received, greed, and sometimes illegal activity.

Quoting from the Romans, "The senators are good men, but the senate is a wild beast." As individuals, the senators are honest; but together, they may be devious at times; and how their work is eventually implemented requires constant vigilance by the people (Blatt, 1970). Politicians as a group cannot always be trusted to carry out the will of the people. Consequently, deinstitutionalization and other reforms in mental retardation will not be achieved by merely letting the politicians follow the evidence to an inevitably proper conclusion. They need convincing, not only to teach them about mental retardation, but also to buck the tide of vested interests, which have other things in mind, and which are willing to pay to achieve their ends, rather than the common good.

Lawyers

Years ago, my heroes in the field were clinicians and scholars. But today, possibly the most visible if not always the most authentic leaders in mental retardation are the lawyers, judges, and legislators. Once, the most intriguing and discussed questions were, for example, whether placement of choice should be the special class or the regular class. Today, the most compelling discussions are whether or not children's rights are violated by placing them in special-restricted environments. Once, Richard Hungerford debated the "functional" occupational education versus the "watered-down" regular curriculum. Today, Thomas Gilhool argues before the United States Supreme Court that an institution should be closed down, that where a child resides (the community or the institution) and where that child goes to school (or if he or she goes) are more primary issues for society to consider than the type of special treatment made available or the content of schooling.

Once upon a time, the most serious and substantial issues in the field of mental retardation were clinical. Today, they are legal. Once upon a time, the prepotent objective was to improve clinical services and opportunities for the clients. Today, for many in the field the objective is to *free* the clients. Hence, as Herr (1979) argued, today we may think about mental retardation as a different field with "new clients." Herr contended that the lawyers, their affiliates, and consorts have been responsible for changing the rhetoric in the field from an emphasis on clinical concerns to legal ones, and from a discussion of what's going on in such places as Willowbrook, Forest Haven, Belchertown, and Partlow to a discussion on whether people are entitled to be in other places. Herr's provocative conclusion, however, is that while there are more legislative and legal avenues open to retarded persons today, there continues to be a serious shortage of trained advocates. He argued persuasively that a legal principle or, for that matter, a legal decision cannot be retained for a client. Clients need lawyers, people to help them. He presented anecdotal evidence to support the contention that while things are much better today, insofar as protecting the legal rights of handicapped persons, great injustices are still perpetrated. He argued that there is a gap between advocacy needs and advocacy resources, and when retarded people seek legal or administrative relief without good counsel, the actual doors to courthouses and bureaucracies remain shut. For the most part, good counsel isn't available to them. Hence, the call for still more lawyers and other legal advocates. Hence, a plea for these "new clients"—"new" in the sense that retarded persons more than ever before need legal, as well as (if not rather than) clinical services.

In spite of Herr's conviction and its popularity today, and in spite of his persuasiveness, while more lawyers would surely open more doors there remains the perennial question: Now that the doors would open, what's inside? How good is it? That is, what exactly is it that we are demanding for our clients? Are we doing them any great favors? And can (must) it be better? To be sure, something was terribly wrong for many years to bring us to the state we're in now, a state created in spite of the work of good clinicians. But without especially castigating the clinicians, why were they oblivious to issues of human and civil rights? Why were the abuses of segregated institutions and schools not regarded as part of the clinician's concern? Herr's concern is exactly right, as is the concern of the other lawyers and those who support modern legal advocacy. But something is also wrong with a society in which each person needs a lawyer to remain safe from harm. Who can dispute today the fact that thousands of people (especially handicapped and other disenfranchised groups) need and should have legal services? What troubles me, though, is that in our rush to provide such services and to guarantee human rights, clinical concerns seem to have become secondary—almost submerged in the wave of lawyers clamoring for open doors and advocates clamoring for open environments.

I will have more to say about this matter in the following section. But possibly because the lawyers are the "new heroes" for the "new clients," the urge to control the pendulum of excitement causes us now to be worried while we once simply said, "Amen." In the final analysis, it will be the responsibility of the larger society to find a place for handicapped persons; and in the final analysis, it will be the clinicians who will be called upon to help ameliorate the learning disorder, to prevent further handicap, and to circumvent that which is believed to be unalterable.

We've learned in mid-20th century America that lawyers must be part of the team. But we must better understand that they can no more replace the family (the primary advocates), the general society (the primary normalizing environment), or the clinicians (the primary treatment specialists) than can the law replace the deed. Lawyers are good at seeing to it that society makes sincere attempts to give people that to which they are entitled. Lawyers, however, have no special preparation or experience to actually deliver on those legal guarantees. And lastly, we should not forget that the need for lawyers is a barometer not of how *just* the world is but how bad it is. In the ugliest totalitarian world possible, lawyers are prohibited. In a merely bad world, everyone needs a good lawyer to fight that bad world. There's something to be said about a world that needs but a few good lawyers to protect the citizens from occasional injustices. That is, we'll have a better world not when we have more lawyers but when we need fewer lawyers. Possibly, even the lawyers themselves look forward to that kind of world. In the meantime, we should be grateful to the Stanley Herrs and Tom Gilhools of society.

Advocacy

What the Golden Rule was to the ancients (and is to those who still hew to the Good Book), advocacy is to the moderns, especially those who seek to serve disabled persons. Almost, but not quite, the concept of advocacy *is* the Golden Rule. While once we were instructed to "Do Unto Others as You Would Do Unto Yourself," advocates today are guided by the proposition that they must work on behalf of another person as if they were working for themselves. In that manner, advocates need not be objective and must not be even handed. Advocates work on behalf of another person whether that other person "deserves" such efforts or not. Advocates must be less interested in serving society than in serving the particular individual for whom they advocate. Advocates must draw a line between their loyalty to the individual they serve and their general goodwill toward all people.

Like the Golden Rule, advocacy is a wonderful concept. But in a fashion, advocacy goes beyond the Golden Rule. While it's one thing to do for others as you would have others do for you, it's quite another thing to work for another as you would work for yourself. In the first instance, you are guided to treat other people as you *expect* to be treated by *them*. That's only decent and reasonable. If you're an advocate, you have agreed to treat another person as you would *treat yourself*—to "buy" into his or her viewpoints, to rationalize his or her behavior, to be as selfish concerning his or her needs as you are concerning your own. Advocacy goes beyond the Golden Rule, because you as advocate are asked not only to treat your client as you can reasonably expect your client to treat you, but to treat him or her as you treat yourself. It's a wonderful concept, but like anything that's wonderful, there may be negative side effects. I once discussed those side effects with colleagues, and then I was sufficiently stubborn and vain to put those ideas in writing. What followed caused controversy and hurt feelings. I knew then that what I had to say about advocacy, while not necessarily precise, was on the track of what needed to be said. Brief excerpts from that commentary are reproduced here:

Dear Friend:

We return to the most disturbing element of the entire advocacy movement—our intolerance. We know so little, but we act as if we know everything. When opponents raise sensible arguments, we shoot them down with slogans. When a perfectly decent family expresses anxiety about 8 or 10 unrelated mentally retarded people moving in next door, we call those citizens unfeeling, godless, and un-American. Ironically, we live by the Golden Rule, but more often we do to others no less than what others have done to the mentally retarded. We must stop that. We have neither all the answers nor all of the righteousness. We are no better and no more righteous than other people. Like the mentally retarded themselves, advocates are people, fragile people, people like those who work in institutions and even run them. If we have any special insights about where people should live and how they should be treated, it is only because we are now smart in ways in which we were once stupid. Our advocacy label is the license to work on behalf of certain others as we would work in our own behalf, but that is neither justification nor authority to infringe upon the rights of others. If we are not careful, there will be advocacy movements created to protect people who have been hurt by certain brands of our advocacy. If this happens, everything else we have done will have been for naught. We have preached that bad ends are not justified by good intentions. Now we must live by the belief that good ends are not justified by callous means. (Blatt, 1979a)

Dear Friend,

Once it took courage to join the "movement" against the institutionalizers, to be an advocate for the retarded, the other homeless, and the weak. Now it takes courage to decline the opportunity to join up. For the last decade advocates have become tough through dishing it out against almost overwhelming odds. But I hope we have not become so tough that we are not strong enough to take it, especially when the criticism is tinged with unfairness and is overstated in the same way that advocates overstate things to make points to hostile mobs.

We need advocates because of the way our political-economic system works. It supposes that if everyone grabs as much as he can, everyone will have what he deserves. However, the poor, the weak, and the handicapped are at a great disadvantage in such a system. These persons have not been able to grab fair shares. Consequently, one solution to their plight is to assign advocates to take for the weak what they cannot take for themselves. The goal to institutionalize advocacy can only be a permanent state of siege between the weak and the strong, the poor and the rich. Those who grab the most for themselves or others come out the winners, but to wish a fair share for the weak is to repudiate the adversary model. As agents of social change we should seek to establish advocacy as a short-range expedient only as long as it is needed to counteract the destructiveness of a society gone wrong—a society where avarice and materialism predominate. As a long-range social goal we should seek to eliminate the need for advocacy or, at the very least, seek to minimize it. The systemic focus of social change should not be the establishment of advocacy networks as routine as fire departments or schools. Rather, the focus should be to reduce the raw frontier ethics of the survival of the strong. A truly civilized society is beyond the need for advocates. We should not have a system that serves the weak, like card players are served by the good or bad luck of who is drawn to advocate. Triage is not sharing.

When we fight for moral issues, we do so with the conviction that we are right. Our conviction is not the same as knowledge that we are, in fact, right. If we fail to understand that our conviction could be mistaken, we may become zealots who are at times stupid and dangerous. The dangerous consequences of being wrong are always present, even when we are aware of the frailness of our conviction. Therefore, we are potentially responsible for wrongs done in the name of justice. This responsibility cannot be dissolved by claiming certainty that we are right. Of course, we are tempted to fake certainty to be brave enough to act, but we should try as hard as we can to remember what we believe and are trying to impress upon others. (Blatt, 1979b)

As happened to so many other ideas, advocacy is now less of an unassailable idea and more of a good issue. It's also a problem. At least in part, the advocacy medicine is a new disease, possibly not as lethal as that which it was created to cure, but a disease nevertheless. Like most medicines, advocacy has its unintended negative side effects. "But even ordinary water can have side effects," so the rationalists advise the alarmists.

While it's been said that a functional test of advocacy is whether or not advocates work for their client as if they were working on their own behalf, it can also be said that, to the degree that anyone works on another's behalf, he or she is depriving that individual of working for himself or herself. This is a conundrum without escape, a circle with no detour. Parents are wonderful when they protect their young, but they are stifling when they give—when they insist upon giving—that same protection to their grown children. The consumer advocacy movement was built on the idea that families of the handicapped would work on behalf of the "cause" as no professionals could, as no ordinary citizens could—in spite of the humanitarianism of those other people. In large measure, that is so.

There *is* a problem, however. We are neither decrying the influence of the consumer movement nor suggesting its demise. Quite the opposite. But there *is* a special problem we must face. Advocacy—whether the consumer "brand" of the mother and father, or the citizen "brand" created by people such as Wolf Wolfensberger—

must bridge the need for disabled people to be protected to the need each person has to be free, to take responsibility, to assume appropriate authority. It could be said that programs for retarded individuals that are long on advocacy and short on responsibility are analogous to programs that have been created and are controlled by benevolent dictators. It's not enough to create something—even something good and decent—for people. Eventually, there must be the element of participation. Eventually, there must be something there that represents accomplishment by retarded persons themselves. In view of the development of such organizations as People First, The Association for Persons With Severe Handicaps (TASH), or the Center on Human Policy, it seems that we are learning to better value participation of handicapped persons—because we can learn from them, but moreover because they can help themselves in ways that other people cannot.

Another problem of advocates—exactly as it is a problem of the hospital administrator (who isn't a physician) or the athletic coach (who never excelled in the sport) or the film hero (who is intimidated by the real world)—is establishment of legitimacy. To advocate for another human being as if you were advocating for yourself is not exactly as if you were advocating for yourself. Everyone understands that it is perfectly understandable—albeit sometimes foolish, misinformed, or silly—to tell your doctor how he should dose you, or your tailor how he should clothe you. However, when someone presumes to tell the "expert" how to dose, tailor, feed, or measure other human beings, then that person is often accused of being meddlesome, a fraud, or a quack. The advocate who must inform the school that it is not properly serving a particular child may be on shaky ground because the advocate may not be "expert" in matters concerning instruction. And for sure, when the advocate informs the court that the hospital did not do right by his or her client, the court may wonder what expert knowledge the advocate has to make such strong and categorical assertions about medical practice. We ridicule the pretentiousness of someone who can't play the violin but believes he or she is qualified to be a concertmaster. To a degree, the advocate must overcome a similar if not identical reaction to his or her claim to speak on behalf of another person. It's a problem, and creates a tension that never quite finds resolution. But it has also been said that out of tension, out of strife, comes resolution. And so we have the paradox of the advocacy system, which is, on the one hand, a creator of tension and irresolution, and on the other hand, a force that can mitigate tension, resolve conflict, and even save lives….

Life With the Decision Makers

As mentioned previously, in 1968, I spent a full year as director of the Mental Retardation Program for the Commonwealth of Massachusetts Department of Mental Health at 15 Ashburton Place, Boston. The experiences I enjoyed (and those I didn't enjoy) are recounted in several of my previous books, especially *Exodus From Pandemonium: Human Abuse and a Reformation of Public Policy* (Blatt, 1970). What follows describes my "life" there, excerpts originally published in the aforementioned book, but most recently reprinted in *In and Out of Mental Retardation: Essays on Educability, Disability, and Human Policy* (Blatt, 1981b).

The Defensive Moat: Sophists' Paradise

A man can get along, quite adequately and for many years, on the elegance of his language and the passion and conviction of his speech. One would suppose that this is the hallmark of the university professor, and so it may be. However, I have observed sophistry and pedantries much more frequently in 15 Ashburton Place and its tentacles than in the halls of ivy. Very few people at 15 Ashburton Place must make decisions, if they do not wish to make them.…Obviously, many choose to make decisions, but they elect to decide and are not required to decide. For some, department activities are one grand round of debating, discussion, more debating, and more discussion. The payoff for sophistry is rather good, considering the investment. Men have been promoted on the passion of their verbal convictions, rarely having been required to influence the life of one child, but having persuasively proclaimed their regard for the lives of all children. Further, the System is such that one learns quickly of the peril of making certain decisions and the impossibility of making others. Rather than torment oneself with the uselessness of trying to "buck the System" (and one hears this time and time again), many men make their peace with it. They give expression to their good intentions, good training, and anger in activities that appear vigorous and dynamic but are empty repetitions, which are heard by no one of any importance or influence, but reassure the speaker that he is doing his job and that he is on the side of the "good" people. (We should not discount the cathartic effect such activities provide the speaker.)

Decision Making and Accountability

Few people are forced to make decisions because few people are accountable for specific programs or activities. Obviously, those people who are accountable for specific activities must make decisions. How are these decisions made? A better question might be, "What causes an individual to make one decision rather than another?" For many months, my experiences at 15 Ashburton Place puzzled me because I was completely unable to "read" the System vis-a-vis decision making. For example, several of what I considered to be very reasonable requests were denied by various business offices without explanation or apparent reason. Other requests were ignored. Still others were quickly and categorically honored to our complete satisfaction. There was no apparent logic to these responses. It seemed as if some mad table of random numbers was at work here, approving one thing, denying another, and ignoring the third. It must be admitted that, in each instance when I did require an explanation for a decision, there was some law or regulation or policy that seemed to lend credulity and wisdom to the decision. However, on other occasions, similar requests—in equal violation of the regulation or policy—would be granted. All one can do is speculate about the basis for decision making at 15 Ashburton Place—as, obviously, one can't read the decision maker's mind and there seems no logical pattern to his activities. My speculations have led me to three insecure and tentative conclusions (1) It is thought much simpler and less perilous to make no decision, or to decide negatively, than to decide positively. (2) The System makes it more satisfying to decide negatively than to decide positively. (3) The process of working with laws, regulations, and policies encourages their utilization to prohibit activities and developments rather than to promulgate such activities and developments.… If a System is based on convictions and standards and precedents that make it easier, less perilous, and more satisfying to make negative decisions than to make positive decisions, to the degree that this assumption is true laws, regulations and policies will be interpreted in the light of their prohibitionary powers rather than in the light of their enabling powers. (pp. 314-317)

The industries in our field are political, defensive, organized, and less interested in the public good than they should be. Even those people on the highest level—the "decision makers"—appear to worry more about how they are getting along than how the clients are getting along, more concerned with their careers than with their clients' lives. Of course there are many exceptions.

What is found among the professional and labor forces in mental retardation is found in *every* industry. Bishops want to be cardinals and cardinals want to be popes. There is a Securities and Exchange Commission because business and industry can't govern their own affairs. Similarly, society demands autopsies, schools are required to appoint committees to deal with issues concerning handicapped persons, construction companies must satisfy building codes. Ralph Nader has become very powerful and very famous. It would be a mistake to conclude from the politics—from the cynicism, from the monopolistic and monolithic practices recounted in this chapter—that the mental retardation industries are particularly venal and particularly in need of reform. I believe that reform is necessary for the same reason that America once decided that the automobile is too dangerous an instrument for drivers themselves to set the speed limit. The purpose of this chapter was not to elaborate on the unique ways our field disregards its responsibilities and abuses its authority. Rather, I want to call attention to these problems because hardly ever are such problems brought to the attention of the student. And when on occasion they are brought to the attention of people in the field, it seems that hardly ever is the "problem" our doing but, rather, that there are "outsiders" who need to be watched, regulated, and punished for their wrong doings. Possibly that's no more than another example of the human condition. But we must expect more from our colleagues in our field. It was Pogo who remarked, "We have met the enemy and it is us." Well, we may have met the culprits, and they may also be…

Reprinted by permission of Steven D. Blatt and the Blatt family.

If People Could Heed Good Advice[16]

Lessons From the Street Lectures

I had a wise mentor who used to harangue me with precepts, homilies and good advice—hardly any of which I heard, much less acted on. But he repeated so often the adage, "The most we learn from history is that we don't learn anything from history," that it stuck in my mind—although I never figured out if it was true or not, or even quite what it meant. Years later, I got the idea that we don't learn much from history because nothing changes. But nothing changes differently today from the way things didn't change before. Thus, people acquire the false impression that things do change, and that it's worthwhile to recount and analyze history—although, inevitably, we don't learn from history. But suppose we would learn from history…what could we have learned from these Street Lectures?

Reading the lectures chronologically, one might see a shift from concern with what needs to be done to interest in how to do something. …So, if these papers reflect reality, the concerns of education professors shifted during the decades between World War II and today from philosophical to practical ones. But what about the lessons to be learned?

A. Education is a serious and complex business. Consequently, it can't be wholly understood by cleaving to a professional orthodoxy or standard academic rhetoric. Education deserves the attention of our best thinkers, not solely the best identified with our field. But it won't be enough for society's other great people to worry about how children learn if we who have more direct responsibility for those children won't listen to advice from outside of our own Establishment. In Ganders' (1941) lecture, he begins by comparing Jesus' aphorism about the truth making us free with Hitler's on the idea that society should create its own truth to serve its own needs. He continues the counterpoint with references not to professionals and scientists, but rather to Mohammed, Confucius, and St. Paul. Inevitably, he gets to the spread of hate across the world and the antidote, democracy. After all, it's 1941. He worries that our people may now be "thinking that a class system based upon hereditary economic privilege has replaced a European class system based on hereditary aristocracy" (p. 10). Forty years ago, Ganders discussed educational inequity and related it to the deeply embedded erroneous idea that war is inevitable. So, how might we avoid future wars? Through better teaching, whereby people come to understand what divides nations. War can be eliminated, but only if we prepare ourselves to embrace the idea of a world organization, only if we are good and intelligent enough to make the idea work.

B. It's been said that what's new isn't true and what's true isn't new. William Cruickshank, the Street lecturer for 1952, may be known today as a conservative in special education. Of course, he's also known as a controversial pioneer of the Learning Disabilities Movement and a policy leader. But if there's a negative connotation to his special education philosophy, at least among certain groups, it's that he has been known to foster separate classes and schools for the trainable retarded child and separate systems for those who do not meet traditional criteria for public school eligibility. But think about what he said in 1952, a time when throngs of professionals were beating the drums for separate classes and schools, and a time when state after state had fallen in line with the demands for mandatory segregated special programs for the handicapped.

> It is our considered judgment that the great majority of children with physical disabilities can and should be made a part of regular class instruction in the schools. We do not mean to go so far as to say there is nothing special about special education. We do mean to say that to our knowledge there are few, if any, adjustments which need to be made in the curriculum of an elementary or secondary school for approximately two-thirds of the physically handicapped children of the nation. There is no special method of teaching reading to the child with poliomyelitis. There is no special method of teaching number concepts to the cardiac which is not also applicable to all other children. Social studies and language arts for the child with a club foot are the same as those for the child not so characterized. Cannot these children then be integrated into the normal social and educational functions of a typical American school? Must they, because they carry a cane, or walk with the aid of a crutch, or ride in a wheel chair, spend their formative years in isolation in special classes or schools where at best, because of the limited number of children, programs are frequently not so rich as for nonhandicapped children? An emerging tenet with regard to the exceptional child thus is that whenever possible he shall be integrated into the regular educational stream of the school system. (p. 11)

The truth is the truth! Sometimes we don't see it easily, or remember it, or understand it—or want to understand it. But the truth continues to crop up, year after year and decade after decade. Cruickshank saw it more than 30 years ago, even when those around him were blinded by their own zeal to do more and more for the handicapped—when it wasn't "more" that some of the handicapped needed.

C. There are always good people and bad people, heroes and villains. Once upon a time, William Cruickshank stood almost alone for advocating integration of the handicapped. Today, he stands almost alone for not advocating integration of the handicapped. Once upon a time Cruickshank went too far, and today not far enough. If we compare his writings then with his writings today, we may see that his position hasn't changed as much as the fact that society's position has changed. Much of that change has been fueled by the black power movement, the women's movement, the wars we've had, and the minority reforms of the post-World War II era. Some of it was due to the propensity we have to get on and off bandwagons. If Andy Warhol says that everyone in the world will eventually be famous for a few minutes, then we must also consider the need for lots of bandwagons to accommodate the ideas of the moment. For example, in his Street Lecture for 1958, Eric Gardner discussed teacher preparation in the context of the new Russian earth satellites. Insofar as American education was concerned, the antagonist of the 60s was Mother Russia with her science and mathematics curricula which demanded more from children—and got more. The antagonist today is our Japanese ally—with his Toyota and Honda cars which are closing our factories and steel mills. Twenty-five years ago, educators proposed to teach our children better so that America would be first on the moon. Today, educators are asked to teach our children better so that America will get on the move again, so that our mills will be running and our workers will be employed. There are always good people and bad people, nations to overcome and others to join. But one factor remains constant: education continues to be both the scapegoat and the panacea for what ails the society. While it has not been without some justification that education has been accused of being a ragtag and fashion-driven discipline, there is another side. And while there may be substance to the charge that education is continually in disarray but always avant-garde, at once superficial and eager to be counted among those who serve science, there is another side.…society is much the better for its teachers and those who lead and prepare them. But I don't have to tell you that.

D. There are big problems and trivial problems. And these don't change very often. DiCarlo's 1959 paper still is contemporary today:

> Fourteen years ago skies over Hiroshima and Nagasaki jettisoned human constructed cargoes of fire, destruction, and death upon a people and land below. Man's genius had penetrated the secrets of the atom, but with his first use of this new force, he compromised his conscience. Man can no longer escape responsibility for the consequences of his research. The new age of atomic energy merged imperceptibly into the hydrogen era. Man had somehow managed to survive through the atomic age in spite, rather than because, of himself. Modern hydrogen stockpiles, thermonuclear weapons and satellites leave the solution of man's survival in serious jeopardy. (p. 7)

I don't know if the way to teach people to be wiser about their own lives and the world they live in is found in DiCarlo's suggested honors courses for our students. But he strikes a sympathetic chord, when he calls for an emphasis on ideas more than technical facts. He lays bare the well-known professional sin—the overreliance on subject matter, on discrete facts, and abstract formulae—which repels the student, and should repel the professor. Let's get to the big problems—the problems which, if not solved, will severely diminish the future society. Ganders (1941) wrote about education as the antidote to war. Today, we write about building better (or bigger) graduate programs. Somehow, I'm persuaded that Ganders and DiCarlo were more on the right track insofar as what education should be all about. I'm also persuaded that we're much more comfortable when we avoid such talk.

E. There never were "good old days." Like DiCarlo's, parts of Sheldon's 1961 paper on reading instruction are as fresh as this year's plethora of reports on the crisis in education:

> Critics of today's schools refer frequently to the excellence of education in the "good old days." Parents boast of how they learned to read, spell and write without difficulty in the first three grades. Employers yearn for the kind of secretary they used to hire—one who not only could spell, but also could correct her employer's errors in grammar and punctuation. Few recall a classmate who failed; instead they remember that anyone who graduated in their class from good old Central High had no difficulty gaining admission to any college in the country. Educators replying to these critics have pointed to vast changes in the social scene which are reflected in the students of today's schools. For example, a population explosion has occurred in the United States. Many communities, geared for years to one thousand school children, now house and educate five and ten thousand, often in inadequate facilities with teachers partially trained and certified for an emergency. The emergency has lasted since 1948

and can now be accepted as a more or less permanent state. (pp. 7-8)

Of course, Sheldon was wrong about the emergency need for teachers, but he was wrong for only a brief time. The shortages are with us again and may become greater than ever, more severe because fewer people will be lining up to take those temporary positions. And admit it! Isn't it comforting to be reminded that today's educational scene is not unique insofar as: parents complaining about how little their children have learned, employers complaining about how little their workers accomplish, and educators complaining about how unsympathetic people are with respect to those who labor in our multicultural everchanging schoolhouses? There never were sufficient resources, even during the golden post-sputnik days. Parents never were satisfied with their children's schooling, and employers always felt that they were not getting their money's worth from the help. What else is new?

There is much we might have learned from those splendid papers, from Harry Smith's (1945) percepts on ethical training to Helene Hartley's (1956) good common sense approach to classical education. She asks what can we do to be "saved," what can we do to penetrate the complacency that infects our schools. And she thinks we might take more care in selecting teachers—not only for those qualities necessary to succeed in the classroom, but also for those which are needed for future leadership. If such papers could have taught us anything, it's probable that those which posed the "why" questions might have taught us things that could have made a difference. Some of these writers were concerned with changing the world—not only the world of education, but a world where there is too much suffering and too much indifference. Possibly they didn't know how to do it very well.

But, possibly, we don't want to know how to do it. What I've been implying is that today's stewards of policy and curriculum in education must be more concerned with radiation and toxic wastes if we seek fundamental improvements in our programs to prevent handicaps. We must be more concerned with U.S. activities in South America if we seek fundamental improvements in civic education. We must be better informed about the reasons why our country's no longer a moral beacon for the world's nations if we are to regain our lost morality. If our teachers and their professors hardly know where Nicaragua is, much less why our government mined its waters and bombed its villages, is there genuine hope that our children will learn why our revolution was fought, what our Constitution guarantees, what this great nation could mean to the world's oppressed people? This is the hard pedagogical question. By comparison, teaching a child to read is simply child's play—albeit important child's play.

How to Change Yourself

Why didn't we heed the advice of those Street lecturers? Why do we hardly ever listen even to good advice? I think we most seriously entertain advice when it speaks directly to our personal interests and needs. It's another thing to tell a person how to change the world, or the schools, or his pupils. Frankly, who is going to believe advice on changing schools or curricula when every bit of it is contradicted by the next expert or, oftentimes, by your own book? It's all so general, so ephemeral, so abstract, so seemingly useless at the moment.

But if I look you in the face and say, "I may have something to teach you about your life," then you might listen. You might even listen to the idea that the only way anyone successfully influences the world is by changing himself. I must admit that the idea of this paper shocks me—for its impertinence and immodesty. And it gives the appearance of being simplistic and, worst of all, talking down to people—which is how advice often sounds. There really is only one word for it: chutzpah. But for two reasons—because it may keep your attention for a while, and because these are the things which I've been wanting to share with you—I'm balancing the probability that some will ridicule what I'm about to say with the possibility that others will let a few of these words remain trapped in their minds long enough to think about them. If what follows is insulting, it isn't intentional. If parts of it are not what you expected, what could you possibly have expected…another argument against institutions or for the university? Some professors make their way by concealing their prejudices, others by revealing them.

A. On Achieving a Balanced Life

1. The first thing I try to do each day is strictly for myself. A person should start the day his own way. If you like to read, then read. If you like to write, write—you'll get promoted and tenured. If you like to run, run. If it's eating well, then eat well. The only thing you shouldn't do at the beginning of the day is go back to sleep, which leads to a second idea. You shouldn't go to sleep at night until you have tried to do something for someone else. For me, there's a certain balance to life when you start things off doing something for yourself, but there is also the responsibility to help another person before you can call it a day. How can a person change himself? By doing something for himself, by doing something different, but also by doing something for someone else.

2. My father used to tell me that if, in your most productive years, you need more than one job, you have the wrong job. I hope each of you becomes a rich, famous, and beloved professor. I think many of you will.

But if an already rich and famous professor has to give that speech, or must take that consultancy because he needs more money or fame, then he has the wrong job. People must figure out how big a cup they need to be happy. That's the lesson to be learned from the Twenty-Third Psalm. The brimming cup runs over because the container is no bigger than its contents. Some people never have a large enough cup. For some people, a caldron isn't enough. Those are the unhappy ones. The lucky ones manage to figure out what cup would just satisfy them and how to fill it. It may be difficult for a young and underpaid professor to take these words from an old and overpaid one. But I actually believe that those who find a vocation—life—in the academy, rather than a career, will also find here riches beyond wealth, and fulfillment beyond even what people dare to dream.

3. A person has to control his schedule, which is by way of saying that one has to control his life. If you could get away with it—and at least most senior professors can—when you're asked to give a speech, check the airlines or the railroad station first. Tell the sponsor when you can give the speech, so you might be able to come and go on the same day, thereby accommodating your schedule and not theirs. How much you charge for a speech should be related to the organization of your life. If too many people want you to make speeches, and you don't know how to say no, or if you have more important work to do in the field or on campus, then ask for a lot of money. That will ease your travel schedule considerably. Of course, good neighbors don't charge friends to give speeches or consult in the neighborhood. That is, unless you need more than one job.

B. On Responsibility

1. Once upon a time, there were many people who aspired to leave the world a better place than they found

it. That idea has enjoyed better days. But its attractiveness is not only in how it may contribute to the lives of others but also to oneself. In the past, I've written papers on how to change the world—another of my indiscretions. Here, I'm speaking about how one can make his or her life better. But, as I keep insisting, these are not unrelated concerns—making the world better, and yourself. Indeed, there are people who have found ways to make their lives more satisfying by helping others. I don't have to illustrate that argument—especially for you—but that won't stop me from continuing the discussion. For example, everybody worries about being expendable: old people, retired people, alienated people, in one way or another all people. Yet, while we worry, we act as if everyone else is expendable. "Sure, take your vacation anytime. We can get along without you." Are we being kind to that colleague? Or, especially at this time of the year, deans and others are wont to say, "Graduates, go forth. You don't need us anymore." Or we advise our friends to retire; they've had enough. They owe it to themselves to fish or read or, as they say, engage in leisure activities. One part of us refuses to admit that people are "replaceable parts." But much of what we say and do suggests that everyone is replaceable. Satisfied people live their lives as if they are not replaceable. And we make others more satisfied if we don't treat them as if we can get along without them.

2. Be prepared to pay your way, for at least two reasons. It's expected, and sooner or later everybody must pay up. Everything is accounted for eventually, and every account must be settled. So what does all this mean for the university? I'll offer an esoteric example. Today the computer is king. The computer is the royal flush of the university. And medieval history? In most university quarters, it's next to nothing. In other quarters it is nothing. But in one important way, there is no difference between the computer and medieval history. Medieval history continues to be supported—where it is supported—because there are university administrators and professors on a campus who know that if that program goes we will forget the Middle Ages. And they are smart enough to know that we have to pay for our memories. What's a computer? A memory. We pay for computers because it's important to have access to the millions of bits of data they are capable of analyzing and storing. We pay for medieval historians because they are capable of analyzing and storing the data on the Middle Ages. Memories are expensive. So, too, are university professors. We require salaries, offices, telephones, duplicating machines, and the other emoluments we've grown to need. That's what professors get. But as is the case with the computer or the medieval history program, the university expects something for its money. As professors, we must return good teaching, good scholarship, good advisement. There's no escaping responsibility.

3. It isn't smart to complain too often. In fact, I think clever people hardly ever complain. Where does it get you? Possibly 10 or 20 times a day someone asks you how you are. Do they really want to know? Of course not. Now, there are a few people who really want to know. Your friends want to know that you're well, that things are going well, that you don't have a care in the world. Those who aren't your friends may want to hear other things. By not complaining, you make friends happy, and others hear what they deserve. There are three bonuses. First, by saying that things are swell, you often believe it yourself. So actually, a person can will himself a happy life—more or less. The second benefit occurs when you genuinely need sympathy and support—because there are times (even in a lucky man's life) when things are so bad and he's so desperate that a sympathetic ear or word will save him from drowning.

When an optimistic person is depressed, everyone is concerned. But when a depressed person is depressed, who will notice it? Third, cheerful people light up rooms and lives. So be happy. Sacrifice your unhappiness for your friends. It's almost the least you could do for them.

4. Smart people don't hold grudges, but they also don't forget who their friends are. Smart people should thank others who help them and praise those who deserve praise. But few of us take sufficient time to express appreciation. That's ironic, especially in our culture, where we cheer the unknown actor or athlete—even when we don't see such people in person—and yet we don't sufficiently encourage our loved ones or dear friends. This is an instance where proper attention could change the world, change our friends, and change ourselves. This would seem to be important. And if we must criticize someone, we should do it face to face, without beating around the bush. It's easier to tell the truth, and I've learned that people don't become deranged when they hear the truth. However, it is permissible to avoid telling the truth in order to avoid unnecessarily hurting someone.

5. Some people have the responsibility to tell the truth. Animals and university administrators—be they deans or chairpeople—should share a common characteristic: telling the truth. Animals have no interest in lying, because they can't lie. But administrators shouldn't lie—unless they must avoid telling the truth in order to spare someone unnecessary pain, which is an idea that bears repetition. When you come right down to it, most administrators have very little they must do. We have to sign official documents, chair a committee or two, and see people. But there's little else that's specifically required of us. Hence, the faculty have a right to expect us to tell the truth. Why don't other people always tell the truth? It's hard to tell the truth to your colleague next door who wants your honest opinion about his paper, or his lecture, or his chances for promotion. That's so difficult as to make honest response an impossibility—unless we have unbelievably gifted colleagues whose virtues shine and whose defects are hardly existent. Consequently, telling the truth must be left sometimes to those people who have few psychological neighbors in the university.

It isn't all that easy for administrators to tell the truth either, but what else do they have to do that's truly important?

6. Always at the bottom of any argument for improving the world or oneself is the idea that the beginning point is me. Start with yourself. Before you seek to change the world, change yourself. Even if there are others at fault, even if the blame is elsewhere, if you don't start with yourself, you avoid the solution and, thus, contribute to the problem. So, when we get down to the essence of things, the suggestions are simple: be yourself but change yourself, make your life better by contributing to other lives. Work hard. And, with a little luck, the future will be good. Of course, one has to believe that there is a design to things, and that the design holds nothing but good for you.

C. On Scholarship

1. As I said, it takes chutzpah to write this sort of stuff. But it also takes chutzpah to write anything for publication. Writers have all sorts of difficulties to overcome. But chutzpah is the two-edged sword encompassing both the problems and the solutions. Writers must overcome their sense of modesty (if they have it), their lack of special talents (with which most of us are doomed to live), their blocks (which we learn to develop), and their intimidation by blank page and silent room (which we never seem to lose). How to overcome?

Just do it. Write every day, a little or a lot. But get the habit—like the jogger, or the eater, or the late sleeper. However, if you jog too much, or if you eat too much, or sleep too late, you're not going to have the time or the energy to write every day. Then you'll complain to friends that you have a writer's block, or to your wife or husband that you're given too much to teach and not enough time to write, or to your students that you're not political enough to get published, and to yourself that the only way to survive is to lie. Really, one's life need not be that difficult. We must simply control our eating and sleeping habits. Or whatever.

2. It's now or never. We wait for the right time to write, to design a new course or to drop an old course (it's been noted that we're more apt to design new ones than drop old ones), to read a book that's been sitting on our night table, to deal with a nasty problem, to confront a nasty person, to get on with doing something about what's bothering us. We seem always to be waiting for the right time. But it's the beginning of the semester and the rush to register students that stops us. Or it's the fall conference schedule that gets in the way, or the Christmas season, or getting over the Christmas season. And then it's Easter, and then spring break, and then the semester is almost over. So why bother? If one is going to do something, it has to be done today—now. Now is always the best time, even when we don't feel quite up to the task.

D. On Improving Oneself

1. Every successful life has time for work, time for family, time for recreational and other pursuits. But possibly, the most satisfying life is one where the seams don't show, where work and family are not compartmentalized—where one's recreation, for example, can actually be reading and writing.

2. We must learn to take chances. Learn to say "yes," even though it's much easier to say "no." Saying "no" obviates the possibility that you were wrong in permitting whatever was asked of you. Saying "no" is usually less expensive than saying "yes." Saying "no" establishes your authority. All those things notwithstanding, only when you can say "yes" is there a possibility that someone is going to be able to do something, try something, change something, help someone. Sometimes, we have to take chances. But we shouldn't take foolish chances. We should be radical with our vision, but conservative with our actions. I love to bring a group together, stir up a good argument, develop all sorts of "impossible" plans, even develop a few that might eventually work. But implementation must, by necessity, be "slow motion," incremental. Radically changing an environment, a program or a curriculum makes people nervous, especially when those people don't "own" those ideas—and change takes time. It's much easier to comprehend an idea than to set it in action. That's by way of saying that it's much easier to think about changing something than actually changing yourself. Who doesn't know that?

3. I don't worry about making mistakes, because I have a belief that I can turn whatever mistake I make to my eventual advantage. For sure, it hasn't always worked out that way. But the facts haven't altered the belief. As a result, I don't get terribly nervous when things go a little wrong. I don't stay up nights worrying about tomorrow's agenda, even when I know I am supposed to be in two places at the same time seeing two "impossible" people concerning a score of unresolvable problems. Somehow, everything gets worked out. My charitable friends think of me as optimistic. Others have harsher explanations. Even they usually don't distract me. It's easier to listen to one's friends than to others. One of the reasons why I don't

hold grudges is that I don't try to remember who my enemies are, what it is they don't like about me, or I them.

The unforgivable tragedy of the German people wasn't that they killed and tortured innocent victims. Only a relative few committed those crimes. It was their utter indifference to the suffering they knew existed. To save Germany required heroic and good people who would no longer be silent. There weren't enough of them, so Germany perished…and they perished. To make America better, I must become better. That's why there's always something in it for the individual when he does battle with the injustices and suffering of the world. But as with Don Quixote, such efforts make it difficult not to look foolish to outsiders and misguided to colleagues. However, it must also be remembered that it's still the impractical visionary whom our children read about and adults revere, while those who ridicule even quixotic chivalry and idealism are invariably forgotten. The individual's life is irrevocably bound to the welfare of the masses, and only good people can save us and, thus, themselves.

I've tried here to connect questions about how to change the world with questions about how to change yourself. I find these to be intimately related, although we don't usually think of them that way. For example, DiCarlo worried about a future atomic war, but he probably didn't feel quite the same way when the first bomb dropped on that summer day in 1945. Then we were saving the world. How did he come to conclude that what was once the cure became the disease? That is, how did DiCarlo change? If we can deal with such questions, we may see better the relationship between altruistic interest—such as when one seeks to change the world, and self-interest—such as when one seeks to change himself. We may see that the beginning context is always the individual. For the world to change, I must change. For others to change, they must first learn how the change can make their lives better. To improve the schools, first the teachers, administrators, and professors must see how they, too, can improve. Possibly, we didn't listen to the good advice of our predecessors because they were silent about how our own lives are altered as society evolves, about how they themselves needed to learn—that is, change.

To summarize, I think a practical key to organizing our lives better is not to put off what we should do today. For example, we should try to answer the mail every day. Ditto returning telephone calls. Of course, it's easier when you have a competent secretary. But what it comes down to is that paying attention to the obvious is the G Factor of the efficient life. There is also a moral key, which is sometimes referred to as a person's ethics—one's reasons, one's principles. How can a person develop moral bearings that are compatible with his soul? I think some of the answers could be found from the work of those early Street lecturers, who tried to comprehend education in the context of a larger, interdependent world. We must not act as if we are alone. We've been alone, but it is neither necessary nor desirable. If I were a betting person, I'd bet that the happy professor has a somewhat manageable desk, a reasonably good conscience, passable self-esteem, a willingness to see connections between altruistic and self interests, a capacity to suffer because others suffer, a world view—and a lot of luck.

I've had more than my share of luck. I'm not ungrateful. Enough.

Reprinted by permission of Steven D. Blatt and the Blatt family.

Afterword

Steven D. Blatt

When Steve Taylor first approached me about publishing a book of the collected works of my father, I had conflicting thoughts. My initial reaction was "great." When I was asked to help with compiling these writings, I said, "My pleasure." Then I was asked to write the last chapter; I began to worry. At first, it was concern that my inadequacies as a writer or, worse yet, a thinker would become all too apparent. It's one thing to say something foolish in the privacy of one's home, in front of students, or, worse yet, in front of one's colleagues. Little would compare to the humiliation of doing so in your father's book.

Then I had a more dreadful thought: Would anyone want to read "old stuff"? Although it might have historical or even sentimental value, are these writings relevant for today's issues? Readers will draw their own conclusions. For me, I have often wondered what Dad would say about today's societal issues. People bomb abortion clinics, killing doctors and nurses, in order to save fetal life. Dr. Jack Kevorkian "assists" people in ending their personal tragedies and sufferings. Certainly, he would applaud the closing of the Syracuse Developmental Centers of the world, but what would he say about the services that have replaced them? Surely he would see progress in the Americans With Disabilities Act, although he would be quick to point out how sad it is that such an act was needed in the first place. Although most of his colleagues would expect him to support the proponents of inclusion, the details of how he would support it or what he would say remain elusive.

Obviously, I believe that these writings are relevant and important. I remember when he was writing the lecture "If People Could Heed Good Advice." He was the dean of the School of Education at Syracuse University and the audience was his faculty. Although I do not have recollections of many of his important speeches, I doubt there were too many he worked on more than this one. This was the only one he asked me to read before he presented it. I don't remember the details of the early drafts, only that I didn't like them. They were confusing and rambling. I am sure he agreed because the final product was so different.

I remember him sitting in the lecture hall, smoking his pipe (certainly a different era than today), waiting for things to start. I doubt his colleagues sensed how much work he had put into his thoughts. Little did any of us realize this would be the last formal presentation he delivered. I have always thought this was one of his best writings. Although he didn't write this until only a few months before he died, it was the basis for his philosophy and his personality. It explains why he did the things he did.

There aren't too many, if any, things I have read more often than "If People Could Heed Good Advice." As I reread it once again, I became convinced that Burton Blatt's writings do have value for today. His advice (his good advice), his writings were good back then and remain so today. Although he often would say and write, "I write for myself," I always viewed that as one of those white lies a parent tells his children. Yes, he did write for himself and took tremendous pleasure from writing. He started each day by going downstairs to his den for a combination of pushups, situps, running in place and writing. This routine would always start by 6 A.M. and not infrequently at 3 or 4 A.M. That time was for him (although for many years it was shared with Gus, our Irish setter). But he also wrote for the reader. He had a need to communicate with his students and colleagues. He felt an obligation to those in the institutions who were themselves unable or never given the opportunity to read, let alone write. Most assuredly, he wrote for those administrators and officials who didn't want to read his writings, but in his mind needed to, they more than anybody. And Burton Blatt wrote because he believed with all of his heart that a society can become great only when it takes care of all of its people, especially those who are too old or too young, those with disabilities and those in need of advocates.

The issues that Burton Blatt wrote about in the early 60s are still present 40 years later. The details of the problems may have changed, but the good advice that he wrote many years ago remain constant. In the preceding pages of this book are thoughts on the right way and the wrong way to interact with another human being. He noted, "To observe sorrow untouched is to cause it to continue." He reminded us of our responsibilities to each other and the benefits from owning up to our responsibilities—benefits to victims, to ourselves, and to society. He implored us to agree that "All men are human beings. All human beings are valuable. And all the rest is commentary."

My father was nothing if not an optimist. He believed that, "The design for each of us holds nothing but good." He wrote in "Aphorisms of a Burned-Out Pessimist,"

The lucky man has a wife who believes
he is a lucky man.
    He has children who, in their maturity, continue to believe he is a good man.
    He has parents who respect as well
as love him.
    And he has brothers and sisters,
and uncles and aunts who do not envy his luck.
    He has everything,
and he has this time to reflect and to understand.

Burton Blatt was indeed a lucky man. He had colleagues and students who valued his presence in their lives. He had readers who read his books. He had the good fortune to work with parents and children and professionals who looked to him for guidance and supported his efforts. He had friends (who were often his colleagues, students, readers, parents and children, and professionals) to share with. Most important to him, he had his family—parents, brothers and sisters, nieces and nephews, my mother and my brothers and me. Although he died before they were born, he also has seven grandchildren.

When my father died at the age of 57, many people remarked on how young he was and how tragic it was for us to lose him. He was too young, and 14 years later I continue to miss him and think about him every day. But I have inherited his optimism—or maybe he taught it to me. In addition to many of the feelings I have for my father, I feel lucky to be his son and have him for my father, to have known him and learned from him, and I feel lucky to be able to read his writings. I know he always did his best to make the world better and we all have benefited from him.

Biographical Sketch of Burton Blatt

At the time of his death in 1985, Burton Blatt was centennial professor (an honor conferred upon the 100th anniversary of Syracuse University) and dean of the School of Education at Syracuse University. Born in New York City in 1927, he received his Ed.D. in special education from Pennsylvania State University in 1956. He and his wife, the former Ethel Draizen, had three children, Edward, Steven, and Michael.

Prior to coming to Syracuse University to assume the position of director of the Division of Special Education and Rehabilitation in 1969, he served as a public school teacher in New York City, associate professor at New Haven State Teachers College, and professor and chairman of special education at Boston University. In 1969, he was presented with a special citation from Massachusetts Gov. Francis W. Sargeant in recognition of his service as assistant commissioner and director of the Division of Mental Retardation during a year's leave of absence from Boston University. He established the Syracuse University Center on Human Policy in 1971 and served as its director until 1976.

Burton Blatt was the recipient of numerous awards by governmental, professional, university, and parent organizations for his service on behalf of people with mental retardation and other disabilities and held a variety of leadership roles in professional associations. In 1974, he received the Humanitarian Award from the American Association on Mental Deficiency, now the American Association on Mental Retardation (AAMR). He was elected to serve as president of AAMR in 1976. He was the author of more than 300 books, monographs, chapters, articles, and reviews.

Remembered for his leadership, warmth, and humor, Burton Blatt's influence at Syracuse University continues to be felt today, 14 years after his death. Both the Center on Human Policy and the Gebbie psycho-educational clinic carry on his work. The Burton Blatt Scholarship Fund is a major source of support for students in the School of Education, and in 1998 the School·dedicated a student center in his memory.

Selected Publications by Burton Blatt

Books

Blatt, B. (1970). *Exodus from pandemonium: Human abuse and a reformation of public policy.* Boston: Allyn & Bacon.

Blatt, B. (1973). *Souls in extremis: An anthology on victims and victimizers.* Boston: Allyn & Bacon.

Blatt, B. (1976). *Revolts of the idiots: A story.* Glen Ridge, NJ: Exceptional Press.

Blatt, B. (1981). *In and out of mental retardation: Essays on educability, disability, and human policy.* Austin, TX: Pro-Ed.

Blatt, B. (1984a). *In and out of books: Reviews and other polemics on special education.* Austin, TX: Pro-Ed.

Blatt, B. (1984b). *In and out of the university: Essays on higher and special education.* Austin, TX: Pro-Ed.

Blatt, B. (1987). *The conquest of mental retardation.* Austin, TX: Pro-Ed.

Blatt, B., Biklen, D., & Bogdan, R. (1977). *An alternative textbook in special education: People, schools, and other institutions.* Denver: Love Publications.

Blatt, B., & Garfunkel, F. (1969*). The educability of intelligence.* Reston, VA: Council for Exceptional Children.

Blatt, B., & Kaplan, F. (1966). *Christmas in purgatory: A photographic essay on mental retardation* (2nd ed.). Boston: Allyn & Bacon. Originally printed and distributed by Blatt in 1966; after many printings by Allyn & Bacon, the 3rd edition was published in Syracuse, NY: Human Policy Press, 1974.

Blatt, B., Ozolins, A., & McNally, J. (1979). *The family papers: A return to purgatory.* New York: Longman, Inc.

Articles

Blatt, B. (1958). Physical, personality, and academic status of children who are mentally retarded attending special classes as compared with children who are mentally retarded attending regular classes. *American Journal of Mental Deficiency, 62,* 810-815.

Blatt, B. (1960). Some persistently recurring assumptions concerning the mentally subnormal. *Training School Bulletin, 57,* 48-59.

Blatt, B. (1961). Toward a more acceptable terminology in mental retardation. *Training School Bulletin, 48,* 47-51.

Blatt, B. (1964). Measuring and modifying behavior of special education teachers. *Mental Retardation, 2,* 339-344.

Blatt, B., & Mangel, C. (1967). The tragedy and hope of retarded children. *Look, 31,* 96-103.

Blatt, B. (1968). The dark side of the mirror. *Mental Retardation, 6,* 42-44.

Blatt, B. (1973a). The monolith and the promise. *Therapeutic Recreation Journal, 7,* 4-32.

Blatt, B. (1973b). On the educability of intelligence and related issues: A conversation with Burton Blatt. *Education and Training of the Mentally Retarded, 8,* 219-227.

Blatt, B. (1974). Sins of the prophets: A short prejudiced history [Editorial]. *Mental Retardation, 12,* 59.

Blatt, B. (1975). The integration-segregation issue: Some questions, assumptions, and facts. *Family Involvement, 8,* 10-14.

Blatt, B. (1981). How to destroy lives by telling stories. *Journal of Psychiatric Treatment and Evaluation, 3,* 183-191.

Blatt, B. (1983). The next hundred years. *Journal for Special Educators, 19*(4), 16-22.

Blatt, B. (1984a). How to change the world without ruining it yourself. *Journal of Learning Disabilities, 17*(8), 506-507.

Blatt, B. (1984b). *If people could heed good advice.* J. Richard Street Lecture Series, Syracuse University, School of Education.

Blatt, B. (1984c). The school of education in a research university. *Journal of Learning Disabilities, 17*(4), 252-253.

Blatt, B., Bogdan, R., Biklen, D., & Taylor, S. (1977). From institution to community: A conversion model. In E. Sontag (Ed.), *Educational programming for the severely and profoundly handicapped.* Reston, VA: Council for Exceptional Children.

Blatt, B., & Garfinkel, F. (1967). Educating intelligence: Determinants of school behavior of disadvantaged children. *Exceptional Children, 33,* 601-608.

Blatt, B., Winschel, J., & Ensher, G. (1977). Institutions for the mentally retarded: A war disguised as a debate. *Journal of Special Education, 11,* 267-273.

Source Credits and Notes

[1] This was published as a Preface in *Exodus From Pandemonium: Human Abuse and a Reformation of Public Policy* (1970). It also serves as a fitting introduction to the collected papers.

[2] Reprinted from *Christmas in Purgatory* (Blatt & Kaplan, 1966).

[3] Reprinted from *Exodus From Pandemonium* (1970).

[4] Reprinted from *Exodus From Pandemonium* (1970).
   On May 2, 1967, the Massachusetts legislature adjourned its formal deliberations at noon and reconvened at one of four state schools for the mentally retarded to pursue a thorough discussion and on-scene observation of the more serious problems confronting these settings. It was their purpose to achieve a deliberate focus on our state institutions in the hope that we might find the resources and talent to solve or ameliorate current problems and, also, prevent these from occurring in the future. The writer was invited to deliver the keynote address to this legislature, as well as to the professional administrative staffs of the institution and the State Department of Mental Health, and the officers of the parent association identified with that institution. This entire project received the full endorsement and participation of all of the aforementioned groups. In light of the writer's belief that the conditions and issues he is concerned with here have national rather than local relevance and have general rather than specific interest, he edited his paper of that occasion for presentation to the membership of the American Association on Mental Deficiency at its Annual Meeting at Denver, CO, on May 20, 1967, and publication in their journal, *Mental Retardation* (October 1968).

[5] Reprinted from *Exodus From Pandemonium* (1970). Some readers, mostly younger ones, may be puzzled about the inclusion of a chapter concerning a summer trip to Germany, in a book on human abuse. Although they have read about Nazi Germany, the Holocaust is about as removed from their lives as the American Revolution is from ours. Those readers, the author asks to accept—on faith—the logic supporting such inclusion.

[6] Reprinted from *The Family Papers: A Return to Purgatory* (Blatt, Ozolins, & McNally, 1979).

[7] These are selections from *Exodus From Pandemonium* (1970) and *Souls in Extremis: An Anthology on Victims and Victimizers* (1973).

[8] Written on October 25, 1969, a day when *Time* (p. 35) and the *Syracuse Herald-Journal* (p. 4) reported on the Canadian government's change in policy regarding the killing of seal pups.

[9] Reprinted from *Souls in Extremis: An Anthology on Victims and Victimizers* (1973).

[10] Based on infrequent involvements with medical school cadaver committees, experiences that the reader may wish to forego. I have observed that certain deceased state school residents are selected for medical study as they were selected for institutionalization, and are treated in death as they were treated in life. On the average, each selected corpse involuntarily contributes 1 year of his eternal life to society before he is permitted his rest; he, of all people, who owes so little to society, from whom society has exacted so much, and from whom society has made his entire life—and now his death—a sacrifice.

[11] This essay was published in the *Journal of Psychiatric Treatment and Evaluation* (1981).

[12] Reprinted from *The Conquest of Mental Retardation* (1987) published posthumously.

[13] Reprinted from *The Conquest of Mental Retardation* (1987) published posthumously.

[14] Reprinted from *In and Out of Mental Retardation* (1981). This essay is abstracted from one originally published in R. B. Kugel and A. Shearer (Eds.), *Changing Patterns in Residential Services for the Mentally Retarded* (1976), under the title "The Executive."

[15] Reprinted from *The Conquest of Mental Retardation* (1987) published posthumously.

[16] Reprinted from *If People Could Heed Good Advice* (1984). The J. Richard Street Lectureship, named after Syracuse University's first School of Education dean, is a lecture series by distinguished School of Education faculty.

REFERENCES

Aaronson, W. J. (1972). *Innovation in special education: Title III ESA.* Washington, DC: Department of Health, Education, and Welfare.

All in the name of science. (1972, July 30). *New York Times,* p. D2.

Biklen, D. (1977). *The elementary school administrator's practical guide to mainstreaming.* Syracuse, NY: Human Policy Press.

Blatt, B. (1956). *The physical, personality, and academic status of children who are mentally retarded attending special classes as compared with children who are mentally retarded attending regular classes.* Unpublished doctoral dissertation, Pennsylvania State University, University Park.

Blatt, B. (1970). *Exodus from pandemonium: Human abuse and a reformation of public policy.* Boston: Allyn & Bacon.

Blatt, B. (1971). *Massachusetts study of educational opportunities for handicapped and disadvantaged children.* Boston: Massachusetts Advisory Council on Education.

Blatt, B. (1973a). The monolith and the promise. *Therapeutic Recreation Journal, III*(4), 4-32.

Blatt, B. (1973b). *Souls in extremis: An anthology on victims and victimizers.* Boston: Allyn & Bacon.

Blatt, B. (1976). The executive. In R. B. Kugel & A. Shearer, A. (Eds.), *Changing patterns in residential services for the mentally retarded* (2nd ed.). Washington, DC: President's Committee on Mental Retardation.

Blatt, B. (1979a). Bandwagons also go to funerals: Unmailed letter 3. *Journal of Learning Disabilities, 12*(3), 11.

Blatt, B. (1979b). Bandwagons also go to funerals: Unmailed letter 4. *Journal of Learning Disabilities, 12*(6), 7-8.

Blatt, B. (1981a). How to destroy lives by telling stories. *Journal of Psychiatric Treatment and Evaluation, 3,* 183-191.

Blatt, B. (1981b). *In and out of mental retardation: Essays on educability, disability, and human policy.* Austin, TX: Pro-Ed.

Blatt, B. (1984). *If people could heed good advice.* J. Richard Street Lecture Series, Syracuse University, School of Education.

Blatt, B. (1987). *The conquest of mental retardation.* Austin, TX: Pro-Ed.

Blatt, B., Bogdan, R., Biklen, D., & Taylor, S. (1977). From institution to community: A conversion model. In E. Sontag (Ed.), *Educational programming for the severely and profoundly handicapped.* Reston, VA: Council for Exceptional Children.

Blatt, B., & Garfinkel, F. (1973). Teaching the mentally retarded. In R. M. W. Travers (Ed.), *Second handbook of research on teaching* (pp. 632-656). Chicago: Rand McNally.

Blatt, B., & Kaplan, F. (1966). *Christmas in purgatory: A photographic essay on mental retardation* (2nd ed.). Boston: Allyn & Bacon. Originally printed and distributed by Blatt in 1966; after many printings by Allyn & Bacon, the 3rd edition was published in Syracuse, NY: Human Policy Press, 1974.

Blatt, B., & Mangel, C. (1967). The tragedy and hope of retarded children. *Look, 31,* 96-103.

Blatt, B., Ozolins, A., & McNally, J. (1979). *The family papers: A return to purgatory.* New York: Longman, Inc.

Burt, C. (1957). The inheritance of mental ability, Bingham Lecture. *American Psychologist, 13,* 1-15.

Civil liberties for what? (1974, August 4). *New York Times,* p. 34.

Collings, G. D., & Singletary, E. (1973, Summer). *Case law and education of the handicapped.* Florida Educational Research and Development Council.

Cruickshank, W. (1952). *The exceptional child in contemporary education.* J. Richard Street Lecture Series, Syracuse University, School of Education.

Department of Health, Education, and Welfare. (1973). *Mental retardation source book* (Publication No. OSOS 73-81). Washington, DC: Author.

DiCarlo, L. M. (1959). *Our educational dilemma.* J. Richard Street Lecture Series, Syracuse University, School of Education.

Ganders, H. (1941). *Education for war and peace.* J. Richard Street Lecture Series, Syracuse University, School of Education.

Gardner, E. (1958). *Tomorrow's graduate school of education.* J. Richard Street Lecture Series, Syracuse University, School of Education.

Gould, S. J. (1981). *The mismeasure of man.* New York: W. W. Norton.

Grossman, H. J. (Ed.). (1973). *Manual on terminology and classification in mental retardation.* Washington, DC: American Association on Mental Deficiency.

Hartley, H. (1956). *The unlaid cornerstone of American education.* J. Richard Street Lecture Series, Syracuse University.

Heber, R. (Ed.). (1959). *A manual on terminology and classification in mental retardation* [Monograph Supplement to the *American Journal on Mental Deficiency, 64*].

Herr, S. S. (1979). *The new clients: Legal services for mentally retarded persons.* Washington, DC: Research Institute on Legal Assistance, National Legal Services Corporation.

Hutchinson, E. F. (1982). Wheelchairs. *The Exceptional Parent, 12*(1), 7, 60.

Jensen, A. R. (1973). Let's understand Skodak and Skeels finally. *Educational Psychologist, 10*(1), 30-35.

Justice at the ready. (1982, June 2). *New York Times,* p. A20.

Lewis, J. F. (1973). The community and the retarded: A study in social ambivalence. In G. Tarjan & R. K. Eyman et al. (Eds.), *Sociobehavioral studies in mental retardation* [Monograph No. 1]. Washington, DC: American Association on Mental Retardation.

A Mattewan audit shows inmates were defrauded. (1974, July 7). *New York Times,* p. 1.

Mental Hygiene News. (1974, May 24). Albany: New York State Department of Mental Hygiene.

McCandless, P. (1979). Build! build! The controversy over the care of the chronically insane in England, 1855-1870. *Bulletin of the History of Medicine, 53*(4), 553-574.

Miami (FL) *Herald.* (1972, May 4).

Milgram, N. A. (1969). The rational and irrational in Zigler's motivational approach to mental retardation. *American Journal of Mental Deficiency, 73,* 527-532.

National Advisory Committee on Handicapped Children: Special education for handicapped children. (1968, January 31). Washington, DC: Department of Health, Education, and Welfare.

National Advisory Committee on Handicapped Children: Better education for handicapped children. (1969, June 30). Washington, DC: Department of Health, Education, and Welfare.

National Advisory Committee on Handicapped Children: Third annual report. (1970, June 30). Washington, DC: Department of Health, Education, and Welfare.

National Advisory Committee on Handicapped Children: Basic education rights for the handicapped. (1973, June 30). Washington, DC: Department of Health, Education, and Welfare.

New York Times. (1974, April 28). p. A1.

Perske, R. (Ed.). (1977). *Improving the quality of life: A symposium on normalization and integration.* Arlington, VA: National Association for Retarded Citizens.

President's Committee on Mental Retardation. (1967, June). *MR '67: A first report to the President on the nation's progress and remaining great needs in the campaign to combat mental retardation.* Washington, DC: U.S. Government Printing Office.

President's Committee on Mental Retardation. (1974). *Silent minority.* Washington, DC: U.S. Government Printing Office.

Robinson, N. M., & Robinson, H. B. (1976). *The mentally retarded child: A psychological approach* (2nd ed.). New York: McGraw Hill.

Sheldon, W. (1961). *Influences upon reading instruction in the United States.* J. Richard Street Lecture Series, Syracuse University, School of Education.

Smith, H. (1945). *A new cardinal objective of American education.* J. Richard Street Lecture Series, Syracuse University, School of Education.

Smith, J. O., & Arkans, J. (1974). Now more than ever: A case for the special class. *Exceptional Children, 40*(7), 497-502.

State Department of Education. (1973, November). *Regents of the University of the State of New York: The education of children with handicapping conditions.* Albany, NY: Author.

Stedman, D. J. (1971). *Current issues in mental retardation and human development.* Washington, DC: President's Committee on Mental Retardation.

Steel, R. (1980). *Walter Lippmann and the American century.* Boston: Little, Brown.

Syracuse Herald-American. (1974, July 7).

Syracuse Law Review. (1972). Symposium on the legal rights of the mentally retarded. *Syracuse Law Review, 23,* 991-1165.

Task Force on Children Out of School. (1972). *Task Force on Children Out of School: Suffer the children: The politics of mental health in Massachusetts.* Boston: Author.

Wolfensberger, W. (1972). *Citizen advocacy for the handicapped, impaired, and disadvantaged: An overview.* Washington, DC: President's Committee on Mental Retardation.

Wolfensberger, W. (Ed.). (1973). *A selective overview of the work of Jean Vanier and the movement of l'Arche* [Monograph No. 1]. Toronto: National Institute on Mental Retardation.

Wolfensberger, W. (1980). The definition of normalization: Update, problems, disagreements, and misunderstandings. In R. J. Flynn & K. E. Nitsch (Eds.), *Normalization, social integration, and community services.* Austin, TX: Pro-Ed.

Zigler, E. (1969). Developmental versus difference theories of mental retardation and the problems of motivation. *American Journal of Mental Deficiency, 73,* 536-556.

About the Editors

Steven J. Taylor, PhD

Steven Taylor is professor of cultural foundations of education, coordinator of disability studies, and director of the Center on Human Policy at Syracuse University. He received his PhD in sociology from Syracuse University in 1977 and held positions at the University of Minnesota and Cornell University prior to returning to the Center on Human Policy where he served as a graduate assistant from 1972 to 1976.

Taylor is the author of numerous articles and has written or edited seven books with colleagues at Syracuse University, including *Introduction to Qualitative Research Methods, The Social Meaning of Mental Retardation, The Variety of Community Experience, Life in the Community,* and *Community Integration for People With Severe Disabilities.* He was the recipient of AAMR's Research Award in 1997 and currently serves as editor of AAMR's journal *Mental Retardation.*

Steven D. Blatt, MD

Dr. Blatt is associate professor of pediatrics and director of pediatric education at the SUNY Health Center in Syracuse, the same institution where he received his medical degree and completed a pediatric residency. He completed a 2-year fellowship in ambulatory and community pediatrics at the Children's Hospital of Pittsburgh. In 1991 Dr. Blatt became the first director of ENHANCE Services for Children in Foster Care, a multidisciplinary, comprehensive, and primary health care program for children in foster care. Dr. Blatt has collaborated with the Department of Health, the Department of Social Services, and other community agencies in improving the health care of medically underserved and at-risk children in Central New York. Dr. Blatt has participated on local, state, and national advisory committees to governmental and child welfare agencies, including the American Academy of Pediatrics, the Center on Human Policy, the Child Welfare League of America, the Permanent Judicial Commission on Justice for Children, and the Onondaga County Child Abuse Citizens Advisory Council.